ENGLAND'S SECRET WEAPON

ENGLAND'S Secret Weapon

The wartime films of SHERLOCK HOLMES

AMANDA J. FIELD

CHAPLIN BOOKS

First published in 2009 by Middlesex University Press

This edition published in 2019 by Chaplin Books

Copyright © 2009, 2019 Amanda J. Field

ISBN 9781911105459

A CIP catalogue record for this book is available from The British Library

Design by Helen Taylor

Adapted for Chaplin Books by Andrews UK Limited
www.andrewsuk.com

Chaplin Books
5 Carlton Way
Gosport
Hampshire
PO12 1LN
www.chaplinbooks.co.uk

221B

Here dwell together still two men of note
Who never lived and so can never die:
How very near they seem, yet how remote
That age before the world went all awry.
But still the game's afoot for those with ears
Attuned to catch the distant view-halloo:
England is England yet, for all our fears —
Only those things the heart believes are true.

A yellow fog swirls past the window-pane
As night descends upon this fabled street;
A lonely hansom splashes through the rain,
The ghostly gas lamps fail at twenty feet.
Here, though the world explode, these two survive,
And it is always eighteen ninety-five.

Vincent Starrett

ACKNOWLEDGEMENTS

I am grateful to Portsmouth City Museum for the opportunity to work on the Arthur Conan Doyle Collection, Richard Lancelyn Green Bequest, from the initial receipt of the boxes through to final cataloguing, enabling me to have early access to many documents; and in particular to Sarah Speller for permission to use some of the stills in the Collection. Also to Ned Comstock at the University of Southern California for making the Universal production files for the films available; Lauren Buisson at UCLA for access to the Twentieth Century-Fox legal files; the Margaret Herrick Library for Production Code Administration files; the British Film Institute library for access to trade and consumer magazines; and Catherine Cooke at Westminster Libraries for access to books in the Sherlock Holmes Collection. Lastly, without the encouragement and enthusiasm of Dr Michael Williams of the University of Southampton, and the willingness of my husband John Bull to watch the Holmes series with me over and over again, this book would certainly not have come to fruition.

CONTENTS

LIST OF ILLUSTRATIONS

Illustration sources and copyright acknowledgements:

The Arthur Conan Doyle Collection, Richard Lancelyn Green Bequest, generously made the following photographs from their collection available: Figs 1–2, 5–13, 15, 21, 23, 25, 27–28, 35–36, 46–47 and 50. A number of illustrations are screenshots (Figs 18–20, 22, 24, 26, 30–33, 37–39 and 41–43) taken by the author; all others not listed above are from the British Film Institute: Stills, Posters and Designs. All images in this book are reproduced for the purposes of critical analysis.

All images from *The Hound of the Baskervilles* and *The Adventures of Sherlock Holmes* are the copyright of Twentieth Century-Fox. All images from the other 12 films in the Holmes series are the copyright of Universal. The art deco room (Fig. 34) is the copyright of the Geffrye Museum and the Booth's Gin advertisement (Fig. 51) is the copyright of Booth's Gin.

Cover image: publicity photo of Basil Rathbone and Nigel Bruce as Sherlock Holmes and Dr Watson in the 1942–1946 series of films from Universal. British Film Institute: Stills, Posters and Designs.

INTRODUCTION

'Here, though the world explode, these two survive,
And it is always eighteen ninety-five'
Vincent Starrett[1]

I t is midnight. Clouds scud across the face of the Houses of Parliament as Big Ben begins its familiar chime. The chime continues while the scene fades out to reveal a Baker Street road-sign lit by a gas flare: as the camera pans along a brick wall, the flare makes dimly visible '221B' elegantly sign-written on the entrance door below. The scene cuts to a close-up of an article in *The Times*, about the arrival from Canada of Sir Henry Baskerville, heir to the Baskerville estate. In a midshot, we see Dr Watson seated comfortably at a library-table, scissors in hand, preparing to clip the item out of the paper. He complains to a pacing, dressing gowned Holmes that he can't understand why Holmes wants all the clippings about 'this Baskerville fellow'. 'My conjecture', replies Holmes, as the camera cuts to his face in profile, 'is that he'll be murdered'. 'Murdered?' echoes a baffled Watson. 'It will be very interesting to see if my deductions are accurate', replies Holmes, sucking contemplatively on his calabash pipe. After some showy deductions about a walking stick, left behind earlier that evening (Watson confidently getting it all wrong, and Holmes affectionately putting him right), the door opens and Mrs Hudson ushers in the stick's owner, Dr Mortimer. 'Mr Holmes', the man says in an urgent tone, 'you're the one man in all England who can help me'.

This scene, from *The Hound of the Baskervilles*, a Twentieth Century-Fox film released in 1939, contains the first glimpse of Basil Rathbone as Holmes and Nigel Bruce as Watson in what would become a long-running series spanning the years of war in Europe. It introduced viewers to a new interpretation of Sherlock Holmes, a character with whom they probably already had considerable familiarity gained through the Doyle stories, previous film and stage 'incarnations', radio series, comic strips, parodies, or a combination of all these. Holmes had been a transmedia figure for more than 40 years when this film

---

1   Starrett, 1942, unpaginated.

was released: in terms of cinema alone, this was his 100th appearance and Basil Rathbone was the 23rd actor to play the character. This meant that audiences would have certain preconceptions of how Holmes should look and behave, and would judge this new interpretation as to whether it represented the 'real' Holmes. Which particular point of origin they would use as a yardstick is, however, debatable: Christopher Frayling has pointed out just how far from the literary 'original' these perceived constructs can stray:

> Frankenstein has become confused with his own creation… Dracula has become an attractive lounge lizard in evening dress; Mr Hyde has become a simian creature who haunts the rookeries of Whitechapel in East London; and Sherlock Holmes, dressed in his obligatory deerstalker and smoking a meerschaum pipe, says 'elementary my dear Watson' whenever he exercises his powers of deduction. Not one of these re-creations came directly from the original stories on which they were based: successive publics have re-written them – filling in the gaps, re-directing their purposes, making them easier to remember and more obviously dramatic – to 'fit' the modern experience.[2]

Although Frayling's comments were written from the perspective of the 1990s, they are equally applicable to the representation of these characters in 1939. Holmes' evolution had been gradual, involving layers of accretions that had built onto the original Doyle creation, such as the deerstalker hat, drawn on the character by Sidney Paget in his illustration of 'The Boscombe Valley Mystery' for *The Strand Magazine* in 1891 (and subsequently taken up by American illustrator Frederic Dorr Steele for *Collier's* – see *Fig. 1*); and the curved-stem calabash pipe, added by William Gillette in his stageplay *Sherlock Holmes* in 1899 because it did not obscure his mouth from the audience as the 'Doyle' straight pipe would have done. David Stuart Davies claims that Eille Norwood, who starred in more than 50 British silent Holmes films in the 1920s, consciously adopted the look and style of Sidney Paget's illustrations; and every subsequent actor was likely to bring along what Robert Stam calls 'a kind of baggage'

---

2 Frayling, 1996, p.13. Thomas Leitch makes similar observations about the accrual of characteristics (Leitch, 2007, p.209).

FIGURE 1 Dorr Steele took Sidney Paget's addition of the deerstalker hat, but used William Gillette as his model for the figure of Holmes.

formed from all the previous interpretations of the role.[3] In each new interpretation Holmes was therefore both the Victorian creation of Doyle and the 'man of the moment'. This was arguably an essential commercial balancing-act if Holmes was to remain believable as the decades passed. Twentieth Century-Fox steered a steady course: though the plot of *The Hound of the Baskervilles* was streamlined to fit 'the modern experience', the film has been acknowledged as preserving something that is, perhaps, even more important than literary fidelity: a representation that accords with the Holmes of the imagination. Many of the qualities with which this iconic fictional detective is associated are present in this short scene. Firstly there is his milieu: London is portrayed through its key signifier, the Houses of Parliament, and the cut from this to the sitting room at 221B Baker Street positions Holmes as another metonym for London. The time on the clock is midnight, a time conventionally of mystery and danger, yet the domestic scene, with both men in their dressing gowns, and the homely figure of Mrs Hudson vetting visitors, shows the house to be a safe refuge. Secondly there is the visual appearance of Holmes, with his lean form, sharp features and curved-stem pipe. Thirdly, there are the manifestations of his character – his friendship with Watson, indicated by his playful teasing when Watson wrongly interprets the clues on the walking stick; his intellectual superiority, as he voices a conjecture that Watson finds baffling; his love of puzzles, exhibited in the pleasant diversion of making deductions about the stick; and his coldness, when he remarks that it will be 'interesting', rather than 'horrifying', to see whether Sir Henry will indeed be murdered. His reputation is also conveyed in this scene: when Dr Mortimer arrives, it is because Holmes is quite simply 'the one man in all England' who can help.

The 13 films that followed *The Hound of the Baskervilles*, however, did not follow the pattern that might have been anticipated from this first exposure of Basil Rathbone and Nigel Bruce in the roles. The series had begun with the detective in his 'true' Victorian period, in a classic detective story adapted from the Arthur Conan Doyle canon. But by 1942, Holmes had become a contemporary figure, enlisted to help fight the Nazis in guns-and-gangsters espionage tales that bore few traces of the original stories. By the time the series ended in 1946,

---

3   Davies, 1976, p.23; Stam in Naremore, 2000, p.60.

the films had retreated somewhat ambiguously from modernity and had strayed first into ghosts-and-ghouls chiller territory and finally into horror. These generic and temporal tensions were the outcome of Hollywood's desire to bridge the gap between the Holmes of the Doyle stories and a figure of modern-day relevance. This book aims to shed light on the way the film industry used such a famous fictional character in this series and offers detailed analysis of the films themselves and their social, political and economic context.[4] It draws extensively on primary sources, including correspondence between Sir Arthur Conan Doyle's estate and the studios, much of which has not been accessible to researchers until now: this archive material is employed not simply to create a factual history of the production and reception of the films, but to engage critically with previous accounts of Hollywood history that privilege either 'film' or 'context' without looking at them as inseparable components of the same discourse.

This series of films is a particularly fruitful site for the exploration of Holmes' identity because it was produced at a time when the historical backdrop was that of world war. Arguably such a pressing context would be reflected or refracted in the way Holmes was portrayed, especially as in 12 of the 14 films he had been transported into the present day, yet the studio carefully positioned him as 'unchanging'. The series brings together a number of other interesting perspectives: the creation of a portrayal of Holmes by Basil Rathbone which was to be regarded for more than 40 years by critics as definitive; the first major American-produced series featuring this quintessentially British character; and the pressures that the classic detective genre was under at the time from the emergence of the hardboiled. The films could be termed a 'series' because of these unifying characteristics, though they do not share the same production company, budgets, or director. The first two films were A-features made by Twentieth Century-Fox and the rest were B-features from Universal; four different directors worked on the series.[5]

---

4   See Filmography for full list of these films.

5   Mary Beth Haralovich has defined the criteria whereby the Universal films may be considered B-features, based on four considerations: the lower budget compared to the Twentieth Century-Fox films; reviews in *Variety* which identified the films as 'programmers'; the fact that Universal considered the films successful despite box-office returns that were lower than for the Fox films; and the choice of a specialist B-movie theatre for the films' US premiers (Haralovich, 1979, p.55).

Commercial and social concerns may have influenced Universal's decision to move the character from the classic detective genre with which he was traditionally associated, into the realm of horror and thriller; and into times other than his own, such as wartime Britain.[6] The genre shifts are worthy of examination because they happened within the same series, thus making it an anomaly within the context of a century of representations of Holmes. The move towards horror/thriller can be positioned within two contexts: Universal's specialisation in the horror genre, and the burgeoning influence on cinema of hardboiled detective fiction – a genre that Erin Smith argues was seen as manly and American compared to the feminised and British classic detective genre.[7] In terms of temporal shifts, because Holmes had been customarily perceived as Victorian, it was difficult for the studio to move him entirely into the contemporary without audiences feeling they had lost the 'real Holmes'. Universal sought to achieve a balance by creating the perception of a 'bubble' within which Holmes and Watson operated so that, whatever was happening around them, inside the bubble it was always '1895', a date symbolising an idealised Victorian world and drawing on nostalgic notions of the past. This 'bubble' is conveyed through the depiction of the spaces they inhabit, the clothes they wear and the way they behave – all of which are slightly out of step with the contemporary. Although Universal emphasised the modernity and topicality of the films ('as timely as today's headlines!' said one advertisement)[8], they also acknowledged the deliberate balance between past and present: one pressbook article quotes executive producer Howard Benedict as saying that the characters would only encounter the modern world when they stepped outside their rooms at 221B Baker Street: inside, it would continue to be the nineteenth century.[9] An area for

---

6   Frayling categorises Doyle's story *The Hound of the Baskervilles* as horror, but the horror is largely in the 'spooky' Gothic tradition whereas the later trajectory of the Holmes film series was towards a visceral, physical horror (severed fingers, pygmies, poisonous spiders, mad doctors wielding scalpels, deformed killers and so on).

7   Smith, 2000, p.84. This British-vs-American distinction has a bearing on the way Holmes is represented in this series, particularly in the war-themed films where he is seen to represent a culture and way of life that American audiences are implicitly told is worth preserving.

8   Advertisement for *Sherlock Holmes and the Secret Weapon* shown in the film's pressbook.

9   *Sherlock Holmes and the Voice of Terror* pressbook.

exploration, therefore, is to what extent Holmes remains a constant: in other words, does a 'nineteenth century bubble' imply a hermetically sealed zone in which he exists unchanged, or does his meaning shift or refract depending on the context? This leads to another interesting point, which is that although existing literature has examined *how* Holmes is represented on screen, there has been little analysis of *why* he is on screen; what qualities he possesses that mean he is 'needed' at particular historical moments – such as when the Allies were fighting the Nazis. A starting point for this question might be the sonnet '221B' about Holmes and Watson written by Chicago-based journalist, author and bibliographer Vincent Starrett on 11 March 1942.[10] As he gazes at a fog-bound Baker Street, he muses on the two men who 'never lived and so can never die':

> Here, though the world explode, these two survive,
> And it is always eighteen ninety-five.

These lines encapsulate three interrelated ideas: unimaginable world change, Holmes' and Watson's immortality, and their imperviousness to these changes. Their survival is clearly positioned as desirable or even necessary, as is their tie to a particular part of the nineteenth century, viewed nostalgically as a time when the world was 'safe' or knowable (unlike, it is implied, the twentieth-century world). It is ironic that people living in 1895 probably considered it to be a period of great change and uncertainty; yet here it is used to indicate stability, and thus is an arbitrary date designed to conjure up an ideal of a vanished, yet recent, past.[11] Joseph Kestner, in his study of Holmes and masculinity, points out that when Doyle's first story, *A Study in Scarlet*, was published in 1887, Britain was still suffering anxieties about a number of defeats in battle including the first Afghan War, the Zulu War, the first Boer War and the Sudanese War.[12] At home, there were other unsettling problems, with a series of

---

10 Starrett, 1942. The full sonnet can be read on the frontispiece. It introduces an American viewpoint of what this quintessentially British character symbolises: as will be discussed below, Holmes had been 'appropriated' early on in his transmedia career by the US.

11 Similar arbitrary dates were to be used for *The Hound of the Baskervilles* and *The Adventures of Sherlock Holmes*. The use of 1895 is interesting in that it happens to be the year that the cinematograph was first exhibited by the Lumière brothers.

12 Kestner, 1997, p.7.

7

events involving law, policing and surveillance including the Jack the Ripper case of 1888 and the police strike of 1890. Yet here Vincent Starrett uses '1895' to indicate stability: perhaps an understandable utopian vision for someone whose country had just joined World War Two. If '1895' is evoked as a period of stability in contrast to 'today', and if one of Holmes' key characteristics is his infallibility, then it could be argued that the quality he symbolises is 'certainty in a time of uncertainty'.

Although Holmes is probably best recognised for his deerstalker hat, pipe, magnifying glass and Inverness coat, he is more than a bundle of visual references. Each time he is represented, he also brings with him a set of values: to what extent these are Victorian values is an issue this book seeks to address. This is pertinent both to the Twentieth Century-Fox films set in the Victorian period, in terms of the mores and values being represented as 'Victorian', and to the Universal films set in the 1940s, in terms of whether Holmes' values have remained absolute, or become a 'wartime morality'.

In making this analysis I am conscious that I am doing so from the perspective of another particular 'historical moment', that of the first decade of the twenty-first century, and that my view will be coloured by the distance of 60 years since their production (and by subsequent interpretations of Holmes on screen).[13] It is all the more important, therefore, to avoid treating the films as ahistorical objects whose meanings are constant and inherent, but as commercial and social artefacts that accrued layers of meaning through the context within which they were viewed. Although it is no longer possible to establish directly how audiences received these films, reception can be reconstructed by examining the devices used to set audience expectations including posters, theatrical trailers, press reviews, and pressbook editorials. Here, Barbara Klinger provides a useful model: in *Melodrama and Meaning*, Klinger showed that the public identity of a film is formed through a negotiation between what appears on

---

13 This is akin to what Janet Staiger calls the 'encrustation' of reception history which can prevent 'a clear perception of what was once… at stake in the evaluation of the movie'. Her comments relate to reception analysis of *Birth of a Nation*, but are applicable more widely in film studies (Staiger, 1992, p.152). My analysis, incidentally, is coloured not just by a distance of time, but also by the fact that it is from a UK perspective, though I deal with British and US marketing and reception, acknowledging that these were the two most important markets for the films.

screen and the discourses that surround it.[14] As will become apparent, this public identity includes, but is not restricted to, the genre to which these films were attributed: contemporary studio publicity and press reviews reveal dichotomies between how the films were promoted at the time and how subsequent critical writing has positioned them, which underlines the importance of treating films as historical artefacts.

This study also goes beyond filmgoing-based discourses to look at wider historical issues which affected production decisions: for example, the rise of the female villain may have been motivated by the desire to appeal to women filmgoers, but was also informed by fears that newly empowered women in the workplace may not want to return to domesticity after the war; the inclusion of patriotic speeches at the end of some of the films was designed to sell War Bonds, but was also a way of drawing attention to the shared heritage of Britain and America by using phrases from Shakespeare and Churchill.[15]

In combination with this contextual approach, a detailed look at the mise-en-scène of the films has been especially useful for identifying temporal and generic tensions. Examples of temporal tensions include the exclusively nineteenth-century volumes which constitute Holmes' 1942 library; the triumph of Holmes' simple magnifying glass over the latest scientific techniques in solving a mystery; and the way costume is used to indicate that Holmes and Watson stem from a different era. Generic tensions appear in the application of techniques borrowed from the horror film, including the low-key lighting and claustrophobic 'framing' which were to become prevalent in film noir; the guns-and-spies iconography of the war-themed films with their speedboats and aeroplanes; and the appearance of the femme fatale, a figure more commonly associated with the post-war hardboiled genre. Even in the Victorian-set films from Twentieth Century-Fox, temporal tensions can be found in the way that North America is positioned as modern and forward-thinking, in contrast to an England that is primitive and superstitious; and generic tensions in the need to foreground a love story without engaging Holmes as one of the protagonists.

14 Klinger, 1994, p.xvi.
15 This 'shared heritage' notion has a bearing on the issue of Holmes' nationality.

To pursue historical accuracy and completeness, primary sources have been an essential resource in researching this book, both as tools for analysis and as the means of correcting misconceptions that have tended to be repeated in a number of popular-market books. This approach was facilitated by early access to the then-uncatalogued archive material in the Arthur Conan Doyle Collection – Richard Lancelyn Green Bequest. This hoard of 40,000 documents, pamphlets, photographs and artefacts on Holmes and his creator – the largest in the world – was bequeathed to Portsmouth City Museum in 2004. The material on dramatisations alone includes 6,000 stills and production shots, dozens of pressbooks, 300 scripts and screenplays, 250 posters and 600 theatre/cinema programmes. Of particular relevance to the production history of the Twentieth Century-Fox/Universal series of Holmes films are the files of original correspondence between Denis Conan Doyle (Arthur Conan Doyle's son and his literary executor), his Hollywood agent, and the major studios, discussing the various Doyle stories available, negotiating contracts, and setting out criteria for use of the Holmes character. Other relevant primary source material is held in the UK by the British Film Institute Library (pressbooks and trade press reviews) and in the US by the University of California Los Angeles (Twentieth Century-Fox legal archives), the University of Southern California (Universal production archives), and the Margaret Herrick Library (Production Code Administration archives). Making use of these primary sources enabled me, for example, to chart the way the posters began to portray Holmes and Watson as powerless, simply by moving their images from the top to the bottom; to show that whereas reviewers classified the films as 'detective movies', the studio preferred multiple indicators; and to demonstrate that it was not (as is commonly attributed) a lack of interest that caused Twentieth Century-Fox to drop the Holmes series, but fear of a lawsuit from the Doyle estate.

In order to understand how Holmes came to be represented in this series, it is important to look at his origins. His first major impact on the British reading public came in 1891, when Doyle's stories began to appear in a new sixpenny monthly called *The Strand Magazine*, and on the American public in 1903 when they were published in *Collier's*.[16] Along with *Punch* and *The Illustrated London*

16 *Collier's* was a broadly similar publication to *The Strand Magazine* and appeared alongside *Redbook* and *Liberty*.

News, *The Strand Magazine* was one of the most popular of what were later known as the slicks (an allusion to their glossy paper) which also included *Pearson's*, *Cassell's*, *Harmsworth's*, the *Windsor*, and the *Royal Magazine*. Until the advent of these low-priced, mass-market titles, only the wealthiest could afford to keep themselves informed about art, literature, travel or society.[17] *The Strand's* publisher, George Newnes, spotted a gap in the market for a glossy, well-produced, illustrated magazine with a high standard of editorial which would appeal to the growing middle class. He also tapped into a burgeoning distribution channel: W.H. Smith's fast-growing network of shops at railway stations.[18] 'When *The Strand Magazine* first appeared', said Newnes, 'British magazines were at a low ebb. American magazines were coming here and, because they were smarter and livelier, more interesting, bright and cheerful, they were supplanting those of native birth'.[19] A brief analysis of the first year's issues indicates both Newnes' formula and the target readership: short stories of between five and 15 pages long are sandwiched between factual articles, celebrity portraits, war reminiscences, practical instructions, and explanations of the way social institutions work. At no point in these early editions does a Sherlock Holmes story appear at the beginning of the magazine or have any prominence, though the vigorous style of the illustrations contrasts with the pen-and-ink sketches or etchings used elsewhere in the magazine. The artist is uncredited other than by his initials on the drawing and, though the myth has grown up that it was Sidney Paget's illustrations that forever fixed an image of Sherlock Holmes in the British public imagination, a number of artists contributed to each Holmes story. The readership of these early issues of *The Strand Magazine*, according to David Payne, were 'largely the lower-middle and middle-middle classes of the cities, the non-intellectual, non-public school, hardworking, rising... people – the first true mass moderns'.[20] Newnes' formula was a successful one: by the end of its tenth year of publication, *The Strand Magazine*

---

17 Such as (in the US) *Century* or *Harper's*, which sold at 25 or 35 cents (Smith, 2000, p.20).

18 The many scenes in the Doyle stories where Holmes and Watson travel by rail – such as when they leave their rooms in Baker Street to catch the Paddington-to-Exeter train to pursue the mystery of 'Silver Blaze' – must have had additional resonance for railway commuters reading of their adventures in *The Strand Magazine*.

19 *The Strand Magazine*, April 1899, vol. xvii.

20 Payne, 1992, p.10.

had published 900 short stories, kept 20 artists in employment and could number among its contributors up-and-coming authors such as Doyle, Kipling, Jules Verne and H.G. Wells.

The Strand Magazine's editorial stance changed little over the years: by the end of the Holmes story-run in 1926, authors' names were given more prominence, short stories dominated the editorial, illustrations were often full-page and illustrators were credited alongside the author. The Holmes stories had taken up prime position, billed on the front cover, and often placed as the opening feature, a measure of their ability to affect sales.[21] The magazine's readership had changed over the years: no longer exclusively the domain of what David Payne calls 'the harried servants of commerce', by as early as 1904 it had attracted intellectuals who had begun 'to read Holmes in order to visit the blessed past'.[22] This touches on a key component of Holmes' popularity: nostalgia. Doyle's stories had always been set just a few years in the past, and although one story published in 1917 deals with his war service ('His Last Bow'), his character never really emerged from the Edwardian period.

Throughout most of The Strand Magazine's lifetime, Holmes was also present for British and American audiences on stage, with the play Sherlock Holmes, written by and starring American actor William Gillette, opening at the Garrick Theater in New York in November 1899 and at the Lyceum in London in 1901.[23] The play was a melodrama which combined blackmail, a damsel-in-distress, a battle against Professor Moriarty and atmospheric London sets. Both productions toured extensively: with Gillette in the lead role, the play visited almost every principal American city over a period of 30 years, and in the UK there were two touring companies, led in the south by Julian Royce and in the north by H.A. Saintsbury who performed the role more than a thousand times (see Fig. 2). This 'coming to life'

---

21 When Doyle in 1893 killed Holmes in a fight with Professor Moriarty at the Reichenbach Falls, legend says that some 20,000 people cancelled their subscription. By 1902, Holmes had been 'resurrected'.

22 Payne, 1992, pp.61 and 127. Payne cites these intellectuals as including T.S. Eliot, A.A. Milne, Maurice Baring, Max Beerbohm, Henry Swinburne and G.K. Chesterton.

23 There had been one representation of Holmes on stage before this, when in 1893 British actor Charles Brookfield wrote and starred in a skit called Under the Clock which ran at the Royal Court Theatre, London. According to the only surviving audio recording (archived on the website youtube.com), Gillette, interestingly, played Holmes with an American accent, thus appropriating him for the US early in his transmedia career.

FIGURE 2
William Gillette, whose 30-year stage run as Holmes exerted a powerful influence on subsequent interpretations.

of Holmes took the character into a new 'moving' medium and exerted a powerful influence on how he was to evolve in subsequent film, stage, radio and print adaptations: Frederic Dorr Steele, for example, was to model his Holmes illustrations for *Collier's* on Gillette.[24]

Holmes had made his transition to film around the same time with two shorts: the trick-photography film *Sherlock Holmes Baffled* (1900) and the Vitagraph production *The Adventures of Sherlock Holmes* (1905). Unlike the Gillette play, these appear not to have had Doyle's blessing: this was given in 1920 when he sold the film rights to most of his stories to the Stoll company. The initial Stoll series (*The New Adventures of Sherlock Holmes*), all directed by Maurice Elvey and starring Eille Norwood as Holmes, consisted of 15 shorts, each lasting 30 minutes, released as a group in 1921 and sold as supporting features to British cinemas *(see Fig. 3)*. Despite what Alan Eyles calls 'dire' reviews, there was a brisk demand for the films and Elvey went on to

24 Gillette asked Doyle whether he would allow Holmes to marry in the play. 'You may marry or murder or do what you like with him' was the telegram in return (Gillette, 1974, p.x).

FIGURE 3 British actor Eille Norwood as Holmes in the Stoll series in the 1920s.

direct a further 30 shorts plus a full-length version of *The Sign of Four*.[25] The films were set in the present day, in what Steinbrunner and Michaels term a 'mild and unobtrusive' modernising, thus establishing a pattern that would continue until the release of *The Hound of the Baskervilles* in 1939.[26]

There were obvious limitations to the effective telling of 'deductive reasoning' detective stories on the silent screen, so it is perhaps no surprise that the next influential representation of Holmes

---

25 Eyles, 1986, p.63.

26 Steinbrunner and Michaels, 1978, p.13.

came through radio, when in 1930 some 35 original Doyle stories were adapted by Edith Meiser. The programmes were broadcast weekly in the US on NBC, initially with William Gillette as Holmes, then from 1939 with Basil Rathbone, the first British actor to play Holmes on radio. This 30-minute series, which ran in parallel to the Rathbone films right through to 1947 in a total of 200 programmes, began with adaptations of the Doyle stories, progressing to pastiches once the original plots had been exhausted. Unlike Holmes on film, the radio series retained a Victorian setting, through a flashback device which enabled the modern listener to make a weekly 'visit' to the ageing Dr Watson (Nigel Bruce) and listen to him as he recalled famous cases from the 1880s and 1890s, into which age the listener was then transported.[27]

There were other film adaptations of Holmes at the start of the talkies era, all with contemporary settings: British actor Clive Brook starred in two Paramount films, *The Return of Sherlock Holmes* (1929) and *Sherlock Holmes* (1932); and from 1931 to 1937, Arthur Wontner appeared in five British films *(see Figs 4 and 5)*.[28] It was Basil Rathbone's portrayal of Holmes, however, that would finally supersede that of Gillette to become seen as definitive. The identification of Holmes with Rathbone was further strengthened by international exposure, with the films released in Britain as well as other important overseas markets such as Latin America. Over the six years that he played Holmes, Rathbone successfully conflated the actor with the character, to the extent that he was more often referred to by the general public as 'Mr Holmes' than by his own name.[29]

As Christopher Frayling reminds us, the figure of Holmes has evolved by being re-presented time and again in different media, and many of the characteristics with which he was popularly associated by the start of the Twentieth Century-Fox/Universal series were not present in the Doyle stories. These accrued characteristics, however, tend to be iconographic: the deerstalker hat and calabash pipe sit

27 The series was not broadcast in Britain, which was not to get a Holmes radio series until 1952, but was made available via the Armed Forces Radio Service.

28 *The Sleeping Cardinal* (1931), *The Missing Rembrandt, The Sign of Four* (1932), *The Triumph of Sherlock Holmes* (1935), *Silver Blaze* (1938). Though the films had a contemporary setting, Wontner's costume included a Victorian cravat that served to ally his character with the late nineteenth century.

29 Rathbone letter to Denis Conan Doyle, 17 November 1951.

FIGURE 4   Clive Brook starred as Holmes in two films (1929 and 1932) with overtly contemporary settings.

comfortably alongside many of the original Doylean attributes such as the keeping of tobacco in a persian slipper, or the securing of correspondence to the mantelpiece using a jack knife. Yet Holmes is surely more than what Payne calls 'a cluster of eccentricities': in order to judge whether the changes which Holmes has undergone are merely superficial, it is essential to look at how his behaviour and

FIGURE 5

Arthur Wontner played a contemporary Holmes in five films in the 1930s, though the addition of a Victorian cravat helped ally the character with the nineteenth century.

values have been portrayed.[30] The Universal films with their contemporary context offer an apposite case study: Holmes may move in a modern world and use cars instead of hansom cabs, but would perhaps still be regarded as the 'true' Holmes if he were shown to have retained the Victorian moral values he exhibited in the Doyle stories. Because the audience's view of each incarnation of Holmes is refracted through the contexts in which he appears, some critics believe that mutation is inevitable: Roberta Pearson, for example, says he is 'relatively easily reconfigured to suit different ideological formations'.[31] On the other hand, the appeal of Holmes may actually be the antithesis of this: that he and Watson, as Sally Sugarman contends, are 'fixed points in a changing age' and that this is the reason for their continuing appeal and longevity.[32]

Despite the number of books written about Holmes, there has been little attempt to define these moral values apart from his

30 Payne, 1992, p.44.

31 Pearson, 1997, p.145.

32 In Putney, 1996, p.ix.

rationality, asceticism, imperviousness to women, and enthusiasm for treating crime as a puzzle.[33] Some critics define him by what he is not: David Hammer, for example, in *Yonder in the Gaslight*, lists the hallmarks of the Victorian–Edwardian age as including a 'spirit of fair play, respect for law, concern for privacy, dogged tenacity, notional respect for women, easy acceptance of the class system', then concludes that Holmes displays none of these.[34] H.R.F. Keating in *Sherlock Holmes: the Man and His World*, concludes the opposite, seeing Holmes as the epitome of the English gentleman, 'as if he had been created for this and no other purpose'.[35] David Payne perhaps comes closest to defining the values of which Holmes is the 'guardian', in a list which does not differentiate between Holmes and Watson, implying perhaps that the two are needed to make a whole. He attributes the following to them both:

> moral and physical courage, ingenuity, integrity, compassion for the weak and innocent, a relish for justice... respect for the social order... the necessity of setting a good example, patriotism, wide-ranging practical competence and, perhaps most importantly, a restrained but profound affection and respect for each other.[36]

His remarks are made in the context of Doyle's stories and therefore pertain to the 'original' creation rather than to subsequent re-presentations. If there is one quality however on which critics agree it is that Holmes stands for certainty: he is the one man to whom people turn in times of trouble. From this certainty flow other traits: he is always at their disposal; vastly more competent than the authorities; accepted everywhere because of his fame and reputation; and an expert in applying rational thought. He moves through an ordered universe where telegrams are always answered and trains run on time. He is at home in any milieu, whether 'respectable' society or the opium dens of Limehouse: he can read the character of anyone from their appearance, yet can himself move undetected in alien

---

33 Some 25,000 books have been published on Holmes, according to Ronald de Waal's 1974 exhaustive 1,500-page bibliography.

34 Hammer, 2000, p.70.

35 Keating, 1979, p.11.

36 Payne, 1992, p.108.

environments. And of course he unfailingly re-establishes the status quo, revealing its rupture to be merely an isolated incident, not an indication of impending chaos. Best of all, Holmes is 'on our side', a notion made explicit in the 1917 Conan Doyle story 'His Last Bow' about Holmes' wartime service[37]; the 1945 'Flanders Field' episode of the radio series, in which Watson recollects them 'doing their bit' in World War One; and in the Universal series of films where he joins the Allies in World War Two to battle the Nazis.

The notion of whose side Holmes is on raises a question about his nationality. In the US, Holmes acquired – against all the odds – a dual nationality, becoming both a metaphor for England and an 'underground American', something which was exploited in the way he was represented because it touched on two important concepts: the nostalgia that is part of Holmes' appeal and the desire for his continuing relevance. The nostalgia, from an American point of view, perhaps comes from what Jack Tracy calls a 'slavish' Anglophilia whereby Americans 'idealise an England in which we don't live'[38] and in which, arguably, no-one ever *did* live. Though the Twentieth Century-Fox/Universal series of films is not uncritical of England, the notion of a 'common heritage' is strongly promoted, particularly in the war-themed films. *Sherlock Holmes in Washington* even lifts some lines from Doyle's story 'The Noble Bachelor', expressing the wish for the day when 'our children [will be]... citizens of the same worldwide country under a flag which shall be a quartering of the Union Jack with the Stars and Stripes'.[39] Doyle was an unequivocal supporter of the US: in 1894 he undertook a lecture tour in America during which he repeatedly expressed the same view as he had put into Holmes' mouth and 'not a single American custom or institution drew an unfavourable comment from him'.[40]

In terms of appropriating Holmes for America, this was arguably already firmly established through Gillette's long stage-run as an American-accented Holmes, and by the NBC radio shows in which

37 Doyle, 'His Last Bow', 1997, p.232.

38 Tracy, 1977, p.x. As Koppes and Black remind us, however, for every 'slavish' Anglophile, there was undoubtedly an Anglophobe, to whom nostalgic representations of Britain were reminders of its less acceptable traits such as the nation of Empire and class divisions (Koppes and Black, 1990, p.224).

39 Doyle, 1982, p.232.

40 Pearson, 1943, p.110.

Dr Watson was clearly shown to have retired to California. By the mid-1940s, with the genre celebrating a new breed of virile American detective who could supplant his feminised British counterpart, it was not surprising to hear America's president, Franklin D. Roosevelt, claim (not entirely tongue-in-cheek) that Holmes was an American who learned his trade there, but 'was too well known in top circles in this country and therefore chose to operate in England. His attributes were primarily American, not English'.[41] What the public did not know at the time was that on 5 August 1942, the President had accepted membership of the Baker Street Irregulars. His joining had been kept secret until the end of the war because there were many 'of little understanding who would have raised their voices in dismay if they had known that this man, President of the United States and Commander-in-Chief of its armed forces, was having inconsequential truck with Sherlock Holmes'.[42] Perhaps even the President needed the reassurance that only Holmes could give on the brink of a world war.

Four key thematic stages can be seen in the development of the Holmes series and this book is structured accordingly. The first stage encompasses the two Victorian-set films from Twentieth Century-Fox, *The Hound of the Baskervilles* and *The Adventures of Sherlock Holmes*. The second concerns the war-themed films of 1942 and 1943: *Sherlock Holmes and the Voice of Terror*, *Sherlock Holmes and the Secret Weapon*, and *Sherlock Holmes in Washington*. The third is marked by the 'ahistorical neverwhere' of the mid-series Gothic films, which include *Sherlock Holmes Faces Death*, *The Scarlet Claw*, and *The House of Fear*.[43] The fourth is categorised by the appearance of the female villain, in *Spider Woman*, *The Pearl of Death*, *The Woman in Green* and *Dressed to Kill*. Each thematic stage is reflected in generic shifts, beginning as classic-detective costume drama, moving into guns-and-gangsters espionage, retreating into ghosts-and-ghouls chillers and then finally flirting with visceral horror. Dividing the films into groups in this way enables them to be treated in roughly chronological order, thus giving some sense of the natural trajectory of the series (an important

---

41   Quoted by Kennedy, 1995, p.64.

42   Bliss, 1945, p.2.

43   The phrase is one coined by Alan Barnes to describe this phase in the series (Barnes, 2002, p.167).

consideration in the fast-moving context of the war), but allows for the overlaying of this with interrogation of the films' shifting construction of genre and time.[44]

---

44 Not all writers acknowledge the thematic shifts in the series: Tom Weaver, for example, includes all twelve of the films in his survey of Universal's horror films, acknowledging that this is a controversial inclusion but arguing that it is defensible 'in the light of the fog-drenched atmosphere and latent chiller contents inherent in a number of them' (Weaver, Brunas and Brunas, 2007, p.5).

CHAPTER ONE

THE GAME'S AFOOT

GENRE AND THE WORLD OF THE 'GENTLEMAN SLEUTH'

'The whodunit par excellence is not the one which transgresses the
rules of the genre but the one which conforms to them'
Tzvetan Todorov, 'The Typology of Detective Fiction'[1]

Half a century after Arthur Conan Doyle wrote the first story, Sherlock Holmes still exerted a considerable grip on the public imagination, attributable not just to his immediately identifiable iconography but to the particular values for which he stood; values which could be summarised as 'certainty in a time of uncertainty'. This concept of certainty is integral to the classic detective genre, in which comfort and reassurance are key elements. This chapter explores these and other elements of the genre, establishing its parameters and how it differs from allied genres such as the thriller. Whereas later chapters will look in detail at the Holmes films themselves for generic 'clues', the aim here is to examine expectations: what contemporary audiences expected from a detective film; how, and why, this differed from a detective novel; and how these expectations tallied with the way Twentieth Century-Fox and Universal promoted the Holmes films. The latter point is especially relevant given Universal's 'modernising' of the character and the straying of the series across genre boundaries. One motivation for this is that the studio was endeavouring to compete with, or counter, the emergence of the hardboiled detective genre. As 'certainty' was an early casualty in the hardboiled film, this is a particularly interesting development.

Looking briefly at the detective genre in literature is an appropriate way to begin analysis of the Holmes films, partly because the character's origins are in literature, and also because that is the discipline whose critical language has most influenced that of film

---

1   Todorov, 1971, p.43.

studies. Literary genre criticism can offer useful pointers in defining the types of narrative expected in a detective story, the behaviour the detective is likely to display, the way suspense is created, the outcome, and the boundaries which the writer must not cross if they are to remain in the detective genre. In transferring these parameters to film, however, it is important to bear in mind that film is distributed and consumed in different ways to novels or short stories, and that therefore the rules for literature may provide only a partial 'fit' for the screen detective. With this in mind, the chapter touches on the development of critical writing about film genre and argues that its reliance on literary theory has resulted in a somewhat narrow approach.[2] This is manifested in two principal ways: the attempt to define genre by examining only 'what is on the screen', and the discarding of all 'aesthetically unworthy' films before any such definition takes place. With the first approach, the film itself is deemed to be the sole conveyor of generic meaning, and other factors such as production decisions, marketing campaigns and reception are excluded. With the second approach, genre theory and history is developed through a very small canon of films – those that are the equivalent of 'literary fiction'. These films are often outstanding precisely because they have broken away from generic conventions and thus do not form a reliable guide to what constitutes a genre.

This chapter looks beyond the films themselves, treating commercial factors, such as studio advertising and promotion (including posters, pressbooks and theatrical trailers), as equal contributors to the genre, and in so doing reveals a much more complex set of overlapping indicators than is to be found in the films alone.[3] For example, given the interchangeability of the terms 'detective' and 'Sherlock Holmes', it is surprising to discover that

----

2   The extent of this reliance can be judged from the fact that, in film studies, the film under discussion is often referred to as the 'text'.

3   Pressbooks (sometimes called campaign books) contained information about the film's plot and its cast, together with a selection of articles on different aspects of the production (such as the stars, the locations, the costumes), and suggestions for local publicity. The pressbooks were distributed by the studio to the press, to provide them with ready-made editorial, and to exhibitors, to give them ideas for promotional tie-ins and allow them to order from a range of pre-prepared advertisements. Jancovich argues that the pressbooks for the series offer a plethora of genre indicators, but it is worth bearing in mind that the only audience for the complete pressbook (and therefore the complete genre 'message') was the exhibitor or reviewer: they were free to choose which items to use, or emphasise, in editorial and local publicity.

none of the films was promoted by the studio as a detective film. All were marketed with multiple 'tags' to ensure the widest possible box-office appeal. Looking at the series from the perspective of marketing is a reminder that the primary purpose of any Hollywood genre was to attract particular groups of cinema-goers and to set expectations for their viewing experience: genre creation was therefore a living activity rather than a retrospective taxonomic exercise.

THE DETECTIVE GENRE IN LITERATURE

For many years, the detective genre remained invisible in literary criticism, principally because it was considered to be 'low' culture. Even Arthur Conan Doyle thought his Sherlock Holmes stories had little or no literary merit compared with his historical adventure novels such as *The White Company*, and he seemed frustrated that the reading public did not agree with him. There were two exceptions to this invisibility: in 1942 the British writer Howard Haycraft attempted to define the qualities that marked a story as belonging to the detective genre rather than to allied genres such as crime or mystery, the key factor being the use of deduction rather than incident. He had little time for the 'slick product of today', but favoured – for its nostalgia and comforting quality – what he called the 'romantic reality' of Sherlock Holmes.[4] The opposite view was put by the American writer Raymond Chandler in his 1950 essay 'The Simple Art of Murder', a condemnation of the English brand of gentlemanly detection that he saw as 'arid formula', and a spirited call for (his own) hardboiled 'realist' approach that acknowledged the seamy side of life.[5] Both these views were coloured by the experience of World War Two. In Haycraft's case, writing during the peak of the war in Britain, this was because 'comfort' was exactly the quality that readers seemed to need. He also drew nationalist connotations from the genre, saying that the Allies loved detective fiction because it exemplified their belief in fair play and justice; it was natural for the Axis to hate the genre because they did not believe in these things. In Chandler's case, writing in world-weary, post-war America, the picture had shifted considerably, the old certainties seemed to have been washed away and people no longer believed in neat endings,

4   Haycraft, 1942, pp.56 and 87.
5   Chandler, 1988, p.14.

trustworthy authority figures or clear definitions of right and wrong.[6]

It took until the 1960s for the detective genre to be analysed in a manner more commonly used to dissect literary fiction. This influential critical text, 'The Typology of Detective Fiction', appeared in a collection of essays published under the title *The Poetics of Prose*. Its author was Tzvetan Todorov, a Franco-Bulgarian literary theorist, who was writing at a time when structuralism (the examination of the underlying logical structures of a work and a discipline closely allied to semiotics) was gaining in popularity across the humanities and social sciences, and particularly in literature. Genres were particularly suited to structuralist analysis, because the essence of any genre is the repetition of a set of elements – narrative, iconographic and so on – across a number of works. In his essay, Todorov praises the very qualities which had previously guaranteed the invisibility of detective fiction in literary criticism; in essence, its repetitive and predictable nature:

> detective fiction has its norms: to 'develop' them is also to disappoint them: to 'improve upon' detective fiction is to write 'literature', not detective fiction. The whodunit par excellence is not the one which transgresses the rules of the genre but the one which conforms to them.[7]

This suggests a completely different critical stance from the established paradigm which had not considered that a 'masterpiece' (to use Todorov's own term) could be a work which exhibited conformity rather than individualism. The stance also, of course, moves the role of the author away from the central position which it had generally been thought to occupy (in art history and film as well as in literature) and instead proposes the perfect genre-work to be the one which is most successful at effacing the author's presence. Todorov's view has since been endorsed by a number of writers: the Marxist Ernest Mandel, for example, expresses admiration for 'mechanical' writers who are able to 'compose, decompose and

---

6   This is not to say that a similar 'war-weariness' did not exist in Britain too, and it is no coincidence that in this period Holmes was largely absent from the cinema screen both in the US and Britain.

7   Todorov, 1971, p.43.

recompose story lines and characters as if on a conveyor belt. The personality of the authors in such cases is relevant only in that it makes them able and willing to write in such a way'.[8] His remarks could easily also be applied to the Hollywood studio system whose B-movies did indeed roll off the production lines as if on a conveyor belt, and in general had their 'authorship' effaced.[9] Other critics, while acknowledging the need for authors to subject themselves to the rules of a genre, find it hard to see it as a virtue. John Cawelti, for example, whose work on literary genre has been widely applied to film, recognises that 'audiences find satisfaction and a basic emotional security in a familiar form' but mourns the way detective fiction transforms 'an increasingly serious moral and social problem into an entertaining pastime', thus revealing a longing for it to break out of its genre constraints and take on the qualities of 'literature'.[10]

If conformity is central to genre writing, then the pattern of its narratives and motifs can be mapped, and used to distinguish one genre from another. Todorov does this in order to separate the whodunit from its close relations, the thriller and the suspense story. The typical whodunit, he says, has a dual story: that of the crime, which usually takes place at the beginning (or even before the story opens) and that of the investigation, which comprises the entire 'real-time' thrust of the narrative. The difficulty with this structure is that the story of the investigation is essentially passive: 'the characters... do not act, they learn', says Todorov.[11] It also means that the detective operates in a 'safe' space, both in terms of his emotional involvement – because the victims are usually unknown to him – and his physical well-being, because his life is never in danger. Todorov contrasts this to the suspense story and the thriller, which retain the crime-then-investigation format, but are more evenly balanced, with the reader 'interested not only by what has happened but also by what will happen next'.[12] In thriller/suspense, the detective loses his immunity

---

8   Mandel, 1984, p.viii.

9   Edgar Ulmer, for example, was what James Naremore calls an 'art obsessed intellectual' in 1920s Germany, but when he came to the US it was to direct the very cheapest of 'pulp' B-movies (Naremore, 1998, p.144).

10 Cawelti, 1976, pp.8 and 105.

11 Todorov, 1971, p.45.

12 Todorov, 1971, p.51.

and becomes vulnerable to emotional entanglement or threats to his life: in other words, where the whodunit is passive and cerebral, the thriller is action-oriented and visceral. Martin Rubin, drawing on Todorov's essay, differentiates the two more precisely when he says that 'in the whodunit, the destination is more important than the route, whereas in the detective thriller there is more emphasis on a journey through a world'.[13] This journey is not the straight A-to-B path of the whodunit but one which 'twists and turns' and 'where one has the feeling of being lost in a maze'.[14] In general terms, this is a difference of nationality, the cerebral whodunit (advocated by Haycraft) being associated with British writers such as Arthur Conan Doyle, and the more visceral thriller (advocated by Chandler) with American writers such as Dashiell Hammett or James M. Cain.

Clearly the hero of the thriller is a very different character from that of the whodunit. Critics seem to agree that the whodunit's protagonist is almost always a gentleman; has a brilliant mind; is a dilettante who regards crime-solving as an intellectual puzzle; displays no emotional involvement in the case; has a character intriguing enough to hold the reader's attention (that is, more intriguing than the criminal); is not particularly interested in justice, only in establishing guilt; and is either British or exhibits British characteristics.[15] Their description reads like a template for Sherlock Holmes.

There are other key conventions of the whodunit, not touched on by Todorov's essay but explored by subsequent critics. These relate principally to the way detective stories reinforce the social order and reassure readers about its stability.[16] Order prevails at the beginning of the whodunit, which often starts in what Cawelti describes as 'the detective's retreat'. The crime signals a disruption to this order and solving it is necessary for the 'harmonious mood of that charming scene by the blazing fire' to be restored, his description immediately conjuring up an image of Holmes and Watson in their rooms at 221B

---

13 Rubin, 1999, p.202.

14 Rubin, 1999, p.27.

15 Mandel, 1984, p.14.

16 These conventions are relevant to the study of how the detective genre transferred to film, because the reassurance of the status quo present in the literary text might be doubly reinforced by the rigours of the Production Code, which did not allow crime to go unpunished, nor the forces of law and order to be mocked.

Baker Street.[17] In other words the utopian ideal of the detective's 'retreat' is shown to represent normality: crime is an aberration which briefly threatens this state and which does not affect the protagonists directly because it is external to them. The type of crime tackled by these whodunit detectives is very particular – not the crimes routinely carried out by the 'criminal classes', but ones which strike at the heart of polite society such as jewellery theft, fraud, blackmail and betrayal. An important aspect of the genre is that the criminal, often a member of the bourgeoisie, should be shown to be a single individual: in this way, the reader is reassured that society is not about to crumble into chaos, while at the same time enjoying a frisson of fear at the prospect. 'The detective story is the realm of the happy ending', says Mandel, pointing out that it is 'bourgeois legality, bourgeois values, bourgeois society' that always triumphs.[18] The underlying message, however, is more ambivalent than Mandel's analysis suggests: the detective, although usually depicted as a gentleman, is (self)-alienated from the bourgeoisie, positing the worrying thesis that the ills of society need the intervention of an outsider to quell them, an idealised police figure in an age when the police were seen as incompetent. Also, there is the unspoken knowledge of the reader that this crime is only one of a whole series that the detective will tackle: any happy ending is but a temporary state. As will be seen later, in analysis of the films from Universal, presenting the Nazis as a series of aberrant individuals for Holmes to vanquish would be a difficult message to sustain.

Todorov believed that although the whodunit, thriller and suspense story could co-exist, the genre was evolving, moving from whodunit towards suspense, a trend which was mirrored in the cinema: in fact, given its cerebral nature and static quality it is surprising that the 'classic' whodunit ever made the transition to film. William Everson, in his survey of the detective in film, remarks on this point, speculating that the two arts of story and film are too far apart. 'The detective story', he says, 'is essentially… contemplative and non-visual' and needed to be supplanted by 'action, excitement and the suavity or quaintness of the detective hero' on screen.[19] This

---

17 Cawelti, 1976, p.83.
18 Mandel, 1984, p.47.
19 Everson, 1972, p.3.

theory is certainly borne out by the evolution of the whodunit film, whose familiar characters, including Holmes, were given a suspense/ thriller spin over time. As Hollywood strove to breathe new life into an old formula, or to attract new audiences, it was to be outpaced by the rise of the hardboiled detective genre, popular in the pulp magazines long before its adoption by the film industry. By the end of World War Two, the classic detective genre both in literature and film had reached the end of its natural life: its future for the next decade or so would lie only in nostalgia (ironically, a quality already inherent in much of the genre and particularly in Sherlock Holmes). The hardboiled detective – as advocated in Raymond Chandler's essay – quickly eclipsed the gentleman dilettante.

BRINGING THE CLASSIC DETECTIVE GENRE TO THE SCREEN

In bringing the classic detective genre to the screen, Hollywood drew – as it did in other genres – on well-established characters from novels and short stories, and initially left the majority of literary genre conventions intact. Screen detectives exhibited the same characteristics as they did in fiction: well-bred, charming, eccentric gentlemen with keen intellects who relished crime-solving as a pastime.

Detective films had been popular from the early days of cinema: as discussed in the Introduction, Sherlock Holmes was on screen fairly consistently from 1900 right through the silent era. By the late 1930s, the whodunit had become a staple part of the double-bill programme on both sides of the Atlantic, with a number of long-running series, nearly all of which were based on literary sources.[20] In addition to Holmes, there were: Boston Blackie, a reformed crook created by Jack Boyle in a 1919 novel and subsequently appearing in *Redbook* and *Cosmopolitan* magazines; Bulldog Drummond, conceived by Sapper in 1920; Charlie Chan, a Chinese detective based on a 1925 novel by Earl Derr Biggers; Ellery Queen, a character backed by more than 40 novels with total sales of over 100 million copies; the Falcon, a spin-off from a Michael Arlen short story about a gentleman-adventurer; the Saint, a debonair crime fighter from the pen of Leslie Charteris; Mr Moto, a Japanese detective created by

---

20 The double-bill or double-feature had come into exhibition practice during the Depression, to encourage cinema attendance by offering more value for money.

John Phillips Marquand; Mr Wong, another oriental sleuth, created by Hugh Wiley for *Collier's* magazine; the Thin Man, a spin-off from a Dashiell Hammett story; the Lone Wolf, based on a 1917 novel by Louis Vance; and Philo Vance, hero of a series of novels by S.S. Van Dine.[21] There seems to be only two not based on literary sources: the Crime Doctor, a sleuth who used psychoanalysis to solve crime, had its origins in a radio series; and Dick Tracy came from a newspaper cartoon strip by Chester Gould. Almost all these characters also had a radio series which ran concurrently with their films. With the exception of *The Hound of the Baskervilles* and *The Adventures of Sherlock Holmes* (both 1939), all the detective-series films of this late-1930s era were B-movies, designed to be screened as the lower-half of the bill to a big-budget A-feature.[22] They might not have had much in the way of prestige – Thomas Leitch believes the detective genre 'never achieved the eminence in Hollywood that it did on the printed page' – but what was notable was their sheer volume.[23] Because the films were issued as part of a series, this embedded the characters, the narrative trajectories and other genre conventions ever deeper into decisions made about production, budgeting, distribution and marketing, and ultimately into reception and public consciousness. In this sense, they were far more influential than A-features which, as Tom Ryall argues, 'were much more subject to the need to vary the conventions, to break the generic rules', unlike B-movies in which the basic conventions or pure form of the genre could be found.[24] Series were also commercially attractive to the studios, building a loyal audience for each film and offering economies of production.[25]

Genre plays a key part in decisions made at every stage in the life of a film, from production to reception, but formal generic labelling is often only given, or rendered visible, with hindsight. In defining

21 Series list from Pitts, 1979, various pages.

22 Brian Taves makes the distinction between 'programmers', films that straddled the A-B boundary and offered recognisable cast names, and 'Bs', that were made in less than 12 days with a case of unknowns (in Balio, 1993, p.317). Taves' comments highlight the nuances of the studio production and exhibition system where a 'better quality' B-movie could sometimes be shown at the top of the bill.

23 Leitch, 2002, p.172.

24 Ryall, 1998, p.334.

25 Series were also popular with exhibitors who were less concerned with 'art' but knew what had been good box-office before.

genre as a concept, the most widespread approach seems to be one of visual and textual analysis in which shared iconographic and narrative elements are said to identify a film as belonging to a particular genre. For example, Nick Lacey lists the 'repertoire of elements' of a genre as being 'characters, setting, iconography, narrative and style'.[26] But this approach tells only part of the genre story because it is a retrospective activity, the analysis of genre rather than its active creation. Much of the work of genre theorists consists of deciding which films fit into particular genres; plotting the historical trajectory of genres, and identifying the emergence of new or hybrid genres. In reality the question of genre occupies a much more complex – and arguably more interesting – territory because it deals with 'live' issues that had a direct bearing on how films were made, the budgets they were assigned, which studio and crew made them, how they were exhibited, the way audience expectations were set, and whether they were fulfilled. Genre should thus be more than a taxonomic consideration and should include factors that lie outside the frame of the camera. Rick Altman offers a valuable indication of the breadth of the genre concept when he identifies its four key roles: as blueprint, a formula which 'patterns industry production'; as structure, which provides a framework for individual films; as label, influencing the way distributors and exhibitors market the film; and as contract, 'the viewing position required... of its audience'.[27]

Often the 'label' (marketing) and 'contract' (reception) elements – essentially the commercial parts of the process – are overlooked in favour of the aesthetic. Thomas Schatz argues that, unlike literature, 'film genres are not organised or discovered by analysts but are the result of the material conditions of commercial filmmaking itself, whereby popular stories are varied and repeated as long as they satisfy audience demand'.[28] His remarks draw attention to what happens when genres are determined retrospectively on the grounds of aesthetics alone: only those films deemed to be aesthetically worthy tend to be used to formulate notions of genre, whereas in fact all commercially made films contribute to its construction and continuance. This selectivity can also result in the hijacking of entire

26 Lacey, 2000, p.133.

27 Altman, 1999, p.14.

28 Schatz, 1989, p.16.

genres to fit specific categories. Thus genres like the 'detective film' have sometimes been analysed only according to the criteria of film noir (a genre invented retrospectively by critics rather than recognised at the time): those that do not fit into this aesthetic category are ignored. Critics like Schatz can then talk about the hardboiled detective film as being one of the 'dominant genres' of Hollywood, barely touching on the vast bulk of studio output, which was more likely – even as late as the 1940s – to consist of the classic detective story containing no visual or narrative elements of the hardboiled.[29] More recently, there has been a move to write about these overlooked 'programmers', but only as exemplars of commercial practice and not as aesthetic products in their own right. For example, Mary Beth Haralovich's 1979 paper analysed the factors that contributed to the Holmes films from Universal being categorised as B-movies, including budget, exhibition pattern and box-office returns. The 'on screen' elements of the films (scripts, sets, costume, lighting, adherence to generic conventions and so on) are referred to only within the context of this argument: thus she argues that the choice of contemporary settings, the 'simple' shooting techniques and the formulaic stories were all budget-driven. In other words, a formulaic story saves money on scriptwriting; and sets and costumes for a contemporary-set film are cheaper than for a period film.[30] Although Haralovich's purpose is to make a specific point about industrial practice, in treating the films as products rolling off a factory-line there is an implicit dismissal of any aesthetic worth. Todd McCarthy and Charles Flynn, who were pioneers in deeming B-movies worthy of discussion (their book on the subject was published in 1975), detect a 'strain of anti-capitalist thinking' running through film criticism which results in a reluctance to give credence to any film whose declared motive is to make money.[31]

Discussion about genre therefore tends to polarise into two extremes. The first is the aesthetic and often ahistorical analysis of a canon of notable films in each genre, an approach that goes hand-in-

29 Schatz, 1989, p.viii. Philippa Gates points to the same type of omission by critics, especially the ignoring of 'the classical detective films that ran concurrently to noir in the 1940s' (Gates, 2006, p.6).

30 Haralovich, 1979, pp.53–7.

31 McCarthy and Flynn, 1975, p.6.

hand with equally selective ideas about which genres merit critical appreciation. These small number of films are analysed and the conclusions extrapolated to represent the whole genre – what Rick Altman, using the language of semiotics, calls the 'semantic' approach.[32] These canons – with the exception of much of film noir – are drawn from A-features. Little consideration is paid to the commercial context of these films. The second extreme is the consideration of the 'genre film' to demonstrate aspects of the commercial workings of the Hollywood studio system or to show, as if in a mirror, its relationship with 'religion, mythology, the social sciences, psychology and anthropology'.[33] Little consideration is paid to the text of these films in terms of aesthetics. The division is therefore clear: art-films are thought to offer an aesthetically rewarding experience and an insight into the mind of the auteur; genre-films have no aesthetic value and are best considered as social artefacts. Along with other classic detective-genre series, the Sherlock Holmes films have largely been grouped into this second category.

There is also some confusion of terminology between 'film genre' (the category or categories to which a film belongs such as 'western' or 'musical') and 'genre film' (a low-budget film which represents a production-line type of studio output). Many, but not all, genre films were B-movies, shown as a second feature in double-bill programmes and which received a fixed rental fee instead of a share of the box-office.[34] The 'genre film' (of which the whole Holmes series is an example), when it has been noticed by the critics, receives the same sort of treatment as anything outside the realm of literary fiction does in the field of literary criticism: Steve Neale notes that genre fiction is considered 'formulaic, stereotypical, artistically anonymous, and therefore artistically worthless'.[35] This preconceived notion of

---

32 Altman, 1999, pp.6–7. In my view, a 'syntactic' stance, the consideration of as many films as possible, still seems to be rare. It may be an uncomfortable one for academics to embrace because the presence of an 'author' has been largely effaced in the genre-film: hundreds of years of approaching literature and art from the perspective of the 'maker' is a legacy that is hard to shake off.

33 Kaminsky, 1985, p.3.

34 Taves points out that the products of a studio's B units could sometimes become unexpected critical and popular successes and be boosted to the top of the bill – this happened with the 1930s Charlie Chan films from Twentieth Century-Fox (in Balio, 1993, p.315).

35 Neale, 2000, p.21.

worthlessness colours the way modern critics view genre films from the classical Hollywood period, but does not necessarily reflect the way these films were produced, marketed and received at the time of release – the artistic standards of production, for example, often exceeding what was required; and influential critics (such as Bosley Crowther in the *New York Times*) giving the same amount of review coverage to the fifth or sixth instalment of the Holmes series as to a prestige picture from a major studio.[36]

Perhaps it is easy for modern-day critics to dismiss or elide genre films because, in the main, they emanated from B-movie units in the second-tier studios such as Universal, which boasted few big stars or well-known directors; or they came from the 'poverty row' studios such as Monogram and Republic. When critics have retrospectively 'discovered' particular genre films that they feel warrant rehabilitation, it is often because of the dominance of auteur ideology. In other words, if a director is felt to transcend the restrictions of the genre and stamp his own authorship on a film, his whole oeuvre will then be lifted out of its place in genre-film history and placed in a special category as part of an established canon.[37] In this way, it will then receive aesthetic analysis from genre theorists – but will probably lose out in terms of its relationship to commercial studio practices. Although Roy William Neill, director of eleven films in the Holmes series from Universal, has been the subject of sporadic praise from reviewers and critics, particularly for his pacing and lighting, he has not yet attracted sufficient attention to warrant his being 'lifted out' in this way, despite his films pushing at the boundaries of the classic detective genre.

SETTING AUDIENCE EXPECTATIONS

The process of labelling, named by Altman as one of the four key stages in the genre process, is a way of communicating information about the film to two main audiences – the trade, who will exhibit

---

36 The films' literary origins, however tenuous a link these became, may have been a factor: Jancovich notes that 'if they were B-productions, they were at pains to present themselves as culturally significant events that maintained a strong connection with literary heritage and tradition' (Jancovich, 2005, p.37).

37 This has happened with, for example, Edgar Ulmer's 1945 film *Detour* which, as James Naremore points out, was made very cheaply and poorly reviewed at the time but was then rehabilitated at the onset of film noir studies (Naremore, 1998, p.144).

the film, and the public, who will pay to see it. Successful marketing by the studios lies in the ability to create the right expectations: this is achieved through multiple media including advertising, posters, local promotional campaigns, press coverage and theatrical trailers, all of which will offer guidance on the film's genre. In this way, exhibitors can predict likely box-office takings and the public can choose with some accuracy which films to see.[38]

A single 'label' for a particular film may have existed behind the scenes of production, but in marketing terms, studios preferred to hedge their bets. In order to appeal to the widest audience, films were given broad designators: whereas in the 1920s most films were categorised as melodrama, multiple descriptors were common by the 1940s, such as 'comedy melodrama, juvenile comedy, or comedy-fantasy'.[39] None of the detective films, including the Holmes series, were labelled as detective in advertisements or posters, a point that Mark Jancovich, in his analysis of the marketing of the series, has noted. The reason for this, he explains, is that 'at least as many people would define a… detective film as a "won't see" as would view [it] as a "must see"'.[40] Thus films either used multiple labels or simply relied on the name of the protagonist to indicate genre. This might appear in the title, such as *Boston Blackie's Rendezvous* (1945) or *Charlie Chan's Murder Cruise* (1940), or – if the title offered no clue – on the poster. Thus in films where Sherlock Holmes' name is not present in the title, such as *Terror by Night* (1946), it still appears on the poster. Citing the literary source, such as by inserting the copy line 'based on characters created by Arthur Conan Doyle', or setting up a tagline, such as 'the master-minds tackle the master crimes', were other ways of implicitly signalling genre, as was the choice of image and typography used.

---

38 In the classic Hollywood period, this scenario was complicated by the inclusion of B-movies on programmes – these B-movies were subject to the same range of labelling activities as for A-movies, but the impact of the message on the audiences was slightly different. For the exhibitor, there was an incentive to maximise publicity because B-movies were hired at a flat rate (so the more people came to see the film, the more money the exhibitor made). For the public, B-movies involved a certain amount of inertia because movie-going decisions were more usually dependent on the A-film that was showing.

39 Altman, 1999, p.19.

40 Jancovich, 2005, p.35.

Less ambiguous indications of genre were available to potential exhibitors and audiences through press coverage: film reviews in trade publications such as *Motion Picture Herald* and *To-day's Cinema* gave each film an unequivocal label, and reviews in consumer media such as the *New York Times* used terms like detective, whodunit, and mystery. Pressbooks too, strongly promoted the films as 'sleuthing' and 'detective'.

The task of communicating genre was made easier when films were based on an established character. For example, Holmes was not only a well-known figure from literature, stage and screen, but at the time of the release of the series, was also featuring in a weekly US radio show with the same actors in the roles. The Holmes name alone was enough to indicate the 'classic detective' genre: in fact, the studio could probably have removed the name entirely, and left just the image of a deerstalker and a curved-stem pipe on publicity material, confident that the same message would be conveyed. Labelling for the series capitalised on this 'prior knowledge' but avoided clear-cut genre-allocations. By studying the terminology used to promote the series, it is possible to chart the trajectory of the classic detective genre across a seven-year timeframe, as it begins to come under commercial pressure from allied genres. In the first films, the publicity acknowledges the characters' names, which in the detective genre have always been more important than the names of the stars; references Doyle as the literary source; and offers an implied adherence to whodunit conventions. It then undergoes an evolution, dropping character names from titles and posters, eliminating the literary references and making increasing use of multiple taglines which indicate suspense, thriller or horror genres. This evolution is examined in detail below.

MIXED MESSAGES: POSTERS, PRESSBOOKS AND PRESS RECEPTION

By analysing the studio-produced posters for the Holmes series, examining wording, typography, images, layout and colour, it can be seen how genre expectations were set for audiences and how, through subtle changes to the posters as the series progressed, expectations were shifted towards the thriller/horror genres, with an added implication of sexually titillating content. By setting these posters into context with the pressbooks issued by the studios, and the generic classifications made by trade and consumer press reviewers, a growing disparity emerges in terms of the messages conveyed.[41] The analysis is divided into the four main phases which characterise the trajectory of the series: the Victorian-setting films from Twentieth Century-Fox; the overtly modern, war-themed films immediately following the switch to Universal; the Gothic ambiance of the mid-series; and the rise of the female villain in the latter years.[42] In each phase, representative material from key films has been analysed: in terms of posters and advertisements, exhibitors would of course have been offered numerous variations. The benefits of such an analysis have been demonstrated by Klinger in her book *Melodrama and Meaning* on the discourses that surrounded the Douglas Sirk films. She points out that factors such as reviews and industry promotions are not just 'out there', existing in a separate space from the film; they produce 'interpretive frames' that directly influence the way the public views the film.[43] The use of pressbooks and of press reviews to provide these 'interpretive frames' seems to be growing (Sarah Street, for example, uses them to establish how British films were presented for US consumption) though too often they are examined in isolation from the film itself and thus the symbiotic nature of the film/discourse relationship is lost.[44] Klinger attributes historians' previous reluctance to engage with film reviews as attributable to an attitude that deemed them 'pieces of failed criticism' rather than valuable examples of the social discourse that surrounded films. Their value for reception studies lies, she argues, 'in their mobilisation of terms that attempt to define how a film will be perceived in the culture at large' and that is precisely how they are employed in the following analysis.[45]

Jancovich, in his article 'The Meaning of Mystery', identified the multiple tags which Universal used to promote the Holmes series

---

41 Newspaper reviewers were independent but were undoubtedly influenced by studio publicity material.

42 For purposes of comparison, representative US posters have been chosen. Posters for different markets, such as Latin America or Europe, often used different artwork, though the conclusions reached in this analysis could equally be applied to these foreign markets, as the publicity followed a similar genre trajectory. I have also been careful to use, wherever possible, the colour posters issued by the studios rather than the artwork provided to exhibitors in the pressbook which was principally for press advertising purposes.

43 Klinger, 1994, p.xvi.

44 Street, 2002, p.2.

45 Klinger, 1994, p.69.

and cautioned that terms like 'thriller' or 'suspense' carried different connotations for 1940s audiences than they do today.[46] My analysis of the publicity material builds on Jancovich's work but broadens the scope to include the two Twentieth Century-Fox films and a wider range of expectation-setting elements such as press reviews, theatrical trailers and the opening credit sequence – all of which carried messages about genre. In addition to what was 'denoted', in terms of images, typography, wording or layout, it is also important to examine was 'connoted' by these elements. These connotations relied on the repeated use of particular devices so that both the device and its 'meaning' became embedded in audiences' minds: viewed negatively, they may be said to have drawn on clichés, but their positive attribute is that they were a 'shorthand' and succinct way of delivering information. Thus a night-time scene conveyed mystery or danger; city fog indicated London; a gothic-looking house on a hill signified haunting or horror; 'dripping' letters presumed murder; and the use of the colour red indicated horror or danger.

The first phase of publicity was for the two A-features from Twentieth Century-Fox, *The Hound of the Baskervilles* and *The Adventures of Sherlock Holmes*. Posters for both films show Holmes in deerstalker cap and Inverness, thus using 'signs' readily recognisable from previous cinema, stage or literary representations of the character. Both show a night-time scene, an accepted indicator of suspense or mystery. In the *Hound* poster *(see Fig. 6)*, which uses Sir Arthur Conan Doyle's name above the title to reinforce the film's literary origins, menace is indicated by the fearful expressions on the faces of Beryl Stapleton (Wendy Barrie) and Sir Henry Baskerville (Richard Greene). Across the poster march the footprints of the hound in red – a colour with horror connotations – while the darkened moor looms in the background. There are no taglines present to elucidate genre and this is possibly because the book, which had sold millions of copies and was still in print, would mean the title was a familiar one. Among the press advertisements for the film, however, are some which 'sell' the plot and therefore the genre in a more overt way, some with as many as five different taglines, including 'living horror prowling ghostly moor' and 'fascinating, spine-tingling, suspense-taut'. It is possible that these advertisements, in carrying so much more genre information,

---

46 Jancovich, 2005, pp.34–45.

FIGURE 6 Arthur Conan Doyle's name is used above the title in this poster for *The Hound of the Baskervilles* to reinforce the film's literary origins.

were intended to be placed in media where awareness of the Doyle novel was low, but where Sherlock Holmes – who appears on the advertisements in traditional costume – was still a familiar figure.[47] Another explanation might be that the studio sought to use multiple taglines to counter any impression that Holmes might be considered dull, old-fashioned or 'yesterday's man'.

In generic terms, US and UK press reviewers classified it as a detective story, murder story;[48] mystery-chiller, thriller-mystery;[49] and crime entertainment.[50] Pressbook copy advises exhibitors to 'play to

---

47 The US pressbook for *Hound* emphasises that Holmes had been on the stage in every major city and that the audiences for the weekly radio show exceeded four million.

48 *New York Times*, 25 March 1939, p.19.

49 *Variety*, 29 March 1939, p.14.

50 *Kinematograph Weekly*, 20 April 1939, p.25.

the chill-and-thrill angle that is so popular with movie fans today' and a certain amount of shock-value is also encouraged: throughout the pressbook and on advertisements, there is repeated reference to the dialogue-line 'Watson... the needle!' Almost all US and UK press reviews mention the novel and the pressbook plays up the literary connection, mentioning the publication of a special tie-in edition of the book featuring a still from the film on its dust-jacket.

By the time *Adventures* was released, the character of Holmes was obviously considered sufficient to 'sell' the film and for the first – and only – time Rathbone appears alone on the poster in a full-length shot: all the posters for subsequent films in the series will depict head-and-shoulders or just a disembodied head. This is an action pose *(see Fig. 7)*, with a traditionally clad Holmes crouched on the windowsill of a castle-like building with iron-bar windows – revealed in the film to be the Tower of London – pointing a gun at an unseen assailant. The pose, together with sinister shadow cast on the wall behind him, is a clear genre indicator of suspense. Rathbone's name now heads the cast-list and is joined

FIGURE 7 The treatment for the poster for *The Adventures of Sherlock Holmes*, showing Holmes alone, is reminiscent of those for the 1920s films.

for the first time by that of Nigel Bruce. The style of the poster, out of step with the rest of the series, harks back to the Holmes films of the 1920s. In posters for *Sherlock Holmes* (1922), *The Sign of Four* (1924) and *The Return of Sherlock Holmes* (1929), all of which emanated from different studios, Holmes is shown alone and is identified through the use of familiar iconography (deerstalker, magnifying glass and pipe). In *Sherlock Holmes*, as in *Adventures*, he is shown as a man of action, facing an invisible enemy who holds him at gunpoint. *To-day's Cinema*, a UK trade paper, picked up on the action theme, saying that *Adventures* portrayed Holmes as a do-er 'rather than the Doyle dreamer and incisive reasoner'.[51] The paper called the film a detective melodrama, with mystery, thrill and sensation. *Variety* avoided categorising the film but acknowledged that it would appeal to 'mystery devotees'.[52]

With the change of production company to Universal for the rest of the series, the posters took on a consistent style which gave Basil Rathbone and Nigel Bruce equal prominence and which elevated the female support, initially to suggest Holmes shielding a vulnerable woman from danger, and subsequently to indicate the power of the sexualised female villain as a threat to Holmes' supremacy. Both types of portrayal have thriller-genre connotations.

The first group of films from Universal were war-themed with overtly contemporary settings: *Sherlock Holmes and the Voice of Terror*, *Sherlock Holmes and the Secret Weapon*, and *Sherlock Holmes in Washington*. In marketing terms, all three have the benefit of the detective's name in the title for easy genre identification, and all three posters feature above-the-title depictions of Holmes and Watson. The protagonists look out at an unseen assailant, Holmes with resolute expression, Watson with trepidation, while heavy shadows behind them lend thriller/suspense connotations. These posters also feature a consistent graphic element: an illustration in modernist style of a key scene from the film, giving a clear indication that the setting is contemporary.[53] For *Voice of Terror*, the illustration is the fight between the Nazi agents

51 *To-day's Cinema*, 20 December 1939, p.10.

52 *Variety*, 6 September 1939, p.14.

53 The illustration style derives from art deco, but also from its subsequent popularisation in 'American streamline', an aesthetic that emphasised modernity, speed, and an affiliation with the 'machine'.

FIGURE 8 Modernist illustrations, such as this one for *Sherlock Holmes and the Voice of Terror*, dominate the posters for the war-themed films.

FIGURE 9 The Nazi villains in their sharp suits and wide-brimmed hats have the appearance of American gangsters in this poster for *Sherlock Holmes and the Secret Weapon*.

(looking like American gangsters with their suits and wide-brimmed hats) and Kitty's gang of East End criminals; for *Secret Weapon* it is the shootout at the waterfront; and for *Washington* it is a plane passing over the White House *(see Figs 8, 9 and 10)*. All these action shots are unambiguous indicators both of genre and modernity, as indeed (with

FIGURE 10 Unambiguous indicators of genre and modernity in the illustration of the plane flying over the White House in the poster for *Sherlock Holmes in Washington*.

the exception of *Washington*) are the titles themselves with their use of the words 'terror', 'death' and 'weapon'. The pressbooks are equally unambiguous: *Voice of Terror*, for example, is called a sleuth/detective thriller and set in the context not just of the Doyle stories but of film genre too, speculating that its release 'may well inaugurate a new cycle of timely detective thrillers'. The updating of Holmes, indicated strongly on the poster in terms of dress, hair and illustration style, is also emphasised in the pressbook, which headlines one of its suggested editorials: 'Saboteurs outwitted by modern Sherlock Holmes' and another as 'Master sleuth returns in streamlined thriller'. Similarly, the pressbook for *Secret Weapon* describes it as a 'streamlined tale' and a 'modernised classic' that is a 'thrill-drama'.

Advertising also gave prominence to the updating. An advertisement for *Voice of Terror* in the trade journal *Daily Film Renter* reads: 'Holmes leaps from his historic reputation to the front-page headlines and excitement of to-day', thus neatly combining modern-day relevance with his Victorian origins, and emphasising action rather than deductive reasoning.[54] His literary heritage was clearly something the studio thought worth promoting and for *Washington* they gained special permission to use Doyle's name in publicity, even though the screenplay was an original story and not based on his work.[55]

Although these films were B-movies on a tight budget, this did not mean the studio paid only minimal attention to publicity: double-page colour advertisements in the trade press were common, and the studio was always looking out for possible book tie-ins, links to the radio series, or other topical events. Terry DeLapp of Universal, reporting on a discussion he had with Denis Conan Doyle, was excited by the suggestion that Denis 'could work out a big thing in Washington for a preview or premier' of *Washington*, including 'a very flossy shindig with the showing of the picture and might even drag in the President in some way'. Denis suggested that a recently found unpublished manuscript by his father might stimulate interest, or perhaps a magazine article on spiritualism, relating the contact Denis had had with his father since death.[56] Studio promotion of these three films was accurately mirrored in the way the consumer and trade

---

54 *Daily Film Renter*, 3 October 1943, unpaginated.
55 Ward letter to Denis Conan Doyle, 22 September 1942.
56 Report by DeLapp, 10 January 1942.

press classified them. Reviewers in the US consumer press called them mysteries, spy movies;[57] sleuth films and detective melodrama.[58] In the trade press, they were described as thrillers, espionage dramas, detective tales, whodunits;[59] melodramas, mystery-dramas, detecting stories, suspense and action films;[60] and detective-melodrama and murder-mysteries.[61]

The series entered a new phase with the release of *Sherlock Holmes Faces Death*: no longer do the films have such a definable contemporary setting, and the iconography and narrative become those of a Gothic horror film. The posters for *Sherlock Holmes Faces Death*, *The Scarlet Claw* and *The House of Fear* reflect this shift in emphasis.

The poster for *The Scarlet Claw*, for example, *(see Fig. 11)* is a striking black and red design with the claw of a giant beast dominating the space and trapping the hapless characters in its grip (with the exception of Holmes and Watson, whose pictures appear out of range of the claw, thus indicating their infallibility). The genre indicated by the claw is horror, but the illustration, which is unambiguously of an animal's foot with bared claws, is misleading, the 'scarlet claw' turning out to be merely a garden tool wielded by a madman. There is no indication of when the action is set. As with all the entries in the series so far, the words 'detective', 'sleuth', 'whodunit' and 'mystery' do not appear on the poster, but do form a prominent part of pressbook editorial. In just one page, the word 'detective' is mentioned seven times, and 'sleuth' – or 'super-sleuth' – four times. The material does also include mentions of the film as a thriller, chiller and mystery, but these descriptions are given within the context of the detective genre. Other elements reinforce this, such as the description of Holmes as a 'mastermind' who uses deduction to solve the mystery. Critics were unconvinced by the horror aspirations of the poster, calling the film a 'mystery yarn'[62] and a

---

57 *New York Times*, 19 September 1942, p.9 and 5 January 1943, p.15.

58 *Variety*, 9 September 1942, p.14, 30 December 1942, p.23 and 31 March 1943, p.8.

59 *Kinematograph Weekly*, 15 October 1942, p.35 and 21 October 1943, p.21.

60 *Motion Picture Herald*, 12 September 1942, p.897 and 3 April 1943, p.72.

61 *To-day's Cinema*, 16 October 1942, p.12, 4 December 1942, unpaginated, and 15 October 1943, p.22.

62 *New York Times*, 19 May 1944, p.12.

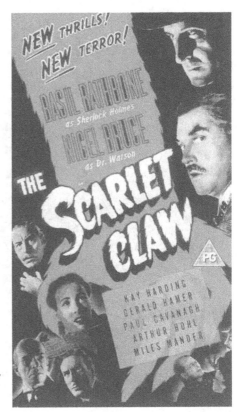

FIGURE 11

The illustration for *The Scarlet Claw* hints at the supernatural, but this is not borne out by the narrative.

'thriller', but 'nothing to harm the youngsters'.[63] They generally shied away from further categorisation and instead catalogued the film's inclusion of 'grisly murders and suspects, fog-shrouded marshes and deserted houses'.[64] The same sentiments appear in the *New York Herald Tribune*[65] and in the *New York Times*.[66] In other words, the film was seen by critics largely as a genre pastiche rather than a genuine horror film. It should be noted that by this point in the series, the name 'Sherlock Holmes' no longer formed part of the title – it had been

---

63 Kinematograph Weekly, 17 August 1944, p.20.

64 *Variety*, 24 May 1944, p.10.

65 *New York Herald Tribune*, 20 May 1944, unpaginated.

66 *New York Times*, 19 May 1944, p.12.

FIGURE 12 Gothic iconography for *The House of Fear*, including the guttering candles and 'haunted house' illustration, suggest that the film is set in the past.

dropped on the release of *Spider Woman*.[67] Another change was that all posters now included a tagline indicating genre: on *The Scarlet Claw*, this was 'new thrills! new terror!'

If the dropping of the 'Sherlock Holmes' name implied a downgrading in the importance of the characters by the studio, then *The House of Fear (see Fig. 12)* marked another such step, with Rathbone and Bruce's names appearing below the title in the poster, a place they would occupy for the rest of the series. Genre indicators are strong, with a picture of Holmes holding a guttering candle; an illustration of a gothic house in the background, and a tagline which reads 'horror stalking its halls!' The poster is dark blue, indicating night. The connotations are thus of a country-house thriller/horror – and of

---

67 This did not happen with other detective film series, such as Charlie Chan. In Sweden and Finland, 'Sherlock Holmes' was retained as part of the title throughout the series; and in the UK *House of Fear* and *Dressed to Kill* retained the Holmes name.

something set in the past. Critics felt the publicity tallied with the product itself, mentioning it as a mystery/sleuthing drama/thriller, with *To-day's Cinema* drawing attention to the 'intelligent deduction' involved, thus placing it squarely in the classic detective genre.[68] The critics pointed to the 'mechanical' nature of the narrative, implying that the film was simply going through the motions of genre adherence and ceasing to engage either with reality or with audience emotions.[69] *Kinematograph Weekly* was alone in relishing the film, as well as drawing attention to the keen sense of humour it displayed, categorising it as a 'murder mystery comedy drama', the first time that the term 'comedy' had been used, despite frequent mention in reviews of Nigel Bruce's comic interpretation of Dr Watson.[70] Shorter reviews might have meant that the press were getting weary of the series, but the studio publicity machine was just as active in promoting the later films as it had been at the beginning: right through to the last film, there were double-page trade-press advertisements and comprehensive pressbooks. Rathbone's star persona as Holmes, despite having seemingly been downgraded on the posters, was further exploited through endorsement advertising: a US magazine advertisement for Stratford Pens featuring Rathbone refers to his forthcoming appearance in *The House of Fear*.[71] Interestingly, in the photograph he is shown with all Holmes' traditional Victorian accoutrements – pipe, magnifying glass and deerstalker hat – the latter, of course, not having appeared in the films since 1939 but clearly thought of as necessary iconography to identify the detective.[72] Universal had originally offered Stratford Pens' advertising agency some stills from the series, chosen by Rathbone himself, but the agency rejected them, asking Harry Ormiston, Universal's manager of exploitation, for 'the old Sherlock Holmes get-up': in other words, it was only the 'Victorian' Holmes that they wanted. Rathbone posed for new shots.[73]

---

68 *To-day's Cinema*, 25 May 1945, p.64.

69 *Motion Picture Herald*, 24 March 1945, p.2,374; *New York Times*, 17 March 1945, p.17; *New York Herald Tribune*, 17 March 1945, unpaginated.

70 *Kinematograph Weekly*, 31 May 1945, p.20B.

71 Stratford Pens advertisement, 15 January 1945, sheet torn from unnamed magazine.

72 A similar illustration was used for Rathbone's endorsement of Booth's House of Lords Gin, and though he appears as himself in a Chesterfield cigarettes advertisement (a tie-in with *Dressed to Kill*), a magnifying glass hovers just over his right shoulder.

73 Cable from Leon to Ormiston at Universal, 25 August 1944.

FIGURE 13 The poster for *Spider Woman* includes horror connotations in the typography and the implication, in the arrangement of the woman's arms and legs within the web, of a woman–spider hybrid.

As the names and figures of Holmes and Watson began to recede in importance on the posters, a new element emerged to challenge them: the dangerous female. The poster for *Spider Woman (see Fig. 13)*, for example, still has depictions of Holmes and Watson above the title, but almost everything else has changed. The tagline is 'mistress of murder', and its placement – next to a drawing of a scantily clad woman reclining in a giant spider's web – carries connotations not just of murder/suspense, but also of sexual titillation, something unsubstantiated by the narrative.[74] Sheri Chinen Biesen, in her book about noir cinema during World War Two, points out that 'studio promotion narratives capitalised on suggesting more than censors would visually allow on screen' and it is true that advertising was subject to less stringent restrictions than the film itself.[75] That *Spider*

---

74 This pose of the 'spider woman' does not occur anywhere in the film itself.

75 Biesen, 2005, p.135.

Woman is a horror film is indicated in three ways: through the title itself; the typeface, which uses jagged-edged, hand-drawn lettering reminiscent of that used on the *Hound* poster; and through the illustration which, in its tangle of arms and legs within the web, implies a woman–spider hybrid. The press spotted the change in marketing approach straight away, with G.E. Blackford in the *New York Journal-American* commenting on the removal of Sherlock Holmes from the billing 'because they thought the Spider Woman would better attract the thrill trade'.[76] While the film itself certainly had horror elements, press reviews still tagged it as a mystery chiller-diller,[77] murder/mystery/melodrama[78] and thriller[79] – the same descriptors as they had used for earlier films in the cycle. Clearly the film itself offered a rather different viewing experience than the marketing would suggest. Indeed, Bosley Crowther told his readers that it was 'no use getting all excited… for this luridly titled picture is nothing more than a new turn with Sherlock Holmes'.[80]

The 'mastermind' tag made its first (and last) appearance on a poster for *The Pearl of Death (see Fig. 14)* which is notable for being the first in the series to drop all direct reference to Holmes and Watson. Instead, a tagline reads: 'the master minds tackle the master crimes'. This is interesting because the tagline makes clear this is a crime picture, which has not been stated in the series before, and that its solution lies in deduction/intellectual reasoning. It is strange that so specific a genre category should be promoted just as the decision was taken to drop the Holmes name. Perhaps the studio felt that, by now, Rathbone and Bruce were so closely identified with the characters that their names and faces were enough for audience recognition, or they felt the appeal of the classic-detective tale was waning and that a different marketing approach was needed. Although the film features a female villain, it is the Creeper who is given prominence on the poster, with a spookily lit, disembodied head. The layout of this poster, the number of taglines replete with exclamation marks, and the use of a cartoon-like drawing of the pearl itself – rays of light issuing

76 *New York Journal-American*, 15 January 1944, unpaginated.

77 *New York Journal-American*, 15 January 1944, unpaginated.

78 *To-day's Cinema*, 14 January 1944, p.22.

79 *Monthly Film Bulletin*, January 1944, p.6.

80 *New York Times*, 15 January 1944, p.11.

FIGURE 14

A pulp-fiction approach to promotion for
The Pearl of Death with multiple taglines,
the disembodied head of the Creeper, and
the cartoonish illustrations of the pearl itself.

from it in carefully drawn lines – display similarities to pulp-fiction
illustration. The approach also signals the film's appeal to an important
B-movie audience – juveniles. This audience was addressed in one of
the promotional advice-sheets for exhibitors, which suggested
cinemas construct a strong box, secured with a padlock, and place it
in the lobby a week before the film was shown. Customers would be
dared to look through a peephole at the pearl of death ('at their own
risk') – a still of the Creeper lit with a green spotlight. Despite the
lack of the Holmes name on the posters, the pressbook urged
exhibitors to use the name heavily in promotion, in particular with
book-store and radio-show tie-ups. The emphasis on detection in the
tagline was clearly felt by the critics to be borne out by the narrative
and the film was described as elegant detection,[81] a detective
melodrama with plausible detective sleuthing,[82] and a 'gumshoe
epic'.[83]

The posters for *The Woman in Green* and *Dressed to Kill* reveal the
growing influence, on the way the series was marketed, of the thriller

---

81 *New York World Telegram*, 25 August 1944, unpaginated.

82 *To-day's Cinema*, 18 October 1944, p.17.

83 *New York Times*, 26 August 1944, p.15.

genre, in the sense of its definition by Martin Rubin as a genre that embroils the detective in the unfolding of the narrative and puts him in moral danger.[84] Although critics and studio publicity had used the term 'thriller' liberally throughout the series, the label rarely was a close fit with the films themselves – and these two films are no exception. What the posters showed was no different from their predecessors: what had changed were the connotations. Taking their lead from *Spider Woman*, women dominate these posters, appearing at the top (the usual place for illustrations of Holmes and Watson) and relegating the two protagonists to a below-the-title position for the first time. This repositioning means that instead of looking down on the action from a position of authority, detachment and omniscience, Holmes and Watson look up to the deadly female, subservient, seemingly in her power – and, thus, embroiled. Subtle changes of expression on their faces from earlier posters reinforce the power-shift.

On one of the posters for *The Woman in Green*, *(see Fig. 15)* Holmes' face wears a slight smile: this, plus the positioning of the tagline 'temptress of pleasure or mistress of murder?' imply a sexual involvement between detective and female protagonist, a familiar enough scenario in the hardboiled detective genre by this time (1945), but one that sets false expectations in the asexual world of Sherlock Holmes. *The Terror by Night* poster *(see Fig. 16)* changes Holmes' expression to an apprehensive one and pins him and Watson into the bottom corner, while the top is dominated by the disembodied face of Vivian Vedder (Renée Godfrey) gleaming in green. On the poster for Dressed to Kill *(see Fig. 17)*, the power balance is much the same, with the poster dominated by the figure of Hilda Courtney (Patricia Morison) in white fur cape and exotic dress, brandishing a revolver and confining Holmes and Watson to a subservient position. One version of the poster bears a strapline across the top: 'queen of a crime cult', the word 'cult' offering a suggestion of deviance, as does the other tagline 'danger in her icy heart', the implication being that this is an abnormal heart for a woman.

The publicity ideas mooted in the pressbook for *The Woman in Green* still include radio-show tie-ups, and joint promotions with pipe shops, but also feature a 'hypnotic' display box for the cinema lobby

---

84   Rubin, 1999, p.194.

FIGURES 15 & 16 In *Terror by Night* and *The Woman in Green*, sexual innuendo is introduced and women begin to assume the dominant position on the posters, eventually pinning Holmes and Watson into the bottom corner.

FIGURE 17

Glamour and deadliness: a powerful combination in the poster for *Dressed to Kill*.

using a still of Hillary Brooke as Lydia Marlowe (catchline: 'from her lips – poison!'); and a suggestion for a mystery woman-in-green lookalike to walk around the town.[85] But this change in marketing stance only goes so far: once the pressbook editorial material is examined, the notion of female dominance disappears. *The Woman in Green* pressbook, for example, features little material about Hillary Brooke, but instead reiterates the usual mix of stories about Rathbone and Bruce, with many mentions of Holmes, Watson, Conan Doyle, detectives/sleuths, deduction, crime and mystery – the appeal is therefore directly to fans of classic detective films. 'Thriller' connotations, in Rubin's sense, are absent.

---

85 The 'hypnotic' display was to consist of a box inside which special photographs of Rathbone and Brooke (which emphasised their eyes) would be placed. A green spotlight would give an unearthly glow and a metronome, with a small lit bulb at its pendulum tip, would move back and forth in front of Rathbone's eyes to create a hypnotic effect.

Critics labelled this set of films in the same way they had always done (the way in which the pressbooks had always encouraged them to do), with *To-day's Cinema* giving them the same 'detective-melodrama' tag the journal had used since *Adventures*;[86] *Motion Picture Herald* pegging them squarely on detection/suspense,[87] and *Kinematograph Weekly* calling *The Woman in Green* a 'comedy-crime-melodrama',[88] the same category it had given *House of Fear*.

In terms of posters and press advertisements, therefore, there arose a promotional disjuncture which sought to minimise the 'Sherlock Holmes' angle while emphasising horror, thrills and sex. This emphasis outpaced the evolution in the films themselves, which were always careful to keep one foot in the classic detective genre even while they strayed across generic borders. This tie to the classic detective genre was arguably essential if Holmes was to remain recognisable as 'the old Holmes'. Posters, however, are designed to attract a potential audience and the wider the generic appeal made, the more likely the film is to draw in new viewers. Emphasising particular elements might appeal to different sectors such as juveniles (as cited above in the promotion for the *The Pearl of Death*), women (in the introduction of glamorous female adversaries, or romantic subplots) and young men (in the emphasis on thrills or horror rather than deduction).

It is worth noting, however, that other classic detective series spanning the same timeframe did not undergo a similar change in marketing. Charlie Chan offers an interesting comparison: like Holmes, the Chan character was adopted early by cinema, with a particularly successful run by Twentieth Century-Fox beginning in the early 1930s, starring first Warner Oland and then Sidney Toler. These were A-features, and their titles which included *Charlie Chan in London* (1934), *Charlie Chan in Paris* (1935), *Charlie Chan in Egypt* (1935) and *Charlie Chan in Shanghai* (1935), indicated the exotic locations as well as the substantial budgets. In 1940 Fox dropped the series, which was picked up by B-movie specialist Monogram. It then ran for thirteen releases through to 1948 and, although the titles still

---

86   *To-Day's Cinema*, 18 July 1945, p.10 and 23 April 1946, p.17.
87   *Motion Picture Herald*, 23 June 1945, p.2,510 and 25 May 1946, p.3,007.
88   *Kinematograph Weekly*, 19 July 1945, p.27.

had an exotic ring (such as *The Jade Mask* and *The Scarlet Clue*, both from 1945), they were all set economically in an unspecified US city. The series thus parallels the Holmes series in a number of respects: there is the same downgrading from A- to B-feature together with a change of studio, a similar number of films, a contemporary setting, the use of a well-established character, and a broadly comparable production timeframe spanning the war years. However, the posters for the Chan films are much more consistent than those for the Holmes releases: the 'Charlie Chan' name appears above the title throughout, whether it forms part of the title or not, and remains in the same typeface; after the switch to Monogram, the actor's name appears and remains above-title; there are no taglines or slogans on any of the posters; the picture of the Charlie Chan character is never relegated to the bottom of the poster; and at no point is a villain pictured larger than, or dominating, Chan. The majority of the posters illustrate a scene from the film and although Chan is pictured once with a female star (Virginia Dale in the 1948 film *Docks of New Orleans*), his role as protector rather than lover is clearly indicated. Many of the posters hint at otherness (images include, for example, an oriental cat, a cobra, a bug-eyed statue, and numerous black/Chinese characters) but – with the exception of the poster for *Black Magic* (1944), which includes a skeleton and a crystal ball – there are no allusions to the horror genre. In this sense, the posters accurately reflect the films themselves, which remained in the classic detective genre, even if they did include a few 'chills' along the way. The consistent style of the posters, however, demonstrates a continuing faith in the pulling-power of the Chan 'brand', a faith that clearly was not mirrored at Universal. It is difficult to assess just how strategic a decision it was to change the way the Holmes series was marketed: the fact that the pressbooks showed no such evolution does suggest that marketing efforts were not strongly coordinated, and that different departments worked with separate briefs. Right until the end of the series, the pressbooks were promoting precisely the same messages about the Holmes films as they had at the start: it was only the posters that had shifted in generic tone. Perhaps the pressbooks, as a written medium, and as the source for journalists' reviews, remained more rooted in the literary origins of the series; or perhaps it was simply that the poster artists were more accustomed to designing material for Universal's horror releases.

The studio had two more ways to set expectations for films, both of which were received once the audience was in the cinema: theatrical trailers, which were designed to make audiences decide to come back and see a particular film, and the credits sequence of the film itself, which acted as a final genre setter.

THEATRICAL TRAILERS: STYLISTIC BRANDING

Each theatrical trailer for films in the series was 75 seconds long, and followed broadly the same format; used the same music (with the exception of the trailer for *Dressed to Kill*); the same 'wipes' between scenes and the same typographic style for its on-screen 'slogans'.[89] There was, therefore, a strong sense of stylistic branding, emphasised by the repeated use of particular words in the slogans. These words helped identify the films as being of the detective genre (murder, baffle, mystery, sleuth), with a good dose of suspense (thrill, breathless), and some horror (grim, weird, stalk, fear, brute horror, blood). These keywords, designed to evoke an emotion, were differentiated typographically from the rest of the slogan, being written in a script font and carrying an initial capital for emphasis (e.g. 'Murder'). It is hard, from the limited number of trailers available, to identify a trend whereby particular elements, such as horror, begin to take precedence. The only noticeable shift occurred in the trailer for the final film, *Dressed to Kill*, which used the presence of a woman villain to sell the film as racy. 'This is a man-trap!' declared the first slogan, over a shot of the villainess in furs luring a victim to his death. Another slogan described it as 'the case that was too hot for Scotland Yard' implying titillating content which was not borne out by the film.

Each trailer followed the same pattern, opening with a series of slogans which appeared over mute footage from the film ('danger at every turn', 'in the balance hangs the fate of a nation!'); then the introduction of ambient sound over a series of crisply edited scenes. These usually included three key moments of Holmes' investigation of the crime: demonstrating his powers of deduction; saving Watson from danger; and being threatened or attacked himself. With the exception of the last two trailers in the series, all concluded with 'star' shots of Rathbone and Bruce before closing on the name of the film itself.

---

89 The analysis is based on trailers for the latter films in the series, earlier trailers not being traceable.

The trailers often referred to the films as baffling mysteries but this was undercut by their revealing of key plot points, which indicates that by the time the audience saw the whole film, they had forgotten the trailer; or that 'howdunit' was actually more interesting to the viewer than 'whodunit'. In the trailer for *Terror by Night*, for example, Holmes and Watson are shown discovering the secret compartment in the empty coffin, something not revealed until 36 minutes into the film; and in *Voice of Terror*, the trailer discloses the identity of the spy.[90]

In common with the posters, the trailers gradually downgraded the prominence of the characters' names. In the trailer for *Voice of Terror*, Rathbone and Bruce were billed as appearing 'in the roles they made famous on the radio network'; by *The Pearl of Death*, there was no cross-reference to the radio shows, but the stars' names still appeared alongside those of their characters; and later in the series, there was no on-screen mention of Holmes or Watson at all, with the slogans referring only to 'fiction's greatest sleuths'.

OPENING CREDITS: A MOOD SETTER

The final task of genre setting fell to the opening credit sequence. Once the Holmes series moved to Universal, it featured a standard sequence used in all 12 films. This sequence was a crucial mood setter for audiences who may already have sat through a variety of material in the same programme that had no generic affinities with what they were about to see – the Holmes films, for example, were frequently shown on the same bill as an Abbott and Costello comedy, and every programme would have included a newsreel and cartoon.

The credit sequence, which uses dramatic, stirring music (the same as for the trailers), begins with swirling fog that fills the screen. We see two pairs of feet, strongly backlit so that the shadows of their feet and legs fall to the foreground. The camera then pans up, past their overcoats, to their faces. Both men wear hats and one smokes a pipe. They stand side by side, looking almost to camera with serious

---

90 Similar plot revelations were made in the pressbooks: a 'review' article in the pressbook for *Sherlock Holmes in Washington*, for example, gives away the fact that the enemy operative has the document all the time 'but is unaware of his good luck'. Bearing in mind that in the days of continuous showings, 50 percent of every audience at every film showing entered the cinema when the film was half over (according to Zanuck of Twentieth Century-Fox, quoted in Behlmer, 1993, p.171), giving away the plot in the trailer or press coverage was perhaps a minor issue.

expressions. When the lines 'Basil Rathbone as Sherlock Holmes' and 'Nigel Bruce as Dr Watson' appear, the men begin to walk slowly across the screen, the camera moving with them, showing not the men themselves but just their shadows on the paved ground. The sequence is full of generic connotations which regular cinema-goers would have assimilated without difficulty. Mystery and suspense is indicated through the dramatic tone of the music, the use of shadows, the fact that the scene takes place at night, and the way the camera initially shows only the feet of the two protagonists. These techniques are used repeatedly in the films themselves, thus tying audience expectation tightly to the product itself. Fog is another indicator of mystery, but is also a powerful metonym for Victorian London and therefore evokes a mythology of the city that would have already been familiar to the audience. There is no indication however, other than the absence of a deerstalker, that the action is taking place in the present day.

When the two men on screen are identified as Holmes and Watson, the genre is clearly one of crime as well as mystery and suspense. It also implies a very particular kind of crime film: the viewer's accrued knowledge of Holmes, from previous films, literature or other media, would offer the promise that this crime may test Holmes' powers, but that he will triumph in the end. Even without prior knowledge of the detective, merely the determined and confident expressions on the faces of the two men, and the old-fashioned, 'establishment' values implied by Watson's wing collar, would offer reassurance that right will triumph. As the two men walk off through the dark, it is clear that this is their 'territory' and the implication is that they are patrolling the streets on our behalf to keep them safe.

Overall then, the opening credits sequence tells the audience that the genre is mystery, suspense or crime; that the protagonists are Holmes and Watson; the setting is London; the likely outcome is that the mystery will be solved; and that the timeframe, though ambiguous, is Victorian. Only the latter is not borne out by the films themselves, though the characters bring with them into the modern era so many aspects of the Victorian that the opening credits could not be said to set false expectations. Retaining the same opening sequence for each of the 12 Universal films may have been driven by budgetary considerations, but the outcome was to reinforce the Holmes 'brand' and its associated values, to give consistency to the series, and to promote unchanging messages about the genre to which these films belonged.

CHAPTER TWO

'WATSON – THE NEEDLE!'

THE APPEAL OF THE VICTORIAN

'They were the footprints, Mr Holmes, of a gigantic hound'
The Hound of the Baskervilles

This chapter examines the first two films in the Holmes series: *The Hound of the Baskervilles* and *The Adventures of Sherlock Holmes* from Twentieth Century-Fox, discussing the films themselves in conjunction with their contemporary discourse. It therefore looks at key aspects of the mise-en-scène together with the films' production history, how they were promoted through studio pressbooks, and their reception by the trade and consumer press. In this way, it demonstrates how the figure of Holmes was portrayed – as a man of action rather than as a cerebral genius – the production decisions that led to this portrayal, and the accrued layers of meaning that contributed to his representation. It offers evidence to show that, despite the fact that these films placed the detective in his 'true' late-Victorian period and that the first was adapted from the Doyle novel, they cannot be considered as a control group against which to judge the subsequent 'modernised' films because generic and temporal tensions are evident throughout. There are, for example, mixed-genre messages, not least that *Hound* was commonly perceived as a horror story even if not, as Julian Johnson of Fox termed it, 'a straight horror story of the Universal brand... but a sort of horror-mystery';[1] and the sets, costumes and character behaviour all reveal 1930s attitudes to, and interpretations of, the nineteenth century.[2]

---

1   Zanuck story conference on *Hound* treatment, 24 October 1938. Christopher Frayling has characterised Doyle's story of the hound as being in the horror genre, but acknowledges that, in the light of the 'real-life horrors' of World War One, such Victorian tales were 'not only tame, but curiously reassuring' (Frayling, 1996, p.215).

2   It could be argued, of course, that this is always the case with Hollywood period films: the temporal tensions in these Holmes films are worthy of detailed examination, however, because of the way the industry was shortly to 'update' the character.

TWENTIETH CENTURY-FOX

In 1939 Twentieth Century-Fox was a new company, formed from the merger four years earlier of Fox Film Corporation and Twentieth Century Pictures; but it had the drive and leadership to put it quickly into third place in the rankings. Fox Film Corporation had been founded in 1915 and built its success on a string of more than 500 theatres, but foundered in the wake of the 1929 Wall Street Crash. It needed a merger to rescue it from receivership: Twentieth Century Pictures recognised the potential, being strong on production but without its own exhibition chain, or such a superlative studio lot as Fox had just constructed at Culver City. Itself formed only in 1933, Twentieth Century Pictures was a partnership between former Warner Brothers' production head Darryl Zanuck (b. 1902) and United Artists' president Joe Schenck.[3] The idea was that Zanuck would make the movies and Schenck would release them through United Artists.

After the merger on 29 May 1935, Zanuck signed up a stable of young stars including Tyrone Power, Henry Fonda, Betty Grable and Shirley Temple, concentrating on biopics and musicals. By 1939 the studio had emerged 'as a leader in popular entertainment that extolled American virtues'.[4] It was also riding on a huge wave of expansion in Hollywood: more than 85 million people were going to the cinema each week and in that one year Hollywood released 600 films.[5] 'It was a year of... the greatest burst of creativity in Hollywood's history' says Berg, with titles including *The Wizard of Oz*, *Gone with the Wind*, *Stagecoach*, *Ninotchka*, *Dark Victory* and *Mr Smith Goes to Washington*.[6] Twentieth Century-Fox had a number of films whose domestic rentals alone brought in more than two million dollars – including *The Rains Came*, *Drums Along the Mohawk*, and *Stanley and Livingstone*. In that sense *The Hound of the Baskervilles* and *The Adventures of Sherlock Holmes* were just two more features in what could be called a glittering year, and it is perhaps not surprising that in the only book-length academic study of the studio (Aubrey Solomon's

---

3   Zanuck had begun at Warners as a writer in the 1920s, working his way up through the ranks to become a story editor and producer.

4   Berg, 1981, p.313.

5   Maltby and Craven, 1995, p.472.

6   Berg, 1981, p.312.

Twentieth Century-Fox: a Corporate and Financial History) they are not even mentioned.[7]

Zanuck was a hands-on production head: he was known as the 'tyrant in charge' according to Solomon, closely involved in scripting, casting, producing and editing.[8] In common with other Hollywood moguls, he appeared to make decisions based on instinct and therefore the apocryphal story that, in a spur-of-the-moment conversation about whether to make a Holmes film, he named Rathbone for the part, is entirely believable. Rathbone (b. 1892) was a veteran of period costume dramas, firstly in his Shakespearean stage career at Stratford-on-Avon and London, and then on screen. Many of his 30-plus films made in the 1930s were period pieces, including *Captain Blood, David Copperfield, A Tale of Two Cities, The Last Days of Pompeii, Anna Karenina* (all 1935), *Romeo and Juliet* (1936), *The Adventures of Robin Hood* (1938) and *The Tower of London* (1939). He was frequently cast as a sophisticated villain, which he cited as one of the reasons he was keen to take up Zanuck's offer to play Holmes – a completely different type of character.[9] He was signed on 25 October 1938 at a fee of 5,000 dollars a week.[10] Though he had no prior association with the detective genre, his lean physique, sharp profile and incisive delivery made him an instantly identifiable Holmes *(see Fig. 18)*[11] and *Kinematograph Weekly* acknowledged that he 'looks and acts the part'.[12] Perhaps the most important quality that Rathbone, and his co-star Nigel Bruce, offered in terms of marketability was that they were perceived as quintessentially British, something that would be repeatedly emphasised by Twentieth Century-Fox. Britishness was the subject of fascination in the US: indeed Bruce (b. 1895) had specialised in portraying bumbling Englishmen

---

7 Solomon gives box-office figures for the largest-grossing films of 1939: it has not been possible to find figures for *Hound or Adventures* either in Twentieth Century-Fox's archives or in the contemporary trade press.

8 Solomon, 1988, p.41.

9 *Hound* pressbook.

10 Twentieth Century-Fox contract, 25 October 1938. He was to receive the same weekly rate for *Adventures*, with a total payment of 35,000 dollars for the film (letter from de Lavigne to Towell of Fox, 12 May 1939).

11 Rathbone's only other detective role was when he once played Philo Vance in the 1930 film *The Bishop Murder Case* to fill a gap in the series when William Powell was absent.

12 *Kinematograph Weekly*, 20 April 1939, p.25.

FIGURE 18 Rathbone's lean physique and sharp profile made him an instantly identifiable Holmes in this early scene from *The Hound of the Baskervilles*.

throughout his film career, and recent roles had included Sir Benjamin Warrenton in *The Charge of the Light Brigade* (1936) and Sir Malcolm Cameron in *Suez* (1938). Pressbook editorials stressed how patriotic both men were, how they always stopped for afternoon tea and how Bruce liked to follow the cricket.[13] Such promotion might be thought of as a studio exaggeration, but seems to have been an accurate reflection of their lifestyle. Both Rathbone and Bruce were prominent members of what Sheridan Morley calls the 'Hollywood Raj', who had arrived during the 1920s and 1930s and who had 'proceeded to establish a colony that was almost a caricature of British life, forming themselves rapidly into polo clubs and cricket teams and [giving] tea parties for each other on Sunday afternoons'.[14]

---

13 The exploitation of this star persona as 'British gentlemen' also crossed over into endorsement advertising. For example, copy accompanying Rathbone's appearance in press advertisements for Booth's House of Lords Gin and for Walker's DeLuxe Bourbon emphasised his gentlemanly and upper-class lifestyle.

14 Morley, 2006, p.5.

In other words, as émigrés they exaggerated the qualities of their Britishness, perhaps out of nostalgia for the life left behind – a life that had already largely vanished in their home country. This aspect makes the colony particularly interesting in the light of the temporal tensions that were to be revealed throughout the Holmes series: it was, metaphorically, frozen in time. Morley says the Hollywood British 'survived in a remarkable historic and geographical limbo, like curators of a stately home suddenly transported... to another continent, complete with furniture and fittings'. It was not, he says, the England of George V that they brought with them, but 'an England of about 1870: the England of Kipling and Queen Victoria'.[15] Morley might well have said, of course, that it was also the England of Sherlock Holmes. In terms of conflation between star and character, it was a perfect fit.

COMMERCIAL CONSIDERATIONS

Although Fox had the Charlie Chan series on their books from 1929 to 1942, detective films were hardly their specialism; nor was the Gothic. Any concerns they may have had about genre, however, would have been overridden by the film's commercial potential. *Hound* was Doyle's best-known story and had been read by 'countless millions'.[16] Solomon points out that studios liked to buy best-selling novels because of their 'built-in title recognition', whereas an original screenplay meant spending on an advertising campaign to raise awareness.[17] *Hound* also offered a number of publicity 'hooks' over and above the central detective story, including the supernatural, a whirlwind romance, an escaped convict, a mysterious Gothic setting, a host of British 'characters' and, of course, the spectacle of the hound itself. All of these made for the type of multiple-label marketing that would enable Fox to attract the widest possible audience. There were other potential spin-offs too: what the pressbook called 'literature's most shocking, spine-chilling mystery story' could be further exploited through special-edition book tie-ins. In the US a 75-cent hardback book from Grosset and Dunlap featured a still from the film

---

15 Morley, 2006, p.5. Interestingly, Morley chooses 1870 as his 'fixed point' rather than the Holmesian '1895' though what is being connoted is essentially the same.

16 *Hound* pressbook.

17 Solomon, 1988, p.95.

on the cover, and in the UK a sixpenny Penguin edition was made available.[18] In addition the studio exploited the close likeness between Rathbone and the Holmes illustrations that had appeared in *Collier's* magazine by offering exhibitors the opportunity to sell reproduction sets of drawings.

Fox was not the only studio to be courting the Doyle estate with a view to producing a *Hound* film. Having successfully secured the rights for 27,000 dollars, W.B. Dorn of Fox wrote to his colleague George Wasson that 'Metro is raising a little bit of hell for our having taken this property from them' and urged all possible speed in working out the legal phases of the deal.[19] Fox had acquired seven-year rights to the property, which meant that no other studio could make a film based on the book until these rights had expired: however, the earlier the project got underway the longer the film could be on release without direct competition. Fox wasted no time: filming started on 27 December 1938 and *Hound* was released by the end of March 1939.[20] There is no information in the public domain about what budget the film was assigned, but making any major picture was fraught financially: even with a million-dollar budget, Fox would only see a profit if the film ran in movie houses for more than 65 weeks.[21] One initial stumbling block was that the Doyle estate had already sold the rights to French and German versions of the story to 12 European countries. This meant Fox would be unable to release the film in those territories and, although France was the only country that concerned them – presumably the most significant in box-office terms – they thought it worth pursuing a solution. By the time of the film's release, in March 1939, they had paid an additional

---

18 *Hound* pressbook.

19 Dorn letter to Wasson, 22 September 1938.

20 Fox shooting schedule dated 17 December 1938 shows 27 December as the first day of filming. The schedule was intense with, for example, one typical half-day's filming covering nine scenes and involving Holmes, Watson, Dr Mortimer, Sir Henry and Clayton, plus extras, hansom cabs, horses, and process/special effects. As the film's release date grew near, A.W. de Weese was prompted to complain to his Fox colleague George Wasson that one day Wendy Barrie had 'reported for makeup at 6.30 in the morning and finished at 10.30 that evening' (de Weese to Wasson, 8 March 1939). Yet the schedule for *Adventures* was to be no less rushed, with scriptwriter William Drake complaining to producer Gene Markey about the extreme pressure he was being put under : 'I'm sure I'd work better if I could get a decent night's sleep sometime' (Drake memo to Markey, 8 June 1939).

21 Solomon, 1988, p.30.

32,500 dollars to acquire the 'worldwide silent, sound, dialogue and talking motion picture rights' – an amount well in excess of what they had given for the original story. [22]

It was not the first time, of course, that *Hound* had been filmed: there had been a number of adaptations, including British films starring Eille Norwood (1920) and Robert Rendel (1932), and at least three German silents: these, together with the novel, meant that the story had become part of a collective popular consciousness. This, however, was the first big-budget Hollywood version and Zanuck anticipated it being 'a most exciting, unusual type of picture'.[23] As well as the appeal of the Sherlock Holmes name, which the pressbook describes as known to 'every man, woman and child', there was a strong cast, the most exploitable of which was not Basil Rathbone as Holmes, but Richard Greene as the 21-year-old romantic lead, Sir Henry Baskerville. This was largely an accident of timing: when the film was released, Greene had just come fifth in a 'king and queen of the movies' poll, despite having been in films for less than a year. That year had built what the pressbook called 'real marquee strength' for Greene and, though the films themselves have not stood the test of time, they were fresh in the minds of audiences. *Four Men and a Prayer*, *Submarine Patrol*, *Kentucky*, and *My Lucky Star* all had a contemporary setting and were released in 1938; and *The Little Princess* was a Shirley Temple vehicle released in 1939 which interestingly – as it immediately preceded *Hound* – had a Victorian setting. It is ironic, therefore, that *Hound* is now best known for launching Basil Rathbone's portrayal of Holmes, which was to have such a powerful influence on subsequent interpretations by other actors.

Acquiring the rights to a literary work was often only the beginning of negotiations with an author or his estate, and although there is no evidence of any stringent conditions imposed on Fox, it was necessary on occasion to reassure Denis Conan Doyle (Arthur Conan Doyle's son) of their intentions. George Wasson of Fox sent a cable to E.P. Kilroe in the New York office asking him to advise Doyle that:

---

22 Metzler letter to de Lavigne, 9 March 1939. Interestingly, *Hound* never did get a theatrical release in Germany: the reasons, according to Michael Ross, are unclear but may well have been the mounting international tensions (Ross, 2003, p.195).

23 Zanuck story conference on treatment, 24 October 1938.

we are planning to use top cast and important director for production. Script... retains all dramatic value of original story and definitely has not been treated in a comedy vein. We are certain we have not burlesqued the story or injured reputation of story or author.... Perhaps Conan Doyle will withdraw objections if you advise present cast Richard Greene, Basil Rathbone, Nigel Bruce, and we are endeavouring to obtain Anita Louise. Also director to be William A. Seiter.[24]

The cause of the problem was a misunderstanding over a clause in Fox's contract allowing for the inclusion of musical numbers in the film. Though it is interesting to speculate what kind of musical numbers might have been chosen for a Victorian 'chiller-thriller' and what effect this might have had on the finished production (adding yet another genre label to its multiple 'tags'), the truth was that this clause – described by Fox in the same telegram as 'innocuous' – was a standard inclusion in all film contracts. What difference the choice of William A. Seiter as director would have made is also worthy of speculation as Seiter (b. 1890) was a specialist in light comedy, with a number of Laurel and Hardy and Shirley Temple films to his credit. The reason he was named by the studio for *Hound* was probably because he had just completed *The Little Princess* with Richard Greene. In the event, the studio assigned Sidney Lanfield as director and Ernest Pascal as screenwriter to the project. Lanfield (b. 1898) also had a background in comedy: he had begun as a gag writer before directing light comedies including *Cheer Up and Smile* (1930), *Hat Check Girl* (1932) and *Sing Baby Sing* (1936), so a Victorian melodrama hardly fitted into his career pattern any better than it would have done into Seiter's. British-born Pascal (b. 1896) seemed a more logical choice. An experienced screenwriter, he began writing stories for silent film in 1923 and had an established track record in period dramas: his most recent script was *Kidnapped* in which Nigel Bruce had starred.[25]

Both Lanfield's directing and Pascal's screenplay were singled out for criticism by a number of contemporary reviewers, with *Variety* finding the direction 'deliberate and steady' and C.A. Lejeune

24 Wasson letter to Kilroe, 3 November 1938.
25 Pascal was also president of the Screen Writers' Guild.

commenting on the 'omissions and commissions of the Hollywood script' that was generally 'accurate in the big things but completely alien in the significant details'.[26] Setting out to create a literary adaptation was, of course, bound to attract comment from those concerned with faithfulness to the original, no matter how successfully Twentieth Century-Fox handled the genre questions. Wherever Holmes films are concerned, 'a strange literalism sets in', says Paul Leggett. 'The slightest changes… are instantly attacked as some sort of heretical tampering'.[27] This view is borne out by contemporary critical comment: Campbell Dixon in the *Daily Telegraph*, for example, reserved much of his disapproval for the 'less than scholarly' nature of the adaptation, especially in terms of alterations to characters, querying why Frankland was portrayed as Scottish and why Dr Mortimer, slender in the novel, was played by a thick-set man.[28] Lejeune felt that Rathbone's performance had suffered because he had been inhibited by the need to 'do right' by such a famous character: 'it might well curb an actor's flight of fancy', she said, 'to know that every line he uttered, and worse, every line he didn't utter, was a household word in twenty-four languages, including Tamil, Talugu and Urdu, and Pitman's shorthand'.[29] The more critical voices were generally those of the consumer press – publications aimed at fans – with the trade press (magazines aimed at exhibitors) open in their praise, possibly because they were keen to stress the promotional possibilities for cinema operators. In the UK, *Kinematograph Weekly* said that the film's strength lay in its fidelity to the original in 'atmosphere, detail, characterisation and period' and in the US, *Motion Picture Herald* wrote that 'the film is so precisely the book, in substance, tone and spirit, that the obvious exploitation cue is for a straight campaign addressed to the millions who have read it and such other millions as may not have got around to reading it but have meant to some time and now, under the circumstances, needn't'.[30]

It was, perhaps, the early choice of Rathbone and Bruce that influenced the casting of British actors for all the main roles including

26 *Variety*, 29 March 1939, p.14; quoted in Lejeune, 1991, p.156.

27 Leggett, 1979, p.26.

28 *Daily Telegraph*, 10 July 1939.

29 Lejeune, 1991, p.155.

30 *Kinematograph Weekly*, 20 April 1939, p.25; *Motion Picture Herald*, 1 April 1939, p.28.

Richard Greene (Sir Henry Baskerville), Wendy Barrie (Beryl Stapleton), Morton Lowry (Jack Stapleton), Mary Gordon (Mrs Hudson) and Lionel Atwill (Dr Mortimer).[31] The only exception was American John Carradine as the sinister butler Barryman. Even this short list indicates just how many expatriate stars were living and working in Hollywood.[32] With an all-British cast, a British story, and studio sets representing London and Dartmoor, *Hound* was arguably a British film with American financing, yet the picture it paints of Victorian Britain embodies a nostalgia for a time and place not its own – an outsider's view. It is tempting to think of this being an American view, but (bearing in mind Morley's comments cited earlier about the émigrés living a 'Victorian' life in Hollywood) it could equally be a British nostalgia for a vanishing world.

The same could be said of *Adventures*: when Graham Greene, for example, saw the film, he welcomed the Victorian setting, taking pleasure in 'that London of cobbles, fast cabs and gaslamps: lost London'. What Greene had missed even more were the values associated with this 'lost London'. Referring to Professor Moriarty, he said: 'It is a pleasure to meet a well-mannered criminal again: we have suffered so long from "Siddown you"... and [now] we are in 1894 and people say "please be seated"'.[33]

This is an interesting comment not just because of the yearning for a gentler age, but in its implied reference to 1930s gangster films with their American, often lower class, protagonists; a pointed contrast to the British detective genre where the protagonist – if not exactly a gentleman – at least behaved like one. Greene's view, however, was quickly to become an isolated one as the detective genre shifted into

31 Wendy Barrie was a late substitute: Anita Louise, an American actress who had starred with Richard Greene in *The Little Princess*, was initially contracted to play Beryl Stapleton, but her contract was cancelled just over two weeks after filming had begun (Fox contract cancellation dated 13 January 1939). Ralph Forbes was first-choice as Stapleton but ended up as Sir Hugo in the brief mediaeval flashback (handwritten note on Ernest Pascal story treatment dated 22 October 1938).

32 British actors (including Boris Karloff, George Zucco, George Sanders, Clive Brook and Colin Clive) had been a mainstay of the horror and detective genres in Hollywood throughout the 1930s. Despite the size of the British colony, it was not easy for Hollywood to import actors: when Fox Film Corp first hired Nigel Bruce in 1933, he had to provide two testimonial letters and demonstrate that he had no police record. The arrangements for this single contract involved some 30 or more letters back and forth making the arrangements (Twentieth Century-Fox archives box FXLR 1028).

33 *Spectator*, 8 March 1940, unpaginated.

hardboiled territory, and took on an American persona. Period drama, often with a Gothic setting, continued to interest Hollywood throughout the 1940s, but it is indicative of the trends in the detective genre that *Adventures* was to be the last film for 20 years that set Holmes in his 'proper' time.[34]

Fox had kept *Adventures* on its books for some years, having bought the rights to William Gillette's stageplay, *Sherlock Holmes*, in 1932. As with *Hound*, the scriptwriter and director assigned to the project were not detective or period-drama specialists: Edwin Blum (b. 1906), who wrote the story outline and first continuity script, had only four years' screenwriting experience working mainly on Tarzan features, and William Drake (b. 1899), who rewrote the script, was at the end of his short screenwriting career. The director, Alfred Werker (b. 1896), had been with the old Fox Film Company since 1928 when he was brought in to re-shoot an Erich von Stroheim film, *Hello Sister*. His Hollywood output is widely viewed as completely unremarkable: media historian Hal Erickson in the authoritative online *allmovie.com* says Werker was 'either a competent craftsman or talented hack' depending on which of his colleagues you consulted, and finds it inexplicable that he managed to produce a film as fine as *Adventures*.[35] Once more, the cast was almost exclusively British, with George Zucco (Professor Moriarty), Henry Stephenson (Sir Ronald Ramsgate) and Ida Lupino (Ann Brandon). Twentieth Century-Fox took pains to ensure that those small details which had been seized on in *Hound*, such as Lejeune's complaint that 'bullfrogs croak on the tor – and they don't call it a tor, either', would not similarly betray the American origins of *Adventures*.[36] Technical adviser Captain Harold Lloyd-Morris sent a stream of memos pointing out, among other things, the correct name of the high court, the hierarchy at the Tower of London, the wearing of plain-clothes by CID officers, the faux pas implicit in Holmes sending a 'lady' downstairs to have a cup of tea with the servant, and the fact that even in 1890 the Tower had electric light.[37] Not all his comments were incorporated. In spite of Zanuck's instruction not to have fog in scenes 'except where it is absolutely

---

34 It was also, of course, only the second film to set him in the Victorian period.

35 Erickson, www.allmovie.com, 30 April 2008.

36 *Variety*, 29 March 1939, p.14; quoted in Lejeune, 1991, p.156.

37 Lloyd-Morris memos to unnamed Fox employee, 1, 2, 5, 13 and 15 June 1939.

necessary', *Monthly Film Bulletin* felt there was altogether too much of it for an English May evening.[38] No-one criticised the direction (*Variety* felt it was nicely paced and clear cut) and although the plot was said to be over-complex in its intertwining of two stories, the clues were 'not made too absurd or too obvious for mystery devotees'.[39] If there was any absurdity, it was relished by some critics: Frank Nugent in the *New York Times* suggested that if audiences derided 'the notion of a club-footed gaucho roaming London's parks at night' or wondered why 'with the "jools" within his grasp, [Moriarty] should prefer to go chasing Holmes over the embrasures of the Tower of London', then the film was likely to leave them lukewarm, 'but as for me, I haven't stopped quaking yet'.[40]

GENERIC CONVENTIONS AND TENSIONS

The narrative trajectories of both films bear all the hallmarks of the 'classic detective genre'. In *Hound*, Holmes is asked to protect the life of Sir Henry Baskerville, who has inherited the family home on Dartmoor following the mysterious death of his uncle. Locals are convinced that the Baskerville family is under an ancient curse and that a legendary hound haunts the moor. Claiming prior business in London, Holmes despatches Watson to guard Sir Henry, but secretly follows them to Dartmoor and conducts his own investigation. Sir Henry is narrowly saved from the jaws of the hound and Holmes unmasks a neighbour, Jack Stapleton, as the killer bent on claiming what he believes to be his true inheritance. In *Adventures*, the two old adversaries – Holmes and Moriarty – both vow to defeat the other once and for all: Moriarty by committing the crime of the century, and Holmes by catching him and seeing him hang. Moriarty sets up a 'distraction case' – a bizarre murder and a threat to a young woman's life – that he knows will intrigue Holmes. Meanwhile, Holmes becomes careless about the more mundane case already entrusted to him by the Tower of London: the safe arrival of a valuable jewel. The theft of this, and much of the rest of the Crown Jewels, is the 'crime of the century' that Moriarty is planning and Holmes only realises it

---

38 Zanuck conference report on temporary script, 31 May 1939; *Monthly Film Bulletin*, January 1940, v7, p.17.

39 *Variety*, 6 September 1939, p.14.

40 *New York Times*, 2 September 1939, p.20.

in the nick of time. He prevents the theft and, in a final struggle, Moriarty falls to his death from the Tower.

As befits the genre, both films are set in England and in the past; *Hound* in 1889 and *Adventures* in 1894.[41] They involve the unmasking of a 'rogue individual' whose removal ensures reinstatement of the status quo, and whose crimes strike at the heart of 'polite society'. The detective remains emotionally detached, treating the cases as a professional puzzle to be solved. In some aspects, however, the narratives deviate from the norms of the genre and thus from Todorov's model. For example, there is no division between the 'action' section of the film in which the murder takes place, and the 'passive' investigation, because the other characters' lives remain under threat, keeping the narrative dynamic. This threat also extends to Holmes, embroiling him physically in the investigation. In addition these films are not really 'whodunits': in *Adventures* the criminal is known to the audience from the early scenes, and in *Hound* so many millions had read the book that the identity of the murderer could hardly have been a surprise: the suspense comes from whether Holmes will be swift enough in his deductions to prevent further crimes. That said, neither film allows the audience to see Holmes' deductive reasoning at work – in *Hound*, he alludes to having done some unexplained research which revealed the existence of an illegitimate heir to Baskerville Hall, and in *Adventures* he is constantly outwitted by Moriarty and only realises the master plan at the last moment. His displays of brilliance are reserved for trivial matters, such as analysing Dr Mortimer's stick. It is as a man of action that Holmes is portrayed, rather than as a cerebral genius as, perhaps, befits the medium: film as opposed to literature.[42]

The studio played up the horror and gothic-mystery crossover aspects of the films. Exhibitors were encouraged by the *Hound* pressbook to offer 'hair relaxer' in the men's washroom because the

---

41 Neither Doyle's story of *Hound*, nor Gillette's play *Sherlock Holmes* on which *Adventures* is loosely based, give a precise indication of date.

42 Zanuck was worried when he read the first continuity draft that 'instead of always being one step ahead of his opponents, they appear to get several steps ahead of [Holmes] at times....We need a great twist where Holmes, in a clever and ingenious way, makes the discovery that Moriarty has manufactured the one crime as a smoke screen for the other and that Moriarty is still in the Tower'. The rewrite, however, did not seem to redress the balance (Zanuck story conference report dated 19 April 1939).

audience's hair would stand on end when they saw the beast, and to provide women with shawls to counter the 'spine-tingling' effect of the tale (all of which rather negates Zanuck's stated wish that 'hokum' be avoided at all costs).[43] *Adventures* was sold with a four-part advertising and poster slogan that read: 'the strange case of the chinchilla fetish... the Traitor's Gate... the fiendish instrument that strangles, crushes, vanishes... the albatross of doom!' This slogan incorporates multiple generic indicators including exoticism ('chinchilla', 'fiendish'), mystery ('strange case', 'vanishes'), horror ('strangles', 'crushes'), superstition ('albatross of doom'), sexuality ('fetish') and even history ('traitor's gate'): only the title of the film itself suggests a traditional detective tale. The first draft continuity script by Edwin Blum had few of these ingredients and was much more of what Zanuck called a 'British cops and robbers' tale with plenty of Limehouse atmosphere in Chinese joss houses and absinthe bars, plus a fog-bound riverboat chase. Zanuck asked for all this to be dropped in order to insert some of the 'deep mystery and tense suspense' that was so successful in *Hound*.[44]

Another way in which the narratives deviate from Todorov's model is that the events take place in 'real time': this allows for dramatic openings that set up the mystery and introduce the key suspects, without using flashback, as happens in the Doyle stories and the radio series.[45] These opening scenes merit a close reading because they reveal many of the genre tensions of the films and offer a representative insight into the portrayal of the Victorian.

In *Hound*, the genre of gothic mystery is indicated right at the beginning, with Germanic lettering for the credits, swirling music, and an on-screen date of 1889.[46] Doyle's novel was also set around

---

43 Zanuck story conference on first draft continuity, 1 December 1938.

44 Blum, first draft continuity script, 3 April 1939; Zanuck first draft continuing script conference report, 19 April 1939.

45 This technique would be used through the subsequent Holmes films from Universal.

46 Unusually, there is music only through the credit sequence and in the early scenes. Its absence from suspenseful scenes on the moor foregrounds the sound – or absence of sound – very effectively. Nollen admired the restraint in the night-time scenes, but felt the lack of a score makes 'the stately pacing of some scenes and the intrusive nature of the romantic subplot even more conspicuous' (Nollen, 1996, p.129). David Stuart Davies, on the audio commentary to the DVD, wondered whether the speed at which the film was made (less than three months between the start of filming and its release) prevented a full score being composed (and says they 'learned their lesson' by the time of *Adventures*).

this time: he wrote it in 1901 but the action takes place somewhere in the second half of the 1880s, the only indicator being the '1884' inscription on Dr Mortimer's stick. Two points are notable here: firstly that 1889 was just one year after the Jack the Ripper murders, interest in which was still consuming the country, but they are never referred to in the film: in other words, the date is fairly arbitrary and merely indicates 'the past'.[47] Secondly it is worth remembering that when the film received its first theatrical release, 1889 was only 50 years before: it is all too easy now, as a viewer in the twenty-first century, to think of it as the 'historic' past rather than the time-equivalent of the 1950s, though in the case of *Hound*, the Victorian era may well have seemed a world away because of the changes wrought by World War One.

Over a slow pan across the moor in the semi-dark, with an ancient gloomy house in the background, a caption establishes the location: 'in all England, there is no district more dismal than that vast expanse of primitive wasteland, the moors of Dartmoor in Devonshire', the word 'primitive' immediately suggesting a link between the landscape and the nature of its inhabitants, as well as a link to the past.[48] A compact opening scene, full of action and atmosphere, sets out the mystery in the form of the death of Sir Charles Baskerville. Over the sound of a hound baying, we see a man running through the night-time fog on the moor, towards the camera. As he enters the gate of the Hall, he passes a dead, blasted tree in the foreground of the shot – a symbol, perhaps, of the blighted fate of the Baskerville family. Clutching at his heart, he falls dead on his face. There are then two dramatic cuts – first to a wild-eyed, unkempt man stealing a watch from the corpse; then to a woman emerging from the Hall's doorway, lantern in hand, and screaming. We know from this opening exactly when and where the action is set, and that this will be a 'chiller' because of the presence of fog, a gloomy house, the moor, death, suspicious characters and eerie howling. We do not necessarily know that this will be a detective film, something gleaned from extra-textual clues such as knowledge of the book or of Sherlock Holmes,

---

47   At the time, a local newspaper had called on Arthur Conan Doyle (then living in Portsmouth) to use his 'psychic powers' to solve the murders (Lycett, 2007, p.142).

48   Marianna Torgovnick describes the primitive as an exotic world which is also a familiar one – often a world from which we (urban dwellers) have been, or feel exiled, and which is peopled by the 'libidinous, irrational, violent and dangerous'. This primitive world is both 'eternally past and eternally present' (Torgovnick, 1990, pp.8, 187 and 188).

as there are no character names on the opening credits. The second scene, which gathers the key players at the coroner's court, introduces the idea that the 'heart failure' to which Sir Charles' death is officially attributed, is a cover up – and that if it is murder, the suspects are probably all in this room. It is not until the third scene that the audience sees Holmes and Watson, these well-known characters placing the story firmly into the detective genre, something that is reinforced by the fact that the entire scene comprises a dialogue demonstrating the powers of deduction.

This is a much more dramatic opening than that of Doyle's story, which begins in conventional 'classic detective' style in Baker Street with the deduction scene. Dr Mortimer arrives at 221B, claims his stick and asks Holmes to investigate the death of Sir Charles – an event that has already occurred and is therefore not 'seen' directly by the reader. This contrasts with the film, in which audiences hear the baying and see Sir Charles' death 'with their own eyes', in seemingly unmediated fashion.

The film was originally to have a similarly 'static' opening. The script marked 'final' and dated 8 December (filming began on 27 December) begins with a conversation between Dr Mortimer and his wife at their Dartmoor home. This tells the viewer that Sir Charles has died, that young Sir Henry is due to inherit Baskerville Hall, and that the Mortimers fear the legend of the hound. This scene, not used at all in the finished film, was to be followed by the 'stick' deduction scene at Baker Street. At no point in the screenplay was it planned to show Sir Charles' death, to reveal the escaped convict so early on, or to have a scene in the coroner's court which would introduce the key characters and cast suspicion on them all.[49] These changes made the film more dramatic, added action and avoided too neat a 'fit' into one particular genre – it is interesting to speculate whether they were made at the suggestion of Zanuck or director Sidney Lanfield. The only conference reports in the surviving production files relate to the story treatment and the first draft continuity: at treatment stage, Julian Johnson of Fox had suggested that because the film was to be a 'horror-mystery', it should begin not in London but 'on the evil spot in the dead of night'. Zanuck was unimpressed with this idea and asked for a scene instead that would show Dr Mortimer relating the

49   Pascal script, 8 December 1938.

hound legend to his wife – in effect, the scene that appears in Pascal's 'final' script.[50] Whether he subsequently changed his mind is not known. 'Interference' from anyone else working on the project would be unlikely, as Zanuck supervised every aspect of film production, down to the finest detail. As Solomon explained:

> every script would be written with Zanuck's strict instructions regarding pacing, character and action…. Producers and directors would be advised regarding the casting of these scripts. Once a film was in production, Zanuck would catch the daily screenings of rushes with the directors. Upon completion of production, he would supervise the cutting of every film.[51]

Two key characters are missing, of course, from the scene in the coroner's court – Sherlock Holmes and Sir Henry – and the delay before they appear on screen builds anticipation and indicates their star status. Holmes is introduced first, with a 'teaser' scene that does not immediately reveal him. After an establishing shot of the Houses of Parliament, with Big Ben striking midnight, the camera cuts to a 'Baker Street' sign, and then to a close-up of a report in *The Times* of Sir Charles Baskerville's death. The camera tracks back to reveal Dr Watson seated at a desk, discussing the article with an unseen man. At first we hear only Rathbone's voice, his clipped British tones instantly recognisable, then we see him pacing back and forth in front of the desk, the camera low so that it reveals only his dressing gown, and his hand as he taps tobacco from his pipe into the ashtray. After some moments, the shot changes so that we at last see Holmes' face, the camera looking upwards to Holmes, just as Watson does from his seat at the desk. It is in this scene that they discuss the stick left by their visitor (with Holmes abiding by Zanuck's wish that he be 'a clever, observing fellow, but not one of those guys who draws rabbits out of a hat'), receive Dr Mortimer and hear about the legend of the hound.[52]

In examining the opening sequences of *Adventures*, it becomes apparent that they offer fewer cross-genre indicators. The credits

50 Zanuck story conference on treatment, 24 October 1938.

51 Solomon, 1988, p.26.

52 Zanuck story conference on *Hound* treatment, 24 October 1938.

sequence uses the same music, allowing audiences to view it implicitly as a series, but this time the typography has no Gothic connotations and the credits run over a silhouette of Holmes with deerstalker, pipe and Inverness coat. In the darkness and the swirling fog, he holds a lantern, and turns slowly towards the camera and back. The film therefore receives its Sherlock Holmes imprimatur from the very first – both in the image and in the title itself, thus branding it as a detective film. This is reinforced by the opening shot of a page from a printed manuscript dated 1894 that names Professor Moriarty as 'the very genius of evil'. At the bottom of the page is the writer's signature – Sherlock Holmes. The film thus sets out its stall as being a battle between the two men.

This time there is no delay in introducing the main protagonists onto the screen. The first scene takes place in a courtroom where a trial is concluding: an impassive Moriarty is in the dock awaiting the verdict of the jury. He is found not guilty, a decision which fills the judge with disgust. At that moment, the door bursts open and in storms Holmes, determined to present evidence that will send Moriarty to hang, but he is too late and Moriarty is set free. The scene is short and contains none of the lengthy display of deduction originally envisaged in Blum's script, in which Holmes demonstrates how Moriarty tampered with the Greenwich clock to create an alibi for himself. By this second film Zanuck realised that Holmes' brilliance 'should be a given and [that] a briefer scene would add pace'.[53] He asked for the film to cut immediately to Holmes and Moriarty emerging from the courthouse into the pouring rain and thereby created what is a highly effective scene. The two men share a cab, and the camera keeps them in midshot as they sit side by side on their way to Baker Street. The rain obscures any outside view so the audience's gaze is focused on the claustrophobic interior and the men's faces. The fact that these sworn enemies politely share a cab distinguishes them as gentlemen: they are clearly not from the 'siddown you' class. The delicious verbal fencing that constitutes the dialogue not only sets up the plot, which is that Moriarty plans to pull off the crime of the century right under Holmes' nose, but demonstrates that to both men it is essentially only a game. Holmes' enjoyment of their parrying is evident: 'You've a magnificent brain,

---

53 Zanuck, conference report on first draft continuity script, 19 April 1939.

Moriarty', he says, smiling blandly. 'I admire it... so much, I'd like it pickled in alcohol for the London Medical Society'.[54] Audiences may have experienced a frisson of excitement at the forthcoming battle but, when Moriarty says 'you're the one man in England clever enough to defeat me' – a twist on Dr Mortimer's line from *Hound* – this fear may be tempered by a rather more comforting thought. After all, this is Sherlock Holmes, who is invincible; it is a classic detective tale, so right is sure to prevail; it involves intellectual dexterity, indicating emotional detachment; and it is safely set in a picturesque past.[55]

Adventures remains much more embedded in the classic detective genre than *Hound*, though it has its forays into thriller/chiller territory with the bizarre nature of the killer, a club-footed South American musician; the exotic weapon; and the 'funeral dirge' diegetic music. This adherence to genre works principally because there are no supernatural elements; the romance is not foregrounded as much as in *Hound*, and – with two plots to interweave – there is little scope for genre divergence.

LOCATION: THE RATIONAL CITY VERSUS THE PRIMITIVE COUNTRYSIDE

Throughout both films, the city is portrayed as the home of modernity and Apollonian rationality, and the countryside as the unchanging site of superstition and irrational behaviour. In the city, each deadly threat has a clear origin: in *Hound*, for example, when Sir Henry's life is threatened, it is from an assassin's bullet; but in the countryside, the threat appears to come from an ancient curse. In some instances (as will be discussed below) parts of the city – such as parks and gardens – are 'appropriated' as countryside to allow the irrational to creep closer to its edges. How the studio portrayed and interpreted these spaces sheds light on 1930s ideas of Victorian England.

The pivotal location that audiences with any knowledge of Holmes wanted to see were the rooms at 221B Baker Street, a space expected to contain all the iconic objects familiar to Doyle readers,

---

54 This line was suggested by Zanuck and used word-for-word in the script (Zanuck conference report on first draft continuity script dated 19 April 1939).

55 The term 'picturesque' was coined in the eighteenth century to describe landscape paintings that emphasised a sentimental aesthetic.

FIGURE 19 The graveyard is described in Ernest Pascal's script for *The Hound of the Baskervilles*, but descriptions of Holmes and of 221B Baker Street are notably absent.

such as the Persian slipper full of tobacco, or the jack knife that fixes correspondence to the mantelpiece. Yet in Pascal's script there is no description of the room. Screenplays usually have only pithy, one-line indicators of settings, and these are present for other locations in the film. The graveyard on the moor, for example, is described as ancient and uncared-for: 'most of the tombstones have fallen down; those remaining are crooked and crumbling into decay' *(see Fig. 19)*. The omission of a description of Baker Street, therefore, is intriguing and it is interesting to speculate whether it was because Holmes was so embedded in the public imagination that it would be 'taken as read' that the set-designers would know exactly what was required in the construction of his sitting room. This theory seems to be borne out by the fact that the script equally gives no description of Holmes and Watson themselves, though other characters are briefly summed up: Jack Stapleton, for example, is noted to be 'an intellectual looking young man, pleasant, professorial in speech and manner.'

On-screen, 221B is a representation of the Victorian refracted through ideas of Hollywood interior design. This refraction is apparent in the first scene at Baker Street in *Adventures*. As Billy, the young servant, is sweeping the landing outside Holmes' rooms, there is a ring at the door, and the camera follows Billy's glance over the carved, white-painted banisters, down into the hallway, where Mrs Hudson is opening the double-width front door to admit Watson. The walls of the wide staircase and hall are painted in light colours, with elegant Georgian- or Regency-style panelling, and there is an elaborate multi-branched gasolier hanging from the ceiling. The hallway and stairs are empty apart from an umbrella stand, a circular mirror and a large oil painting *(see Fig. 20)*. Inside Holmes' sitting room – a vast space – the decor is very different from what one might expect from the 'high Victorian' period, even though all the detective's accoutrements are present. The furniture is dark and heavy, and the mantelpiece has a characteristic Victorian fringe, but the space is uncluttered, the walls are the same light-painted panelling as the

FIGURE 20 A grand and gracious staircase to Holmes' rooms, in *The Adventures of Sherlock Holmes.*

hallway, and there are blinds at the windows rather than curtains. This set offers an interesting contrast to that which would be constructed for the Universal films which, although purporting to show Holmes in the 1940s, was to look much more overtly Victorian than the set used by Fox to depict the 1880s. The Fox set for 221B also offers a slightly different perspective on Holmes' character: here he is clearly a gentleman and a fairly well-to-do one. He moves with the times – for example, every book on his shelves looks new, whereas in the Universal films his books are battered and ancient, the implication being that he belongs to the past. The connotation of these gracious, ordered rooms is that London is the home not just of the gentleman, but of rationality. The Georgian or Regency style, a product of the Enlightenment, took its inspiration and motifs from the classical, another age associated with Apollonian rationalism. In the US this architectural style was known as Palladian, Jeffersonian or Grecian: it enjoyed a revival in the 1930s, rendering Holmes' sitting room not only 'period' but fashionable too.[56] The link between the set design and rationality is an explicit one, because the only extended scenes of on-screen deduction take place at 221B, firstly in Holmes' analysis of Dr Mortimer's stick in *Hound*, and then in his first scene in *Adventures*, where he is conducting an experiment to determine which note on the musical scale is intolerable to the housefly.

It might be argued that Twentieth Century-Fox simply made use of the standing sets available on their extensive backlot, and it is true that the majority of the locations used for the two films bear similar traces of Regency design: in *Hound*, the Stapletons' house on Dartmoor is an (unlikely) opulent, double-staircase mansion with classical urns in niches, a huge contrast to the mediaeval architecture of Baskerville Hall; and in *Adventures* Ann Brandon's palatial family home is clearly part of the reconstruction of an entire London square that Fox had built for *Berkeley Square* (1933). Yet these were big-budget A-features for which existing sets could have been extensively customised: the fact that they were not suggests two possible motivations, one concerning historical accuracy and the other

---

56 The term 'Jeffersonian' comes from the name of the US president, Thomas Jefferson, who designed a number of buildings in neo-classical style, influenced by Italian Renaissance architect Andrea Palladio. The style was popular in the US between 1790 and 1830 but enjoyed a revival from 1895 through to the 1930s.

concerning the psychological meanings these sets convey. It is quite probable that neo-classical architecture was chosen simply because both films are about 'the past' rather than a 'specific past', which would accord with Zanuck's view that 'nobody buys tickets to see authenticity; they go to be entertained'.[57]

A more interesting theory is suggested by Juan Antonio Ramirez's contention that buildings in the neo-Classical style were felt by Hollywood to be too austere to 'serve as environmental vehicles for romance, passion, and other emotionalised qualities' on which commercially successful films depended.[58] Yet they were chosen here and it is tempting to suggest that they were intended to give the viewer some insight into the personalities of the people who inhabit them: Holmes, who is a 'calculating machine' rather than a human being, and Stapleton, the intellectual who will kill to achieve his ambitions. Stapleton's house not only stores his scientific collection of local flora and fauna but appears to act as a bastion against the intrusion of the irrational, illustrated in the scene of the seance which is brought to an abrupt conclusion by the baying of the hound outside. However, the analogy can only be applied so far, because there are aspects that do not fit this pattern: Ann Brandon, for example, is a romantic, even melodramatic, character and the classical opulence of her family home probably points only to wealth rather than to austerity of emotion.

Both films present particular locations as 'unchanging' by separating them from the contemporary either geographically or psychologically. In *Hound*, it is Dartmoor and Baskerville Hall that are coded as timeless, primitive places because of their isolation and the way they are haunted by the memory of evil deeds. In *Adventures* it is the Tower of London, cut off by fog from the rest of the city and bound to a centuries-old set of traditions, as well as the gardens where Lloyd Brandon and his sister Ann are pursued by the murderer.

The opening title card of *Hound* warned that Dartmoor was a 'primitive' place, and its role is made even more explicit in the script, in which there is a note that reads: 'it must be borne in mind that the moor with its foreboding atmosphere is the real "heavy" in our story. Every effort should be made in the shooting... to emphasise the

---

57 Behlmer, 1993, p.217.
58 Ramirez, 2004, p.170.

FIGURE 21 Filming *The Hound of the Baskervilles* on the cyclorama sound stage.

eeriness of this strange terrain'.[59] Fox art director Richard Day, chief assistant Hans Peters and a crew of 98 artisans spent seven months constructing a 300 by 200 feet moor on the studio's 'cyclorama' stage *(see Fig. 21)*.[60] The pressbook claims that the studio sent three experts to Dartmoor to gather data and then to decide what would have been different 'in Victorian times'. To emphasise the set's authenticity, the pressbook also relates a story about Richard Greene becoming lost on the 'moor' during filming and having to call out for someone to help him find his way out, a story repeated in many press editorials.

---

59 Pascal final script, p.47. Holmes and Watson, of course, travel from the city to Dartmoor by train: Lynne Kirby argues that, because the train was the 'defining vehicle' of the urban experience, stepping from a train into the countryside is like 'stepping into an altogether other world': the journey can be temporal as well as spatial (Kirby, 1997, p.136).

60 Shooting schedule, 22 December 1938.

Though the story was probably just a publicity stunt, it does help code the moor as a sinister place cut off even from the workaday surroundings of the rest of the studio. Baskerville Hall itself is described in Pascal's script as 'just as it was in 1650': its rooms are lit by candle sconces, ancestral portraits line the walls and the long dining table is overlooked by a vast inglenook fireplace.[61] This enables a credible flashback to the age of Sir Hugo, for a scene in which he and his companions enjoy a roistering evening around the very same table. The fact that the audience 'sees' the events that happened 250 years ago elides the difference between past and present. It is also, of course, instantly recognisable as a typical horror-genre setting, thanks largely to Universal having established the 'creepy old house' look in their 1930s horror films.

In *Adventures*, the Tower of London has similar connotations (partly, perhaps, because it had appeared earlier that year in a Universal historical horror film starring Basil Rathbone and Boris Karloff): here the ancient, battlemented building, seen only at night, recalls childhood tales of royal prisoners, executions and, of course, the crown jewels.[62] In the midst of the modern Victorian city, the Tower's keepers wear an archaic uniform, and keep intruders at bay not by gates, but by a moat and portcullis. The isolation of the Tower in the fog, and its role of protecting England's royal heritage, separates it from the contemporary, as effectively as does the physical isolation of Dartmoor. In addition to using the Tower to evoke a space that stands apart from the modern city, *Adventures* codes the murder of Lloyd Brandon and the attempted murder of his sister Ann in this way, by having them take place not on the streets, but in large London gardens thick with trees and undergrowth. During a prolonged chase sequence, Ann constantly battles with branches that lash against her face, and roots that trip her up, rendering the gardens of the gracious mansion an uncivilised, jungle-like space.

The only locations that seem to show London as an unambiguously nineteenth-century city are the exterior street scenes,

---

61 The vast proportions of Baskerville Hall accord with a Hollywood convention which Ramirez has commented on: although English buildings of this period would have had low ceilings, Hollywood consistently portrayed them as lofty spaces, partly because technical difficulties made representing ceilings difficult, but partly because of the 'desire to reinforce the public's fascination with that "importance" so obviously associated with palatial residences' (Ramirez, 2004, p.84).

62 *The Tower of London*, 1939.

FIGURE 22 Lamplighters, fog and cobbles form the Victorian London of the imagination in *The Adventures of Sherlock Holmes.*

where cobbles, crowded streets, galloping hansom cabs, lamplighters, rain and heavy fog conjure up an 'authentic' feel of the Victorian *(see Fig. 22).* This is, of course, the London of the imagination: the Hollywood art director W.C. Menzies once said that an exact reproduction of a place could be achieved by filming on location, but replacing it with a set in the studio would give 'the impression of the street as it exists in your mind, slightly romanticised, simplified and over-textured'.[63] In postmodern terminology, this 'over-texturing' would be referred to as 'hyperreality': something even more real than the street itself because it connects with the viewer's pre-existing idea of what it should look like. There is surprisingly little of London on screen in *Hound:* in fact there is only one significant exterior scene,

63   Quoted in Ramirez, 2004, p.86.

when Sir Henry leaves 221B and is covertly followed down the street by Holmes and Watson. In *Adventures*, much more is made of the city, and presumably this set is what the pressbook refers to as being 'the largest tarpaulin-covered set without inside supporting poles in the history of the film industry', some 234 feet by 240 feet.[64] The sense of Victorian London is particularly well conveyed in the scene where Holmes, dashing to the Tower to thwart Moriarty's robbery of the Crown Jewels, commandeers a hansom cab and races it through the night-time streets, tilting dangerously on every corner.

COSTUME: BRIDGING THE HISTORICAL GAP

To examine costume for temporal indicators is to negotiate ground as tricky as the Grimpen Mire. Costume drama is, as Pam Cook points out, 'notoriously inauthentic', not necessarily through a cavalier 'Hollywood approach' to history, but simply because 'costume plays a crucial role in the duplicity of the historical film'.[65] In other words, it goes with the territory: if historical drama is to engage emotionally with its audience, it has to bridge the gap between past and present, and costume is a key way of achieving this. The romantic leads in a film are often the subject of this 'bridging' attempt and, while minor characters can be shown as unequivocally period in dress, the principals often wear contemporary fashion that simply makes a gesture towards 'the past'.

With the Holmes films, the balance is slightly different: Holmes and Watson are the main protagonists and, as they personify the Victorian, they need to be shown in identifiably nineteenth-century dress. They do indeed exhibit a strict observance of what constituted 'proper' city and country attire.[66] In the rooms in Baker Street, they wear smoking jackets; in the city streets they wear top hat, wing collar, morning suit, waistcoat and gloves, with Holmes carrying a silver-topped walking cane *(see Fig. 23)*. In the country they wear tweed suits or Norfolk jackets and Holmes dons his Inverness and

---

64 Studio publicity departments were apt to make these claims regularly, as Ramirez points out. The café in *Café Metropole* (1937) was said to be one of the largest interiors ever constructed, and the same was said about the nightclub in *Top of the Town* (1937) (Ramirez, 2004, p.109).

65 Cook, 1996, pp.6 and 75.

66 Many times in subsequent Holmes film adaptations, such as *Murder By Decree* (1979), Holmes would be shown wearing his deerstalker in the city – or even to the opera.

FIGURE 23 Rathbone and Bruce in 'proper' nineteenth-century city wear in *The Adventures of Sherlock Holmes*.

FIGURE 24
Old and new worlds meet in *The Hound of the Baskervilles*, with Sir Henry (Richard Greene) in seemingly contemporary costume representing the rationality of North America and Dr Mortimer (Lionel Atwill) in full Victorian regalia, signifying the Europe of superstition.

deerstalker. In *Adventures*, there is theoretically no reason for the deerstalker, as all the action takes place in the city. But in areas 'coded' as being separated from the city, such as the gardens where Ann Brandon is chased by the murderer, and the Tower of London cut off by the fog, it is significant that Holmes wears his country attire.

Temporal tensions can be clearly seen in the costume of the romantic subplot characters (Sir Henry and Beryl Stapleton in *Hound*, and Ann Brandon and Jerrold Hunter in *Adventures*) who wear an amalgam of period and contemporary costume. The contrast is particularly noticeable in *Hound* when Sir Henry arrives in England by ship and is met on the quayside by Dr Mortimer *(see Fig. 24)*. Sir Henry is described in the script as 'an attractive young Canadian with the freshness of the West about him', a phrase suggestive of the frontier or of someone at the 'cutting-edge'.[67] As he walks down the gangway, Sir Henry disengages himself from a number of young ladies who have evidently enjoyed his company on the voyage. He wears a three-piece suit, tweed check overcoat and a 1930s-looking collar and tie. He carries a trilby-type hat, is clean shaven and has a short-back-and-sides haircut. Dr Mortimer, on the other hand, wears a top hat, morning suit, wing collar with cravat, round-framed eyeglasses and a full beard with curled moustaches. Both the context (the fashionable young women) and Sir Henry's appearance position him as the romantic lead and indicate that he emanates from a more modern world – North America – that will have little truck with ancient superstitions. Dr Mortimer is marked as being from another era: not a single person on the crowded quayside is dressed like him, and only one other person wears a top hat, despite this being conventional city wear in 1889.

A similar contrast is evident between Beryl Stapleton and Mrs Mortimer, the latter clad in overtly Victorian costume with fussy black hats, dark dresses with high ruffled necklines, and jet jewellery, rather reminiscent of later portraits of Queen Victoria. This costume is essential for her credibility as a medium, able to conjure up the spirit of the late Sir Charles Baskerville. Beryl Stapleton's dress, however, is intended to be of interest to contemporary women in the audience who might want to acquire something similar: this is borne out by the pressbook's 'fashion notes' column, which reveals that Wendy Barrie – who played Beryl – achieved her 'wasp waist'

---

67 Pascal final script, p.33.

FIGURE 25 The pressbook for *The Hound of the Baskervilles* features a 'fashion notes' column which reveals how Wendy Barrie (playing Beryl Stapleton) achieved her 'wasp waist'.

through the use of stays. In her first appearance in the film, at the coroner's court, she wears a 1930s version of Victorian costume: a short, fur-collared cape with a large velvet bow, and a matching fur hat set at a rakish angle. A number of shots in the film foreground her costume, in particular the scene where she meets Sir Henry when out riding: as she dismounts, the camera remains behind her, silhouetting her against the moor and thus emphasising that 'wasp waist'. Her clothes are dark and tailored – a belted, velvet-collared jacket with puff sleeves, a white blouse with cravat-like fastening, a long, narrow, dark skirt and a small-brimmed hat *(see Fig. 25)*.

Like Sir Henry, who wears suits which are indistinguishable from 1930s dress, Jerrold Hunter, the romantic interest in *Adventures*, wears a modern-looking three-button suit; and like Beryl Stapleton, the costumes worn by Ann Brandon – though more elaborate than the country outfits of *Hound* because of the city setting – offer an 'idea' of the Victorian.[68] They carry connotations too: when Ann receives

FIGURE 26 Ida Lupino as Ann Brandon in *The Adventures of Sherlock Holmes* wears a Victorian hat, with a fashionable bird ornament, its arrow-like shape marking her out as the next victim.

the threat to her life, she wears an outfit with a fashionable hat, veiled at the back, and topped with a bird, echoing the 'albatross' death-threat drawing but also pointing upwards as if it were an arrow for the murderer, singling out his next victim *(see Fig. 26)*.

---

68 The costumes were clearly intended to be a focus of attraction for women in the audience. Director Alfred Werker expressed concerns as to whether Fox might be criticised in allowing Ann to be seen in a 'stunning evening dress… so soon after her brother's death' but no changes were made (memo Werker to Markey dated 12 June 1939).

Bearing in mind the later development of the series, it is interesting to observe a number of points: that Jack Stapleton, in *Hound*, wears a Norfolk jacket, an Edwardian item that is precisely what Holmes will wear in the 'modernised' 1940s films from Universal; that in both films Mrs Hudson's costume of floor-length skirt, white apron, fob watch, and brooch at her throat, is also precisely what will pass for 1940s costume in the later films; and that Professor Moriarty's dress in *Adventures* is very similar to what he will wear as a Nazi helper in *Secret Weapon*. Holmes, incidentally, also wears the same smoking jacket in *Hound* and *Adventures* as he will wear for the rest of the series, despite a 50-year time gap in the setting of the films.

Both films, although ostensibly portraying the Victorian, convey a number of layers of 'the past' through costume: the quasi-contemporary, in the dress of the romantic-interest characters; the 'true' Victorian, in the dress of Holmes and Watson and the older/country characters; and a vaguer, more folkloric past. In *Hound*, the latter is achieved through the flashback that accompanies Dr Mortimer's tale about the ancestral owner of Baskerville Hall. In this flashback, the costumes of Sir Hugo and his drinking cronies are a Hollywood version of the mediaeval: immaculately white Puritan collars, belted tunics, tall suede boots, and neatly trimmed Van Dyke-type beards *(see Fig. 27)*. The scene works, nevertheless, because the audience is seeing the characters through Dr Mortimer's reading of the document, a device conveyed visually by showing them in vignette, with part of the document remaining visible around the edges of the frame. Not that historical accuracy would necessarily have been Fox's priority, but rather – as Tino Balio argues in discussing the studio system – that the scene conformed to 'commonly accepted norms of authenticity'.[69] A rather less romantic glimpse into an indefinable past is offered in *Adventures* through the figure of the South American murderer, whose costume is a folkloric one of gaucho-style wide-brimmed hat, striped poncho, wide-legged trousers and boots. As a member of the band that plays at the garden party this appearance is one of delightful spectacle, but in the chase scene, it becomes 'otherness', a more frightening concept and one that is emphasised by the camera, never showing him in full shot, but only in glimpses of his moustachioed face, his club-footed boot, and

---

69 Balio, 1993, p.87.

FIGURE 27 A Hollywood version of the mediaeval in the flashback scene from *The Hound of the Baskervilles.*

the deadly bolas strung at his waist. 'Play it for all the eeriness and suspense that you can', instructed Zanuck at a script conference.[70]

MORES: RE-PRESENTING THE PAST

In analysing temporal tensions in the films, it is important to engage not just with elements of the mise-en-scène, but also with the way in which the narrative suggests how people behaved in the period being depicted. Just as costume can be a conscious amalgam of the contemporary and the past, it would be dangerous to assume that, simply because a film is set in the nineteenth century, it offers an insight into Victorian behaviour and mores. In attempting to portray the past it is more likely, as Antonia Lant argues, to invite audiences to make comparisons with their own present.[71] Cook goes even

70   Behlmer, 1995, p.25.
71   Lant, 1991, p.5.

further in terms of intent, saying that 'the historical film re-presents the past *for the purposes of* the present and the future' (my italics).[72] Quite how much the 'present' intruded into the lives of the people who made these films is, however, arguable. One Twentieth Century-Fox writer and producer, Philip Dunne, says that the films made during Zanuck's reign 'emphasised courage, self-reliance, honor and integrity. These are Victorian virtues, and Darryl's mind-set, like my own, was essentially Victorian'.[73] This would indicate that perhaps Zanuck brought his own sensibilities to the films he made.

Two distinct 're-presentations' of the Victorian occur in *Hound*: the seance led by Mrs Mortimer, and the closing scene of the film where Holmes asks Watson for 'the needle'. Both these undergo changes in their path from the Victorian period to the 1939 cinema screen. The seance, for instance, does not exist in Doyle's novel and was the invention of the screenwriter, as indeed was the character of Mrs Mortimer. So well does it fit our notions of the Victorian, however, that it has been used in subsequent adaptations, including the 1959 Hammer Films version and the 2002 television drama starring Richard Roxborough. The scene is an effective one with the room apparently lit only by the flickering fire, which produces huge shadows. The camera shows a close-up of each face in turn as Watson, the Stapletons, Frankland, Sir Henry, and Dr Mortimer join hands and watch Mrs Mortimer enter a trance. The seance is brought to an abrupt close when the eerie howling of the hound is heard right outside the window. Spiritualism was popular in the late Victorian period and Doyle was its foremost advocate – a fact that would probably have been well known to the 1939 cinema audience.[74] Although Doyle's most public championing of spiritualism came later in his life, sparked by the death of his brother Innes and his son Kingsley at the end of World War One (another period when spiritualism experienced a surge in popularity), biographer Andrew

---

72 Cook, 1996, p.67. John Davis, in his analysis of Warner Brothers' 'foreign policy' makes a similar point, arguing that *The Private Lives of Elizabeth and Essex*, for example, released in November 1939, highlighted the debate between the isolationist Elizabeth and the interventionist Essex, thus expressing the prevailing American mood (Davis, 1972, p.280).

73 Behlmer, 1995, p.xv.

74 Only nine years earlier, following Doyle's death, 6,000 spiritualists had packed out the Royal Albert Hall, their express aim being to summon the presence of the author's spirit – an empty chair was placed on stage ready (but in vain) for his appearance.

Lycett has revealed that Doyle termed himself 'a believer' as early as 1887.[75] It seems almost an omission, therefore, that though Doyle touched on supernatural themes in his stories, these never included the fashionable ingredient of seances, perhaps because the 'supernatural' was always debunked by Holmes – and Doyle would have been loathe to expose any medium as a fake. Filmmakers, on the other hand, could see the dramatic potential of such scenes. Including the seance in *Hound* helped reinforce the notion that the mystery was supernatural rather than the work of one of the characters in the room, cemented accepted notions of Victorian mores, and perhaps also contained contemporary resonances, alluding to the uncertainty in Europe as the threat of a new war grew ever-closer.[76]

The last few seconds of *Hound* are the most talked about of the entire film. Having rescued Sir Henry from the jaws of the hound, and denounced Stapleton as the murderer, Holmes announces that it has been such a strenuous day that he will now turn in. At the doorway he looks back at the assembled company and says 'Oh Watson – the needle' and strides out. Watson ducks his head slightly, to signal a certain resignation rather than any disapproval, and picks up his medical bag. The theme music swells and the film ends. Alluding to cocaine addiction – something with which readers of the Holmes stories would have been familiar – is a surprise in a film made during the Production Code era. There has been considerable debate over the history of this line of dialogue (which is present in the 2005 DVD remastered version of the film): whether it was initially withdrawn and, if so, when – at script stage at the request of the PCA, in the released version of the film, or only in certain territories. It was written into the script early in the film's development by Zanuck himself. At a story conference in which Pascal's 'treatment' was discussed, Zanuck made detailed suggestions

---

75 Lycett, 2007, p.130.

76 It is also worth bearing in mind that because film releases were phased, beginning with first-run theatres and then spreading out to provincial cinemas, some British audiences did not see *Hound* or *Adventures* until after the outbreak of war – in Small Heath, Birmingham, for example, *Adventures* was not screened until May 1940 and, though its teaming with a 'three mesquiteers' episode, *Riders of the Black Hills*, would indicate that the entire programme was not to be taken too seriously, the wartime context would certainly cast a new perspective on the Victorian mores shown in the film (source: Birmingham cinema programme in Arthur Conan Doyle Collection – Richard Lancelyn Green Bequest).

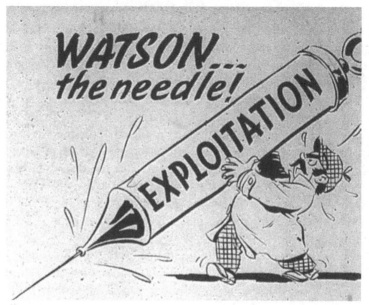

FIGURE 28 The pressbook for *The Hound of the Baskervilles* makes much of the 'needle' line, including this cartoon of Dr Watson placed above the section devoted to promotional ideas for exhibitors.

(the report listing these suggestions runs to 21 pages) on plot, tone, character and incident. He specifically says that the film should end with the words 'Watson, the needle' and that Watson should reply 'Yes, Sherlock'.[77] Pascal subsequently wrote this into his script, though Watson's reply was dropped.

The process by which films were cleared by the Production Code Administration (PCA) began with submission of the script. A letter from Joseph Breen of the PCA to Col. Jason Joy of Fox shows that the script was submitted well before filming started. Breen asked for a number of small changes to be made but made no mention of the 'needle' dialogue.[78] Completed films were then analysed by the PCA using a standard-format, tick-box chart which made it easy to spot possible Code infringements: in addition to a plot summary, characters were listed and divided into 'prominent' or 'minor' and

77 Zanuck, report of conference on treatment of *Hound*, 24 October 1938.
78 Breen letter to Col. Joy, 9 December 1938.

ticked as to whether they were 'straight', 'comic', 'sympathetic', 'unsympathetic' or 'indifferent'. Key professions (such as doctor, judge, minister and policeman) were noted, as were the types of crime portrayed and the 'fate of the criminal'. There was also space to note the consumption of liquor, the number of occurrences and where these took place. The form had no box for 'narcotics use': thus the analysis chart of *Hound*, compiled by George Shurlock and Douglas Mackinnon of the PCA two weeks before the film's release, mentions that Sir Henry drinks a glass of brandy at the end of the film – but says nothing about Holmes' 'needle'.[79] Depiction of narcotics was certainly an infringement of the Code, and the PCA was, only three years later, to ask Universal to remove reference to opium smoking in *Sherlock Holmes and the Secret Weapon*.[80]

It would seem that the line remained. Certainly, the pressbook makes much of the 'needle', with a page of promotional ideas boldly headed 'Give it the needle, Mr Showman!' and another featuring a cartoon of Dr Watson carrying a giant syringe *(see Fig. 28)*.[81] It was also present in the film seen by many reviewers. *Motion Picture Herald*, for example, saw a preview at Grauman's Chinese Theatre and reported that the 'first and last reference' to the needle, 'comes in the final line of the dialogue'.[82] Yet subsequently, it seems, the needle disappeared. By 4 May, columnist Dorothy Manners was writing in the *Los Angeles Examiner* that 'as a concession to the censors, the astute British detective is here seen without his narcotic needle'.[83] So when was it withdrawn? Arguably, this could have been the work of local censor boards who also had a role, via the Motion Picture Producers and Distributors of America, in approving films. The PCA archives include a number of reports on *Hound* from these local boards, but all approved the film 'without elimination', the only exception being British Columbia which wished to delete the reference to the

79 Analysis Chart, Shurlock and Mackinnon, 14 March 1939. Shurlock was later to succeed Joseph Breen as director of the PCA.

80 PCA letter to Pivar, 6 May 1943.

81 Changes often came too late for pressbooks: the campaign book for *Adventures* shows an altogether different, and more grisly, drawing of the albatross and states Holmes' music-hall song as being 'A Walk in the Park'.

82 *Motion Picture Herald*, 1 April 1939, p.28.

83 Quoted in Haydock, 1978, p.115.

needle.[84] It is possible that what remains in the archive is not a complete set of local board reports (there is no report for Great Britain, for example) and that other territories made similar cuts.

Subsequent critics disagree as to whether the line was retained or not. William Everson, writing in 1972, expresses 'pleasant surprise' that 'while this film was a product of the conservative Production Code-dominated years, we were still permitted to hear Holmes ask Watson for the needle'.[85] Ron Haydock, writing in 1978, says that when the film went into release, the line 'was blipped from the soundtrack' and not reinstated until the theatrical re-release in 1975.[86] David Stuart Davies, in his 2005 audio commentary on the remastered set of films issued on DVD, asserts that its deletion had only been for the British market and that the line was reinstated in the 1960s. Whatever the true situation, it is clear that what was acceptable on film was very different from what was acceptable on stage. In William Gillette's stageplay *Sherlock Holmes*, for example, the character's addiction is explicitly shown. In the published script, based on the 1929–1930 tour version, a stage direction reads 'inserts needle in arm' and the dialogue makes it clear that the substance is cocaine.[87] The inclusion by Zanuck of a direct reference to Holmes' drug-taking (something that is mentioned in five of the Doyle stories, but not in 'The Hound of the Baskervilles') may have been intended to avoid an anticlimax at the end of the film, as Stapleton's presumed death in the Grimpen Mire is not shown, the film ending with the rest of the characters gathered in a room at Baskerville Hall; or it may have been simply to emphasise another one of Holmes' many eccentricities, one in this case particularly associated with him as a Victorian literary character.[88] It is a reference that will not occur in the Universal films, indicating that the 'distancing' of a period film allows for the portrayal of mores that might not be acceptable in a contemporary Holmes.[89]

---

84 British Columbia censor board report, 6 July 1939.

85 Everson, 1972, p.16.

86 Haydock, 1978, p.115.

87 Gillette, 1974, p.82.

88 Cocaine is mentioned in *The Sign of Four*, 'A Scandal in Bohemia', 'The Five Orange Pips', 'The Man with the Twisted Lip' and 'The Adventure of the Yellow Face'.

89 The only exception is an oblique reference in *Sherlock Holmes and the Secret Weapon*

★

For a first venture into a Victorian Holmes portrayal, Twentieth Century-Fox's two films were influential, critically well received, and established Rathbone and Bruce in their roles (a pairing reinforced by their weekly appearance as Holmes and Watson in the NBC radio shows).[90] They were to usher in what Leggett calls 'a plethora of Victorian horrors' throughout the 1940s including *Gaslight*, *The Lodger*, *The Undying Monster*, *The Verdict*, *Bluebeard*, *The Picture of Dorian Gray*, and *The Shewolf of London*, all of which Leggett believes 'owe[d] a good deal to the success of Twentieth Century-Fox's Hound'.[91] Yet, having pioneered the taste for the Victorian (or tapped into an emerging interest), Fox was to drop the idea of a series and it would be three years before Holmes was seen on screen once more.

As contemporary critics noted, the studio may not have adhered to the 'letter' of Doyle's stories, but they did to the spirit. The character of Holmes was recognisable in every aspect: brilliant, eccentric, arrogant and enigmatic, with a strong personal sense of justice, and an affection for Watson that throws into relief his emotional detachment from the rest of mankind. When he is idling in Baker Street he is the 'urbane, mellow man of the world, with plenty of wit and the nonchalance of perfect confidence'.[92] When he is hot on the trail of a clue he is 'transformed into a dynamo. Every move is quick, sure and significant and his whole manner is that of a hound that has been given the view-hulloa!'[93] This familiarity – Holmes as the embodiment of particular, enduring qualities – is the real key to the films' success. Dr Mortimer sums up exactly what Holmes stands for in the closing speeches of *Hound* when he says:

---

when Holmes and Moriarty are discussing torture. On hearing Holmes' suggestion of a slow draining of the blood, he says: 'the needle to the end, eh Holmes?' a reference clearly missed by the PCA.

90   Rathbone was said, by actress Gladys Cooper, to receive 1,500 dollars for each of these half-hour weekly radio shows (quoted in Morley, 2006, p.179). The shows began on 2 October 1939 and were broadcast in the US and Canada.

91   Leggett, 1979, p.27. The genre had already been alive and well in Britain during the 1930s with films such as *The Ghoul* (1933), *Sweeney Todd* (1936) and the 1932 version of *The Lodger* which predated Hollywood's remake.

92   Drake comment in Zanuck story conference on first draft continuity script, 19 April.

93   Blum, first draft continuity script dated 3 April 1939 (this stage direction is absent from the final script).

'we've admired you in the past as does every Englishman.... Knowing that in England there is such a man as you gives us all a sense of safety and security. God bless you Mr Holmes.' Such sentiments, particularly in their patriotic evoking of 'England', would become the *leitmotif* of the Universal films that followed.

CHAPTER THREE

THIS BLESSED PLOT, THIS ENGLAND

HOLMES AND THE WAR

Watson: 'Things are looking up, Holmes.
This little island's still on the map'.
Holmes: 'Yes. This fortress – built by Nature for herself.
This blessed plot, this earth, this realm, this England.'
Sherlock Holmes and the Secret Weapon

I n the two years following the release of *The Hound of the Baskervilles* and *The Adventures of Sherlock Holmes,* Rathbone and Bruce – though absent from the screen – continued to play the same parts in their weekly radio series, which bridged the gap between past and present by having a Hollywood-dwelling Watson reminisce about his cases with Holmes. When the characters returned to cinema in 1942, neither this approach, nor that of the costume drama was chosen: the setting was contemporary and the genre was espionage. Three factors had driven the change: America had joined the war; Hollywood had enlisted its star characters in the service of the Allies; and the crime genre itself was rapidly evolving. This chapter looks at the first three films in the Universal series, examines the rationale for a 'modernisation' of Holmes, and assesses how complete (or otherwise) was its execution. This analysis reveals the temporal tensions layered throughout all three films, and the delicate balance whereby Holmes retains some of his Victorian attributes, yet becomes contemporary enough to be a credible force in the war. This balance was essential if Holmes' 'core meaning' – to represent certainty in an uncertain world – was to remain intact. The chapter also examines the films in the context of wartime censorship guidelines, the star personae of the two British leads, the role of Holmes as 'England's secret weapon', and the mixed responses from the press to the updating of the character.

SECURING A NEW CONTRACT

After making two successful Holmes films in quick succession, Twentieth Century-Fox might have been expected to continue the series, but they did not. This has been attributed (by all the leading Holmes-on-screen writers including David Stuart Davies, Michael Druxman, Steinbrunner and Michaels, and Alan Barnes) to a lack of interest on the part of the studio, but my examination of the correspondence between Denis Conan Doyle (co-executor of the Doyle estate), his agents and lawyers, reveals a more complex picture. The sequence of events is not easy to unravel, given that the Doyle estate had a UK agent, Rudolf Jess, who employed a representative in Hollywood – Paul Kohner – who in turn was working with (and sometimes in competition with) the Orsatti agency. The job of these agents was to sell as many Doyle properties to Hollywood as possible, individually or in 'bundles', at the best price. All these players had one eye on the commission they would earn: Denis Conan Doyle, meanwhile, was seeking to deal direct in order to avoid paying commission altogether.[1]

On 23 August 1932, Fox had bought the rights to two Doyle properties: 'The Hound of the Baskervilles' and 'A Scandal in Bohemia'.[2] Because they wanted to include material from the stageplay, 'Sherlock Holmes', they had also made an agreement with its author, William Gillette. The agreement included permission for Fox to make an unlimited number of versions, adaptations or sequels to the material contained in Gillette's play. Fox therefore felt they had bought unlimited rights to the character with no need to pay royalties to the Doyle estate or to consult them on what films they were planning. The Doyle estate at this stage seemed unaware of the potential problem. Even before filming had begun on *Hound*, Paul Kohner was attempting to sell more Doyle stories and was not put off by a letter from Julian Johnson, head of the story department at Fox,

---

1 Denis and Adrian Conan Doyle are described by Andrew Lycett in his biography of Doyle as 'spendthrift playboys' who regarded their father's estate as a 'milch-cow' to fund their expensive tastes in cars, chateaux and women. He also says they 'took pleasure in making things difficult for anyone who tried to write about their father' – this would include, by extension, the film companies (Lycett, 2007, p.438).

2 Kohner letter to Orsatti, 25 January 1939. This letter quotes the terms as being 37,500 dollars, though this conflicts with information in other Fox inter-office memos which give the initial figure as 27,000 dollars.

that 'Mr Zanuck is definitely not interested' at this time.[3] He wrote to Gregory Ratoff at Fox urging him to commit to a follow-up: 'if the two characters of Sherlock Holmes and Dr Watson click in the Baskervilles, it seems a cinch that a series of these two characters should be a tremendous box office attraction'.[4] He added a veiled threat at the end, to the effect that if Fox didn't buy more Doyle stories, others would and it would be those studios that would benefit from Fox's efforts. He evidently held out little hope of Fox changing their minds, as a month earlier he had offered 'The Sign of Four' and other Doyle stories to United Artists, Warner Brothers, Universal, M-G-M, Columbia, Paramount, Selznick, RKO and Republic.[5]

Fox were able to make threats of their own in response. Julian Johnson wrote to Paul Kohner to clarify that the reason Fox had no interest in buying any more stories was because 'we already own the famous play'.[6] This galvanised Denis Conan Doyle into action as he was worried that Fox would simply go ahead and produce their own Holmes series without any further reference (or income) to him. He instructed Frank Orsatti to offer all available Holmes stories to a number of other major studios in order to secure a more watertight deal and to pre-empt anything that Fox might do – something that Kohner was already engaged on.

By the time *Hound* was released in March 1939, Fox had softened its attitude slightly. In a letter that is revealing in its assessment of what was seen as Holmes' limited box-office appeal, Julian Johnson wrote to Kohner that:

> Mr Zanuck feels, and rightly I think, that we must never do a Sherlock Holmes 'series'. The stories are old, the characters are old, and the public's interest in them is again stirred up only by seeing an unexpected revival of a once-familiar subject. Therefore we are probably all right if we do a Sherlock Holmes story occasionally but if a series were announced, it would probably kill the whole thing.... If we could come to the right arrangements,

---

3   Johnson letter to Kohner, 30 November 1938.
4   Kohner letter to Ratoff, 12 December 1938.
5   Kohner letter to multiple addressees, 4 November 1938.
6   Johnson letter to Kohner, 24 December 1938.

we might do another pair of Sherlock Holmes stories next year
– or we might do only one.[7]

In describing the stories and characters as 'old', the implication is that
Holmes was 'dated': not quite old enough for a classic literary
adaptation, but old enough for audiences to have largely forgotten
him – an interesting comment bearing in mind that Holmes had not
been absent from the screen for more than two or three years at a
time over the previous 20-year period.

Three-days later, Johnson amended this by saying that it would
be wise to wait to see how *Hound* performed at the box office before
promising anything.[8] He makes no mention in any of this
correspondence of the production of *Adventures*, which was to be
released in September. Despite their ostensible lack of interest in
Holmes, Fox were busy behind the scenes trying to protect their
interests and scupper a deal that the Doyle estate were setting up with
M-G-M. On 26 February 1940, the estate's lawyers, Fitelson and
Mayers, wrote to Fox asking them to 'formally agree in writing to
refrain from producing, exploiting, advertising or in any manner
interfering with the exploitation, production and distribution of any
other picture or pictures based in whole or part upon the Sherlock
Holmes material, title and characters'. The letter was basically a
'frightener': although Fitelson and Mayers criticised Fox for
'commercial rivalry upon a plane below the morals of even the
market place', suing them would rely on proving that the studio was
acting fraudulently.[9] In other words, the Doyle estate would need
evidence that Fox had told M-G-M that they had Holmes films in
the pipeline when they did not. The estate's lawyers advised them
not to pursue the case and, indeed, to be prepared to pay Fox a
nominal sum should the deal with M-G-M come to fruition. In the
event, neither a lawsuit nor a pay-off was necessary. On 6 September
1940, Fox backed down and agreed not to make any further Holmes
films without negotiating the rights with the estate.[10]

---

7   Johnson letter to Kohner, 8 July 1939. It is interesting that Fox considered that 'a pair' of
    Holmes films in 1939 and another pair in 1940 were not enough to constitute a 'series'.

8   Johnson letter to Kohner, 11 July 1939.

9   Fitelson and Mayers Memorandum Opinion No. 2, February 1940.

10 Fitelson and Mayers letter to Doyle, 6 September 1940.

Tying up an agreement with M-G-M proved more troublesome than anticipated and there were dozens of letters and cables back and forth between agents, M-G-M and the Doyle estate trying to agree terms. While the studio was still making up its mind, Frank Orsatti met with producer Lester Cowan to discuss making between two and four Holmes pictures a year, to be written by Edith Meiser (who was also writing the radio scripts) and Reginald Denham, directed by William Cameron Menzies, and released through either Columbia or Paramount. The offer was for 5,000 dollars per picture plus five percent of the profits: Rathbone and Bruce were already said to be on board.[11] Denis Conan Doyle, though frustrated by the delays, was still keen to wait for M-G-M, saying: 'Mr Mayer has been interested in the idea of a Holmes series for over two years – surely by now he should be able to make up his mind on the matter'.[12] He attempted to keep Rathbone on the hook by telling him there were four separate deals in prospect, the best being a 'very big deal with M-G-M which might be extended over a period of as long as 10 years... [but which] is not yet consummated'.[13] Reluctant to let the Lester Cowan proposal go entirely, Denis Conan Doyle made a counteroffer of 15,000 dollars per picture and, when this was not taken up, revised it to 7,000 dollars per picture plus five percent of the gross.[14] By 16 June, he had had enough, and fired Frank Orsatti because he had represented the estate since August 1939 'without any concrete results whatever'.[15] No more was heard of the M-G-M deal, and a subsequent show of interest from Warners via the estate's new agents, Myron Selznick and Co., also came to nothing.[16]

It was not until 8 January 1942 that a firm deal was on the table, this time with Universal, for a seven-year exclusive arrangement for the use of any of the Doyle short stories, plus the right to devise their own using the Holmes character.[17] The studio proposed making three

---

11 Orsatti letters to Doyle, 2 and 9 December 1940.

12 Doyle letter to Orsatti, 6 December 1940.

13 Doyle letter to Rathbone, 29 December 1940.

14 Doyle letter to Orsatti, 11 December 1940; Doyle letter to Orsatti, 1 March 1941.

15 Doyle letter to Orsatti, 16 June 1941.

16 Warners were interested in two pictures a year but were put off because of concerns about US copyright laws which seemed to suggest that rival studios could make competing features without recourse to the Doyle estate.

17 The fact that it was Universal with whom the deal was eventually struck is slightly ironic, as it was Universal who gave Paul Kohner, a Carl Laemmle protégé from Czechoslovakia,

films in the first year for a 10,000-dollar-per-film payment, with subsequent years at 12,500 dollars per film. They would be required to make three films a year in order to retain the rights. Denis had some concerns about Universal's wish to write their own stories but was reassured that Universal would never cast Holmes 'in criminal, comical or ridiculous roles' and that there would be a limit of one original story per year.[18] Similar restrictions had initially been put on the radio series, which began by having to use Doyle stories exclusively, then to restrict original material to one in every three programmes: eventually this stipulation seems to have been relaxed – understandably with the series running to more than two hundred episodes.[19] On 23 January 1942, Selznick told the estate that the deal with Universal had been sealed and on 24 February the contract was signed.[20] The only further stipulation was that, at the suggestion of the Doyle estate's lawyers, Universal were asked to agree 'not to permit the character of Sherlock Holmes or Watson to die or be killed in any of the pictures produced by it'.[21] It was an easy decision to make: clearly Universal envisaged a long run of films.

Unlike Fox, Universal (with Columbia) was not in the top league of theatre-owning studios, and while this meant it did not suffer too much in the wake of the anti-trust legislation, neither did it command the budgets or the distribution to enable it to make many prestige productions. Clive Hirschhorn, in his history of Universal, characterised the studio's annual output from 1937 through to 1946 as being 'a couple of prestige Deanna Durbin pictures, several low-budget horror films, a few outdoor adventures, two Abbott and Costello offerings and as many quickie musicals as possible'.[22] He is dismissive of Universal's plots, calling them corny and unimaginative, and assesses the cast and crew as 'second rate'. This is not a view shared by other writers: Schatz, for example, sees Universal's production strategy as shrewd, in the way they concentrated on 'low-grade

---

a start in the movie business as a publicity agent for the foreign press along with a young man called William Wyler.

18 Selznick cable to Doyle, 14 January 1942.

19 Denis Conan Doyle letter to Fitelson and Mayers, 30 April 1941.

20 Universal Studios agreement, 24 February 1942.

21 Fitelson and Mayers letter to Denis Conan Doyle, 13 June 1942.

22 Hirschhorn, 1983, p.98.

features and sub-features', always looking for standardisation and formulae, and being quick to fill the gap which had opened up when the majors cut back on B-movie production.[23] Deanna Durbin was, of course, big box-office with a series of hit films for Universal from 1937 onwards; and Abbott and Costello were, by 1942, the number-one box-office draw.[24]

If there was a gap in Universal's programming, it was a lack of B-movie detective series. Its closest rival, Columbia, had a portfolio that included Boston Blackie, The Crime Doctor, Ellery Queen and The Lone Wolf; and RKO, one of the 'big five' studios, had The Falcon and The Saint. Sherlock Holmes was therefore a logical addition to Universal's stable and, given the existing popularity of Rathbone and Bruce in the lead roles both on screen and on radio, a pretty safe financial proposition. The radio series had gone from strength to strength: according to Alan Barnes, 29 broadcasters across the US signed up for the 1939–1940 run but by the second run, this had grown to 53 radio stations.[25] Rathbone was secured by Universal at a flat-rate-per-film of 20,000 dollars and Bruce signed a contract at 850 dollars a week, rising over the four-year option period.[26] The three films planned for the first year of the contract were *Sherlock Holmes and the Voice of Terror*, *Sherlock Holmes and the Secret Weapon*, and *Sherlock Holmes in Washington*. All three would be set in the present day and feature war-related plots. In the first, Holmes would unmask a German agent at the heart of the British government; in the second, he would pit his wits against Moriarty to keep a newly developed bombsight out of Nazi hands; and in the third he would recover a piece of microfilm hidden by a kidnapped British agent. A tight budget would mean extensive use of the studio's standing sets, clever incorporation of stock footage and a rigorous schedule. *Washington*, for example, had a 150,000 dollar budget, 20,000 of which went to Rathbone, 3,666 to scriptwriter Bertram Millhauser and 8,900 on sets. The film was shot in 15 days.[27] Good directing and design meant

23   Schatz, 1997, p.352.

24   The Holmes films would frequently occupy the lower half of the bill to Abbott and Costello, giving them high visibility and a large audience for a B-movie.

25   Barnes, 2002, p.153.

26   Universal contract with Nigel Bruce, 9 February 1942.

27   Assistant director's report, July 1942.

that the economies were not obvious – and the sitting room at 221B was impressive in its attention to detail.[28]

HOLMES JOINS THE WAR EFFORT

The decision to bring Holmes into the present day, and to do so in a fairly robust way, was allowed for in the agreement between Universal and the Doyle estate, which permitted the studio to:

> adapt and change [the Doyle] stories to the fullest extent including the right to use the fullest latitude in changing and adapting such stories, their characters, themes and incidents, to translate, rearrange, *modernize*, add to or take from their literary and/or dramatic material.[29]

Universal was to do all these things, to the extent that it is hard to correlate the films with any of the Doyle stories except through small elements or subplots. One particular transformation was not, however, within their power and that was to change the nature of the principal characters. The agreement specifically states that in all the films, 'Sherlock Holmes and Dr Watson shall be characterised in the same general way in which they are characterised in the said Sherlock Holmes stories'.[30] In this, the Doyle estate kept a measure of control over the 'brand' and provided Universal with parameters within which to work: if the key to Holmes' longevity was indeed his unchanging nature, this might have been to the studio's advantage.

Whose decision it was to have a present-day setting has been the subject of conflicting claims, with some writers, including David Quinlan, crediting Roy William Neill.[31] As Neill was not appointed director until the second film, a more likely answer was executive producer Howard Benedict. Why such setting was chosen is perhaps a more interesting question. Steinbrunner and Michaels suggest that it was the advent of war in Europe that made the 'turn-of-the-

---

28 Shots of a train derailment in *Voice of Terror* were borrowed from the 1933 production of *The Invisible Man*; and Bertram Millhauser's script for *The Pearl of Death* refers to using 'corvette stock' for the ship at sea: Millhauser, 28 March 1944.

29 Universal agreement with Conan Doyle Estate, 24 February 1942. Italics are mine.

30 Universal Agreement with Conan Doyle Estate, 24 February 1942.

31 Quinlan, 1983, p.215.

century Holmes of the misty Fox films seem so hopelessly dated'.[32] Matthew Bunson also feels that the grimness of war meant that 'the last thing the audience wanted to see was a movie full of dark fog-shrouded alleys and bloodthirsty murderers' – though arguably, a Victorian setting might have been a form of escapism in itself.[33] Whereas both these interpretations cite audience expectations as being behind the decision, Haralovich offers a different perspective, that of the economics of B-unit production and points out that a modern setting was less of a drain on the budget because it made 'better use of available sets and costumes',[34] a view repeated by Schatz and by Davis.[35] This is a difficult argument to sustain because of Universal's easy access to an array of standing sets of European buildings, with a distinct historical feel (even if it was hard to tell exactly what period they were supposed to represent); and because the decision was made to construct the interior of 221B Baker Street in considerable detail as a Victorian sitting room.[36]

Neither the economic nor the audience-driven argument tells the whole story because they view the series in isolation rather than looking more broadly at what was happening in the industry. I would suggest that two factors are important here: an evolution in the crime genre and a realisation that existing screen characters could be co-opted to help with the war effort. Although individual writers have advanced part of this argument, there has not been an examination of the whole. Guy Barefoot comes close, in his book *Gaslight Melodrama*, when he looks beyond Haralovich's claims, without dismissing them, to observe the rise in popularity of the 'paraphernalia of the modern' in the crime genre, with an emphasis on guns and cars. In tension with this, he identifies a second popular strand: that of the gentleman amateur detective and of Holmes in particular, which pulls in the opposite direction – and which presumably leads to the impossibility of simply 'dropping' Holmes or of throwing away every one of his Victorian connotations.[37] This tug

---

32 Steinbrunner and Michaels, 1978, p.85.

33 Bunson, 1995, p.207.

34 Haralovich, 1979, pp.53–7.

35 Schatz, 1989, p.353; Davies, 1976, p.69.

36 Universal did in fact make extensive use of these standing sets.

37 Barefoot, 2001, p.52.

of war between old and new would be seen throughout the Universal series and would work most effectively when a contemporary setting was 'connoted', rather than 'denoted' too literally, allowing Holmes to retain enough elements of the Victorian for him to 'float' back and forth between eras, and keeping temporal realities sufficiently distant to enable the audience to construct their 'own' Holmes – much as they did in listening to the radio series.[38]

However, the opportunity to mobilise such a universally recognised figure as Holmes, with his connotations of reassurance and certainty, was surely unmissable. What's more, Holmes was British and could be used, as Blackie Seymour points out, as 'England's secret weapon'.[39] He could help build the notion of a shared culture, whereby the US was not just 'helping out' Britain by having entered the war, but defending a common heritage. A contemporary setting would make this appeal a direct one.

In creating war-related plots for Holmes, Universal was hardly breaking new ground: since the attack on Pearl Harbor and the US entry into the war in December 1941, propaganda had shifted from covert to overt, and everyone from Tarzan to the Dead End Kids had been drafted. In *Tarzan Triumphs* of 1942, for example, Nazis parachute into Tarzan's kingdom; in *Rio Rita* (1942), Abbott and Costello stumble on Nazi agents passing messages through radios disguised as apples; and in *Keep 'Em Slugging* (1942), the Dead End Kids foil a Nazi spy ring. In the detective genre, such a transfer was straightforward, with criminals easily turned into foreign agents and spies: in *Enemy Agents Meet Ellery Queen* (1942), Queen wards off a Nazi diamond-stealing plot; and in *The Falcon Strikes Back* (1943), the Falcon uncovers a war-bond racket. Giving so many of the detective series a war theme was not just a 'patriotic' move by the studios, but a shrewd reaction to audience demand for both detective films and films about the war. It had started with literature, as Haycraft points out in his 1942 book on the detective genre: in London at the height of the Blitz, people fled underground each night for protection – where they spent much of their time reading:

38 The outcome was the creation of what Naugrette terms as a world that was 'invraisemblable mais possible' (Naugrette, 2005, p.126).

39 Seymour, 1987, p.46.

What volumes, asked curious Americans from the comfortable security of their homes, could men and women choose for their companionship at such a time? The answer was soon forthcoming in dispatches from the beleaguered capital, telling of newly formed 'raid' libraries set up in response to popular demand to lend detective stories and nothing else.[40]

Giving a war theme to an already popular screen genre would capitalise on this upsurge in popularity, but studios had to proceed with some caution, as war-related film content was tightly controlled by the US government's propaganda agency, the Office of War Information (OWI). The OWI worked closely with the Hollywood studios, not only issuing guidelines and vetting scripts but even writing dialogue for key scenes.[41] Shortly after its formation in June 1942, the OWI asked filmmakers to consider seven questions before embarking on any production:[42]

1. Will this picture help win the war?
2. What war information problem does it seek to clarify, dramatise or interpret?
3. If it is an 'escape' picture, will it harm the war effort by creating a false picture of America, her allies or the world we live in?
4. Does it merely use the war as the basis for a profitable picture...?
5. Does it contribute something new to our understanding of the world conflict...?
6. When the picture reaches its maximum circulation... will it reflect conditions as they are... or will it be outdated?
7. Does the picture tell the truth or will the young people of today have reason to say they were misled by propaganda?

Despite the 'worthy' connotations of these guidelines, the OWI and Hollywood found that profits and propaganda could sit reasonably comfortably together, because the audience were as hungry for war-themed films as they were for escapist entertainment. This did not

---

40 Haycraft, 1942, p.v. The popularity of detective fiction, presumably containing 'bloodthirsty murders', rather contradicts Matthew Bunson's assertion cited above.

41 Koppes and Black, 1990, p.vii.

42 Quoted in Koppes and Black, 1990, p.69.

necessarily mean that all Hollywood films about Britain or with British characters met with OWI approval: they were particularly keen to avoid stirring resentment of US support for Britain by reminding audiences of class divisions and Empire. 'This baffled many in Hollywood', says Mark Glancy, 'who knew that the Britain of empire and class was the only Britain that Americans were interested in'.[43] In some ways, the complexity of the censorship environment, with studios having to please both the Production Code Administration and the OWI, was restrictive. In others it allowed considerably more freedom than before, partly because the two regimes often contradicted each other in their rulings, and partly because where the PCA discouraged 'crime, violence, sex and political content', the OWI actively encouraged the showing of war-related crimes and violence 'to stiffen patriotic resolves'.[44]

SPEAKING FOR 'CIVILISATION'

Bringing Sherlock Holmes into the modern world to rally for the Allied cause was a move requiring some sensitivity. The pressbook for the first of the Universal series, *Voice of Terror*, features a letter from Denis Conan Doyle *(see Fig. 29)* saying that 'the modern setting was a daring experiment which has succeeded admirably' and that this is 'incomparably the best Sherlock Holmes film ever made'.[45] Doyle's willingness to endorse the films may, of course, have stemmed from the fact that he was a beneficiary of the sum paid for the rights (and indicate his relief at finally finding a studio to take up the options), though he seems to have written unprompted to Universal about both *Voice of Terror* and *Washington*.[46] James R. Luntzel of Universal, in a letter of 18 August 1942 to Denis Conan Doyle expressing thanks, says that his letters 'are just what we needed to complete our advertising campaign for the two pictures' and that the endorsements will 'do much to create added interest in behalf of the pictures on the part of many Sherlock Holmes fans throughout the country'. Another article in the pressbook points out how the studio has tried not to

---

43   Glancy, 1999, p.186.

44   Biesen, 2005, p.48.

45   As all Holmes films prior to 1939 had been given a 'modern setting', the 'daring' quality referred to by Denis Conan Doyle refers perhaps to the overtness of the modernisation.

46   There are no traceable letters from the studio requesting his endorsement.

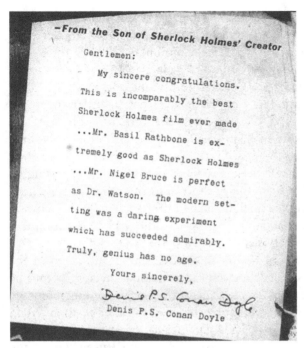

—From the Son of Sherlock Holmes' Creator

Gentlemen:

My sincere congratulations. This is incomparably the best Sherlock Holmes film ever made ...Mr. Basil Rathbone is extremely good as Sherlock Holmes ...Mr. Nigel Bruce is perfect as Dr. Watson. The modern setting was a daring experiment which has succeeded admirably. Truly, genius has no age.

Yours sincerely,

Denis P.S. Conan Doyle

FIGURE 29 Page from the pressbook for *Sherlock Holmes and the Voice of Terror*, with an endorsement of the modernising from Denis Conan Doyle.

offend these same fans, by leaving 221B Baker Street 'exactly the same' and allowing the modern world only to intrude when Holmes and Watson step outside.[47] These articles in the pressbook indicate both a defensiveness about the updating and an ambivalence: the fact that the deerstalker and pipe are absent from the films, but present as logos throughout the pressbooks, is another indication.[48]

Elsewhere in the pressbook, the editorial is more bullish, with almost every headline (such as 'streamlined thriller', 'modern sensation') stressing modernity. Producer Howard Benedict is quoted as saying that a modern Holmes is plausible because all his work is

---

47 Ironically, Universal made the rooms look even more Victorian than in the two Twentieth Century-Fox 'period' films.

48 *Hollywood Reporter* found it hard to believe that 'even an up-to-date Holmes would forego his famous pipe for cigarettes. Benedict may hear from the Baker Street gang about such an unnecessary liberty. Ordinary audiences will not notice it' (*Hollywood Reporter*, 25 March 1943, unpaginated).

done with his brain rather than with gadgets and that 'brain-work is just the same now as it was in the Victorian era'. This is an interesting comment in view of the fact that the plotlines of the first three films of the series each hinge on a modern gadget: in *Voice of Terror*, a time-delay broadcast; in *Secret Weapon* a bombsight; and in *Washington*, a piece of microfilm. The pressbook says that in order to ensure modernisation would be a success, the producer, director and scriptwriter agreed to make no changes to the characters of Holmes and Watson: Universal thus seem to have recognised that it was their immutability that made these characters so enduringly appealing.

One senses that bringing Holmes into the present day (where, indeed, apart from the Fox films, he had always resided on screen) was less controversial than involving him in the war. One prominent newspaper film critic, Bosley Crowther of the *New York Times*, expressed surprise that Universal 'should take such cheap advantage of the present crisis to exploit an old respected fiction character'.[49] Once he had overcome this initial repugnance, however, he got much mileage and humour out of the situation – his role was, after all, to entertain as well as to help readers decide whether to see a particular film. He enjoyed the way Universal had given Holmes and Watson 'the blessing of eternal youth and set them to chase Nazi villains in the war-consumed London of today with the same hale and vigorous tenacity as they showed towards opium smugglers years ago'.[50] Others were not so sure: the *New York Herald Tribune* noted the 'longing for the gaslit era' apparent in Rathbone's eyes, and the British fan-magazine *Picturegoer* said that he would be an ideal Holmes 'if the plays were put in period instead of being rather ludicrously brought up to date'.[51] The trade papers, on the other hand, voiced no real criticism of the updating: the UK journal *Kinematograph Weekly* said it was 'all to the good';[52] *To-day's Cinema*, after some initial wariness, said it was a shock but would not bother audiences;[53] and *Motion Picture Herald* believed

---

49 *New York Times*, 19 September 1942, p.9.

50 *New York Times*, 5 January 1943, p.15.

51 *Picturegoer*, 12 December 1942, p.7.

52 *Kinematograph Weekly*, 31 May 1945, p.20B. This echoes the 1920s reader's letter to *Picture Show* cited earlier complaining that the Stoll series of Holmes films had brought the character up to date.

53 *To-day's Cinema*, 19 December 1945, p.11.

that audiences would find the transformation enjoyable.[54] All seem to have suffered from amnesia as to the previous updating of the character throughout the Holmes films of the 1920s and 1930s, and have remembered only the Twentieth Century-Fox films of 1939.

Even if cinema-goers missed the advance publicity setting out the studio's rationale for modernising Holmes, an on-screen post-credit caption was there to reinforce the message: 'Sherlock Holmes is ageless, invincible and unchanging.... In solving the significant problems of the present day he remains – as ever – the supreme master of deductive reasoning'.

Two words here are key: Holmes may have been transported into the 1940s but he is 'unchanging' (in other words the studio intended him to stand for, or signify, much the same as he did as a 'Victorian' detective); he is also 'invincible'. In bringing Holmes into the present day, Universal had discovered a powerful and arguably unique psychological weapon: in a time of uncertainty and fear, there was only one person who could provide a cast-iron guarantee that the Allies would prevail – not Winston Churchill, but Sherlock Holmes. So powerful was his association with infallibility that the studio initially called the first film in the series *Sherlock Holmes Saves London* and the second *Sherlock Holmes Fights Back* (with Holmes as a metonym for a beleaguered England).[55] Adding a patriotic speech at the end of each film put the finishing touch to exploiting the potential of Holmes' persona as a leader who would ensure an Allied victory.

In the first *(see Fig. 30)*, the speech was an exact transference from Conan Doyle's story 'His Last Bow' which dealt with Holmes' service in World War One:

There's an east wind coming... such a wind as never blew on England yet. It will be cold and bitter, Watson, and a good many of us may wither before its blast. But it's God's own wind, none the less, and a greener, better, stronger land will lie in the sunshine when the storm has cleared.

---

54 *Motion Picture Herald*, 12 September 1942, p.897.

55 These title changes apparently happened late in the day: a publicity still of Kaaren Verne, who played Charlotte in *Secret Weapon*, was issued by Universal with the *Sherlock Holmes Fights Back* title (photo in Richard Lancelyn Green Bequest). Another working title for *Voice of Terror* was *Sherlock Holmes and the Voice of Fear* (script dated 28 July 1942).

FIGURE 30 Holmes delivers the 'East Wind' speech at the end of *Sherlock Holmes and the Voice of Terror*. Kitty's dead body, which he has stepped over to reach the steps, lies unregarded.

In the second, the speech was taken from two (non-adjacent) lines from a speech in Shakespeare's *Richard II*:

Watson: 'Things are looking up, Holmes. This little island's still on the map'

Holmes: 'Yes. This fortress – built by Nature for herself. This blessed plot, this earth, this realm, this England'.

And in the third, from Churchill's speech to the US Congress on 26 December 1941, just nineteen days after the attack on Pearl Harbor:

It is not given for us to peer into the mysteries of the future. But… in the days to come, the British and American people for their own safety and the good of all will walk together in majesty and justice and in peace.

In this way, Holmes was seen to speak for England – or indeed for civilisation. It is hard to imagine any other fictional character being able to carry this off; and it was helped, of course, by Rathbone's star persona: he was a prominent member of the British colony in Hollywood and a campaigner for War Bonds.[56] The pressbook for *Washington* reports that Rathbone and Bruce hurried to finish filming so they could take part in a bond-selling rally in Texas, New Mexico and Arizona, their previous rally having raised four-million dollars in just one hour. To reinforce the conflation of Holmes and patriotism, there were War Bonds advertisements at the end of each film, immediately following the patriotic speech. Reputedly, US reaction to the 'East Wind' speech in *Voice of Terror* was so favourable that similar speeches were commissioned for the next four titles.[57] Churchill's words used for the 'hands across the sea' speech at the end of *Washington* would have been very familiar to American audiences as well as those in Britain, as an anthology of Churchill's speeches was at number one position in the US best-selling-books list in the summer of 1941.[58] Quoting Churchill or Shakespeare was also a way of verbally underpinning the foundations of a culture which was being rocked by uncertainty (and offering a reassurance that this culture would continue). Jean-Pierre Naugrette points to the scene in *Secret Weapon* in which Shakespeare, Dickens and Poe are named when Holmes is finding a suitable hiding place in his bookcase for part of the bombsight, and argues that in this way literature becomes 'une arme secrète, un corpus de références utilisable contre l'ennemi'.[59] On a more prosaic note, the pressbooks often included editorial about Rathbone and Bruce breaking off from filming in order to take afternoon tea, the kind of reference that Antonia Lant sees as reminding people of the 'idiosyncrasies of local culture' under

---

56 Richard Dyer reminds us that a star's persona needs to be read against the background of the specific historical moment: using Douglas Fairbanks as an example, Dyer argues that Fairbanks' charisma was related to the way he played the 'average contemporary American' and was thereby a reassuring presence in the period of American neutrality at the start of the war in Europe (Dyer, 1998, p.31).

57 *Secret Weapon* having already been completed, the 'blessed plot' speech was added afterwards, according to Blackie Seymour in *Classic Images*, August 1987, p.46.

58 Cull, 1995, p.178.

59 'A secret weapon, a group of references that could be used against the enemy' (Naugrette, 2005, p.127).

threat from the war, and thus building national identity.[60] In these films, however, the referencing goes one step further and identifies Holmes as the embodiment of this culture.

Subsequent critics have been less kindly disposed towards the propaganda of these messages. William Everson, writing on the detective film genre, calls it 'patronising and embarrassing'[61] and Michael Pointer, while acknowledging that it was understandable 'in a period of patriotic near-hysteria' that Holmes should be seen doing his war service, felt that 'only the Hollywood that produced the blonde-in-the-bomber type of epic rubbish could have conceived the three films that ensued'.[62] Neither critic considers how this propaganda might have been viewed through the eyes of a nation at war and perhaps – in the case of Britain – a nation sitting in the cinema while bombing raids were going on all around them. Steinbrunner and Michaels, however, sense the poetry of the closing speeches, noting the 'throat-catching charm' of the East Wind speech[63] and Barnes remarks on its magnificence: 'propaganda, yes, a Triumph of the Will, no. But some sort of triumph all the same'.[64]

These 'hands-across-the-sea' propaganda messages were considered important: Denis Conan Doyle expressed the view that the films could do much to 'further Anglo American good will'[65] and Nigel Bruce was quoted in the US pressbook for *Washington* saying that the film was 'doing much to create a greater understanding between this country and Great Britain'.[66] But there were other subliminal messages that have gone largely unremarked: one is the nature of the enemy Holmes pursues in these films. If Holmes is serving the Allied cause, then it follows that his enemy will be the Nazis. This involves an interesting departure from the usual pattern of the classic detective genre, in which crime is assignable to one

---

60 Lant, 1991, p.48.

61 Everson, 1972, p.19.

62 Pointer, 1975, p.82.

63 Steinbrunner and Michaels, 1978, p.93.

64 Barnes, 2002, p.155.

65 DeLapp of Universal, meeting report, 10 January 1942.

66 Morley also points out their historical value, in that 'a history of Anglo-American relations in the Second World War could be derived from these Holmesian codas' (Morley, 2006, p.195).

errant individual. In a war, the enemy is like the hydra – in cutting down one, a hundred more spring up to take its place. This is not a comforting concept and, perhaps because reassurance is crucial to the genre, the storylines seek to address it. First, in *Voice of Terror*, Holmes roots out the one 'bad apple', an imposter in the British establishment; then in *Secret Weapon* reveals – somewhat triumphantly – that Moriarty (a single, identifiable but somewhat mythical figure of otherness) is behind the Nazi plot to steal the bombsight. The equation of Moriarty with the Nazis did not stretch the bounds of plausibility: Haycraft, writing before the release of these films, had drawn exactly the same analogy, characterising the Allies as 'the countrymen of Sherlock Holmes, and Lecoq, of Rouletabille and Father Brown, of Philip Trent and Poirot' who are facing the 'too grimly real Moriarty of Europe'.[67] In fact, Haycraft takes these metonymic qualities even further, arguing that those countries which enjoy detective fiction are on the side of logic, fair play and justice: those which do not (the Nazis withdrew all imported detective fiction from German bookshops early in 1941) are undemocratic and of an alien nature.[68] As to the role of America in the war, Haycraft felt that its entry was inevitable because once the 'countrymen of Sherlock Holmes' were at war, 'no neutrality of the spirit was possible in the land of Dupin, Uncle Abner and Charlie Chan'.[69]

Another subliminal aspect to the propaganda messages of these films is the fact that Holmes is an emissary from another age. James Parish and Michael Pitts argue that the films are successful precisely because they bring into conflict 'opponents of distinctly different eras and opposing codes of operation and ethics'.[70] The underlying message in all three films is that the Allied cause is synonymous with Victorian values and that Holmes is the embodiment of these values.

A CURIOUS MIX OF 'OLD AND NEW'

The three 'war' films comprised Universal's first-year options, with two loosely based on Doyle stories (*Voice of Terror* on 'His Last Bow'

---

67 Haycraft, 1942, p.318.

68 This strand of thinking appears in the Tarzan poster which shows noirish Nazi figures depicted as alien intruders in a 'natural' – and therefore Allied – landscape.

69 Haycraft, 1942, p.318.

70 Parish and Pitts, 1974, p.431.

and *Secret Weapon* on 'The Dancing Men') and the third (*Washington*) an original, scripted by Lynn Riggs and Bertram Millhauser. They were all made within an extremely tight timeframe and therefore, although nominally a series, show no evolution in character, narrative trajectory or attitude to the war. The studio's intention was to release one film a month between September and November 1942, but for reasons that are unclear, this did not happen. In the US, *Voice of Terror* came out in September as planned, but it was February 1943 before *Secret Weapon* was released and April before *Washington* came to the screen. There were no such delays to *Secret Weapon* and *Washington* in the UK, though *Voice of Terror* was delayed for a full year before release, finally coming to cinemas in October 1943. This may have been because of censorship problems: the plot concludes with Holmes unmasking the head of British intelligence as a Nazi spy, and Alan Barnes justifiably wonders 'how [it] could ever have been passed for public exhibition'.[71] No such concerns were raised in the US by the Production Code Administration when they first read the script: they were concerned only that East End girl Kitty should not be seen as a prostitute. Although war-related issues lay outside the confines of the Production Code, they had certainly expressed views on national sensitivities before, for instance questioning in *Hound* whether 'there will be any difficulty with this story in England... in regard to the characterisation of the demented convict'.[72] It can be assumed, therefore, that the year-long delay in releasing *Voice of Terror* in the UK was a decision made by the UK censors. Such delays may not seem particularly significant but in the context of the fast-moving events of the war, they would inevitably change the way the films were received. One of the strengths of low-budget B-movies was their speed of production: in wartime this enabled studios to meet the OWI guideline on ensuring pictures were not outdated when they reached their maximum circulation. A year's delay in the UK also meant that the film missed the peak of the wave of popularity for war-themed pictures, which began to decline in 1943.

The three films, then, can in a sense be seen as a single entity – as Holmes' war films. They share the same characters, narrative thrust and themes, but they do not share the same director (John Rawlins

---

71 Barnes, 2002, p.155.

72 Breen letter to Col. Jason Joy at Twentieth Century-Fox, 9 December 1938.

directed the first and Roy William Neill the other two); nor the same director of photography (Woody Bredell worked on *Voice of Terror* then was succeeded by Les White); nor the same scriptwriter (Lynne Riggs and John Bright were followed by Edward T. Lowe, W. Scott Darling and Edmund L. Hartmann, and then by Bertram Millhauser). All three films share the curious mix of 'old and new' remarked upon by Barefoot, and hover uncertainly between modernity and the Victorian.

This dichotomy is revealed principally in settings, iconography, costume, and the presence/use of technology, but also through the assumptions made, and attitudes expressed, by the main characters in relation to Holmes and Watson. All three films open with the same fog-bound credits sequence which sets expectations of a period drama, following which there is an abrupt shift as the action begins and positions the setting as the present day. The explanatory on-screen wording about the timelessness of Holmes does little to prepare the viewer.

Voice of Terror begins with a map of Europe bearing a super-imposed graphic of a wave-emitting radio mast *(see Fig. 31)* and a

FIGURE 31 The newsreel-style opening to *Sherlock Holmes and the Voice of Terror.*

voiceover that would have been immediately recognisable by contemporary audiences as alluding to Lord Haw-Haw, the British fascist William Joyce who worked for Goebbels, broadcasting messages to Britain: 'this is the voice you have learned to fear. This is the voice of terror'.[73] As he speaks, predicting a string of Allied disasters, the shadow of the mast moves across the Continent like an invading army until it reaches Britain. This opening shot gives way to a montage sequence that cuts between various groups of wireless listeners including working-class men in flat caps gathered around the radio in their lunch break; nurses; professionals; and middle-class men smoking cigars in their clubs. The 'voice of terror' forms a constant background to this montage, which includes scenes of dams collapsing and ships being torpedoed: exactly the events that the voice seems to predict. The sequence ends with a close-up of the headline on the front page of a fictitious newspaper, *The London Bulletin*: 'Terror campaign grows in frightfulness'. Period is thus unequivocally established as the present day and this lack of ambiguity is possible because Holmes is not present in this opening sequence. His first appearance is midway through the second scene, at the offices of the 'Intelligence Inner Council' where the temporal messages become more mixed, the presence of a giant radio set and more live broadcasts of the voice mitigating the distinctly Victorian costume of the public-school types that comprise the council. Outside the building, as Holmes and Watson depart for Baker Street, reminders of the contemporary setting include the presence of sandbags and the fact that their driver is a Wren.

Washington has an equally contemporary opening with a shot of a 'London Terminal Transatlantic Airways' sign, which economically conveys both location and destination. The scene cuts to a huge plane – a symbol of modernity – about to take off. It is clearly wartime, with check-in staff in tin helmets vetting passengers as they pass through. Shots of the plane in mid-air are inter-cut with scenes inside the modern cabin. A stopover in Lisbon – the route through neutral Portugal used throughout the war – is indicated only by a flight

---

73 According to a Production Code Administration document of 20 February 1942, the first 'working title' of the film was in fact *Sherlock Holmes vs Lord Haw-Haw*, a title which remained until 28 April when it became *Sherlock Holmes Saves London*, then *Sherlock Holmes and the Voice of Fear*, before finally settling on its release title.

board, and soon an aerial view of Washington's most well-known landmarks becomes visible as the plane descends.[74] Thus both *Voice of Terror* and *Washington* are not only set in wartime, but they are directly concerned with the war and this concern is the immediate generic indicator. In *Washington*, the plot is set up quickly: a group of Nazi sympathisers, desperate to obtain a secret document, snatch the British agent they suspect is carrying it. The genre messages are therefore ones of war or espionage and this is sustainable because, once again, Holmes is not present in these opening scenes. When he does appear, it is on his home territory at 221B Baker Street. These still-Victorian surroundings, prefaced by a shot of another Victorian icon, the Houses of Parliament, form a pointed contrast with the US modernity that will pervade the rest of the film and serve to position England (and Holmes) as consonant with unchanging tradition. Holmes is not seen again in England in this film – even the closing sequence, which might have returned to London in line with classic detective genre tradition, takes place in an open-top car in Washington. This anchors Holmes very firmly to the present day: one of the reasons for the subsequent retreat of the series from modernity might be that the studio thought they had gone too far.

Secret Weapon is slightly different, with more ambiguous generic and temporal indicators. The film opens with a 'Switzerland' caption over a scene of the Alps, before cutting to an aerial view of a village nestled in the valley, then to a room where a man in the shadows watches a stooped figure in the street below walk into a bar. The night-time scene and the establishing shots of the watching man indicate the genre as 'mystery' but give no clue as to whether the setting is contemporary. The following scene, in the bar's bright interior *(see Fig. 32)*, does little to clarify this, offering a folkloric vision of Continental Europe that could be set anytime in the previous century. A musician in traditional Swiss costume plays the xylophone, customers play draughts, waitresses in dirndl skirts serve steins of beer, and the stooped man – a bookseller – plies his trade. It is made clear that we are in the present day when the 'bookseller' tells two men at

---

74 Stock shots dating from the 1930s were supplemented by new footage of the Washington Monument, the Lincoln Memorial and Washington airport, commissioned via Universal's newsreel department with the permission of the US Department of the Interior and the War Department (Feld letter dated 31 August 1942 and Gartside letter to Universal dated 29 August 1942).

FIGURE 32 A folkloric vision of Europe in the opening scenes to *Sherlock Holmes and the Secret Weapon.*

a table that he has orders from the Führer to obtain the 'Tobel bombsight' before England snatches it. This is the only one of the 'war films' in which Holmes is present in the opening sequence, and therefore the temporal ambiguity is entirely appropriate. He is, of course, the 'old bookseller', something the audience is allowed to deduce for themselves by the fact that he professes not to be familiar with the name of the detective who England is sending to get the bombsight ('Homes?' he asks) and is thus surely the only person in the world not to have heard of Holmes. His presence immediately affects genre expectations, with 'mystery' becoming refined to 'detective'. Despite the background of war throughout the film both in theme and visual clues, *Secret Weapon* never achieves the same modernity as *Voice of Terror* or *Washington*. This may be because the villain against whom Holmes must battle is not a Nazi spy, but his age-old adversary, Moriarty. It is also because *Secret Weapon* has three scenes in the Victorian environs of 221B whereas *Voice of Terror* and *Washington* have only one.

FIGURE 33 Holmes' 1940s but essentially Victorian sitting room at 221B.

BAKER STREET: A VICTORIAN 'TIME WARP'

Set in contrast to all the indications of the contemporary is Holmes' Baker Street sitting room *(see Fig. 33)* which is more overtly Victorian than the Regency-style Twentieth Century-Fox set, except for the discreet addition of an electric table lamp, radiogram and telephone. The fact that Holmes' calabash pipe and his magnifying glass reside on top of the radiogram help 'reclaim' this modern piece of technology for the Victorian.[75] Careful analysis of the set reveals that everything else in the room is Victorian: the walls are darkly panelled in wood, there are heavy velvet curtains and net curtains at both windows, all the furniture is in dark wood, and there is a Persian-style carpet on the floor. There is an enormous amount of Victorian-style furniture crammed into the room: in the centre is a large dining table which is also used for books and papers, and on which rests

---

75 Items are visible in *Washington*.

Holmes' violin and (in *Secret Weapon*) a magic lantern projector. There are three dark leather armchairs, a leather settee, a balloon-back chair with tapestry upholstery, an escritoire desk, a breakfront bookcase, freestanding and built-in bookshelves, numerous bobbin-legged side-tables, a chiffonier, and a number of dining chairs. In addition there is a stand filled with fancy-handled Victorian umbrellas, a coat stand and hat rack, numerous hunting-dog pictures on the walls, Art Nouveau reading lamps, a candle in a fancy brass holder, a fireside companion-set, and a copper warming pan. Lastly, there is the usual paraphernalia associated with Holmes: a make-up table for putting on disguises, a globe on a stand, a scimitar hung on the wall, a sword-and-shield wall decoration, and a full-scale laboratory on a side-table. Clearly visible in a shot in *Washington*, neatly incised into the wall next to the bookcase, are the letters 'VR' in bullet holes – for 'Victoria Regina' – hardly an inscription that a 1940s Holmes, living in the reign of George VI, would have made.[76] Interestingly too, all the books in the bookcase are ancient and battered: clearly Holmes has owned these for a long time. Are we to believe that such an incisive mind which is at home with the latest technological developments, would own not a single up-to-date book? Or perhaps his books are a metonym for Holmes himself, forever rooted in the Victorian.

'Set-dressing' – the supply of furniture, paintings, rugs and accessories – was a specialist studio job, carried out once a set was built and painted. Set dressers, as Antonio Ramirez points out, were especially important in B-movies, where the same set had to be used in different films. 'It was often enough,' he says 'to move the furniture around, put up some different curtains or a new painting, a vase, a lamp, grillwork etc to make the set seem like a new place. So doing, the set dressers saved the studios much money', just as revamping parts of Universal's 'European village' by adding a door, window or chimney could transform the look.[77] Although Ramirez's comments may make set-dressing sound as if its only aim was to create a different appearance at low cost, every choice made about the objects placed on a set was a conscious one, designed to convey the personality of its inhabitant, the mood of the film, or the prevailing 'brand' of the particular studio.

---

76 A post-facto justification is made for this in *Sherlock Holmes Faces Death*.
77 Ramirez, 2004, pp.69 and 103.

Although there is no description of the Baker Street rooms in Lynn Riggs and John Bright's script for the first of the Universal series, *Voice of Terror*, studio publicity stresses that the interior had been deliberately left as a Victorian sitting room, and indeed there is a strong contrast between Holmes' rooms and those of the people he visits. In *Secret Weapon*, for example, Tobel's girlfriend Charlotte lives in a flat in central London but this vast Beverley Hills-style space is furnished in a modern, classic, uncluttered style with clean lines (white woodwork, light-coloured upholstery and pale furniture, including a white piano). Even Moriarty's lair is shown to be elegant – traditional without being Victorian. It is worth noting however that, whereas Holmes' rooms would have looked the epitome of the Victorian to American eyes, contemporary British audiences would not necessarily have thought them particularly out-of-step with wartime reality. Although suburban new homes and purpose-built flats might have looked more like *Fig. 34* with its streamlined art deco

FIGURE 34 A typical modern art deco room of the same period.

furniture, Holmes lived in furnished 'digs' rented from Mrs Hudson, who is presumed to be a widow taking in lodgers to make ends meet (a common situation in central London). Many of these 'digs' would have been unchanged since the turn of the century and – were it not for the presence of Holmes and his close symbolic ties with the Victorian – these rooms might have looked to audiences to be simply a bit old fashioned. Certainly, they would have seemed more 'realistic' to British audiences than their portrayal in the Clive Brook films *The Return of Sherlock Holmes* (1929) and *Sherlock Holmes* (1932), where they resembled a large modern American hotel suite on several levels.

So powerful is the association of Holmes with the Victorian, that some writers misremember the Universal series, glossing over the more obvious aspects of modernity and remembering only the period details. Jim Harmon, for example, says that 'much of the time [Holmes and Watson] were only in their rooms at 221B Baker Street, or in dripping docks infested by rats, human and rodent. Then time stood still, and it might as well have been the old London that Doyle wrote of'.[78] Yet the war is present around them in all three films, visible in the taped windows at the ministry offices, the sandbags on the pavement, the piles of brick rubble that they delicately step around, the dimmed headlights of cars, the bombed church, and the respect for the blackout. It is, however, a strangely distanced war. Holmes and Watson never take refuge in a shelter, or join crowds of people heading for the safety of the Underground; the sirens never wail, and the sound of approaching enemy aircraft is never heard. These films, suggests Naugrette, may mobilise a famous literary figure in the context of the war, but are in no way films about the war itself or the way it affects the daily lives of the population.[79] The only 'live' act of war they witness is the burning of the docks in the East End, which they watch from the balcony of the ministry offices in *Voice of Terror*, and even that has a slightly unreal quality as it follows similar scenes of acts of destruction which happen 'off set' and which are shown in newsreel-style footage, unwitnessed by any of the main characters. This distancing has interesting parallels with America's experience of the war in Europe, which was understood mainly through newsreels, in contrast to Britain's first-hand experience of

78 Harmon, 1975, p.5.

79 Naugrette, 2005, p.133.

the Blitz. The war is even more distant at 221B and makes its presence felt only once: when a tin-helmeted policeman briefly enters in *Voice of Terror* to remove Gavin's body, like an emissary from another age. Otherwise, life proceeds as normal, with afternoon teas, boiled eggs, tobacco, music on the radio, and service from Mrs Hudson.[80]

COSTUME CLUES

Even when not at 221B, Holmes and Watson always carry traces of the Victorian with them through their costume. Throughout the three films, they are neither entirely contemporary in their dress, nor entirely old fashioned and this subtle mix makes the characters plausible in their modern setting while retaining the connotations associated with their 'proper era'. The costume designer for the Universal series was Vera West who also worked on many of the studio's horror movies including *House of Frankenstein* (1944), *She-Wolf of London* (1946), *Mystery of Marie Roget* (1942) and *The Mummy's Curse* (1944) many of which had a Gothic setting. This, however, does not entirely explain the characters' appearance. Whereas West designed Rathbone's clothes which were then, according to a Universal press release, 'kept under lock and key in... a special section in Universal's wardrobe building reserved for trademarked garments of certain celluloid figures', Nigel Bruce wore his own clothes. The only item the studio provided was his bow tie (a claim borne out by the film cost sheets).[81] It was common industry practice for male actors to provide their own costume, unless they were appearing in a period picture, but Bruce's dress says as much about the conflation between star/character, and his previous typecasting as a bumbling English gentleman, as it does about the positioning of Holmes and Watson as midway between the Victorian and the contemporary.

In *Voice of Terror*, clever use of costume helps smooth the disjuncture between the fog-bound credits sequence and the opening montage of modern war-torn Europe. In the scene in the ministry office, the top-ranking intelligence officers wear a mix of costume

---

80 In this way, 221B exists as a kind of parallel universe sealed off from the rest of the world. Vivian Sobchack uses the concept of a parallel universe in writing about film noir: the world she describes is the exact antithesis of that of Holmes and Watson, being a world of anonymous, transient spaces where the notion of 'home' is completely absent (V. Sobchack, 1998, p.160).

81 Universal press release, 26 January 1945.

FIGURE 35 Holmes' Edwardian collar worn with a 1940s suit, an indication to viewers that he is still the 'old' Holmes.

styles: Sir Evan wears cutaway coat and morning trousers, Sir Alfred wears wing collar and bow tie, and others wear naval uniforms or modern 1940s double-breasted suits with soft collars. Such a mix was unusual for the year: a photograph of Churchill's War Cabinet of 21 men shows everyone in three-piece suits, with only one man wearing a wing collar and no-one in a cutaway jacket.[82] Equally, Neville Chamberlain – dubbed 'The Last Edwardian' – was still wearing cutaway coats in this period, and the dress would have connoted tradition as well as 'establishment'. To the American audience, more importantly, it connoted 'British'. When Holmes and Watson enter the room, Holmes looks the image of the city gentleman in his dark suit and tie, bowler hat and gloves, but he wears a stiff, round-cornered Edwardian collar which marks him as being from another

---

82 Illustration in Costantino, 1997, p.67.

era – the 'old Holmes' with whom cinema-goers are familiar *(see Fig. 35)*. Watson wears the style of dress he will wear predominantly throughout the series: wing collar, bow tie, jacket, morning trousers, waistcoat with watch chain, and bowler hat.[83]

Throughout the film, Holmes and Watson retain elements of a late-Victorian look: at 221B Holmes wears the same smoking jacket he wore in the Twentieth Century-Fox films, then when he goes out, he changes into a Norfolk hunting jacket with half-belt. This tweed jacket, a style introduced in the 1880s but still worn in the 1940s, was essentially country wear. The pressbook for *Washington* describes it as an 'up-to-the-minute Victory suit without cuffs', the Victory Suit being an American invention of the War Production Board, though this one seems more redolent of the Victorian than the 1940s. Perhaps its 'hunter' connotations are a way of replacing the item of dress most associated with Holmes – the deerstalker. Early in the film, a light-hearted scene at 221B reassures the audience that, despite the transition to the modern day, Holmes is the same person he has always been. As he and Watson leave the sitting room, reaching for their overcoats from the stand, Holmes picks up his deerstalker, only to be rebuked by Watson who says: 'Oh Holmes, you promised'. Holmes picks up a modern trilby instead. The deerstalker remains on the coat stand throughout the series.

In contrast to Holmes and Watson, the dress of the 'men from the ministry' gradually becomes more modern: for example, by the end of the film, Sir Alfred, first seen in wing collar, is wearing a pinstriped double-breasted suit, striped tie and slouch hat. There is therefore a transition to modernity for these secondary characters that cannot be paralleled by a similar transition for Holmes and Watson because the values they represent are rooted in the previous century and this needs to be made clear in their visual representation. Pointer felt that the modernising of Holmes' appearance was 'reasonably good' – by which he seems to mean reasonably plausible, because he adds that 'the English settings seem to hover uncertainly around the 1920s, as did the men's clothes'.[84] In considering the ambivalence in the 'modernising' of Holmes and Watson, it is worth noting that it is not just the characters' heritage which pulls in the direction of the

---

83 With the exception of *Washington* in which his costume is noticeably more modern.
84 Pointer, 1975, p.86.

Victorian, but the star personae too. Through the two Twentieth Century-Fox films, and the ongoing radio shows, Rathbone and Bruce were already strongly identified with a Victorian Holmes and Watson and both actors were noted for playing in period pieces: of the 20 Rathbone films immediately prior to the Universal series, 13 were costume dramas including three set in the nineteenth century.

The use of costume in *Secret Weapon* follows a similar pattern to that in *Voice of Terror*, though all minor characters wear unambiguously modern dress throughout. The start of the film offers a 'soft' introduction to modernity in the Swiss bierkeller, and the Victorian touches in the main characters have also been toned down slightly: Holmes still wears an Edwardian jacket but sports a windswept hairstyle that is at once unlike the slicked-back look of the Fox films, yet strangely Byronic (it prompted a *Punch* cartoon on 20 January 1943 captioned 'The Locks of Sherlock') and Watson wears an ordinary collar and tie for much of the second half of the film. It is interesting to note, however, that for Moriarty's first appearance, a transition to the modern was felt to be too sudden: he appears in wing collar, cravat tie, and three-piece suit with watch chain. This indicates that he is not a 'new' enemy, nor even an ordinary one, but a force of evil that is eternal, that can spring up again out of its time.

With *Washington*, Universal took what Steinbrunner and Michaels called 'the ultimate step' in modernising Holmes, because the settings 'were no longer crooked Limehouse streets or English manor houses, but the United States capital in wartime'.[85] Although Holmes retains his Norfolk jacket, all other traces of the Victorian are erased and, in particular, Watson's transition from Britain to America is coded as being one from the past to the present: from the moment he steps onto US soil, he wears modern dress and enthusiastically embraces American culture in everything from milk shakes to Flash Gordon comic strips. Indeed, cultures that are not American are shown to be strongly associated with the enemy: the kidnapper of the British agent, for example, runs an antique shop selling Egyptian, Chinese and Moorish artefacts – symbols not just of the past but of otherness. Such symbolism is used in another wartime detective film, *The Falcon in Danger* (1943) in which the villain, who has a German accent, is also an antique dealer, with his otherness highlighted through the nature of the goods in which he trades.

---

85 Steinbrunner and Michaels, 1978, p.100.

FIGURE 36 Holmes displays his familiarity with modern technology, such as this soundwave monitor in *Sherlock Holmes and the Voice of Terror.*

AT HOME WITH TECHNOLOGY

At no point in these films is Holmes shown to be uncomfortable with modernity and, indeed, he regularly demonstrates his knowledge of, and competence with, technology. In *Voice of Terror* he uses a soundwave monitor attached to the radiogram at 221B in order to discover, by plotting a complex and unexplained graph, that the 'voice' broadcasts have been pre-recorded. Close-ups of this monitor, with its buttons, dials and soundwave display, feature in a prolonged scene *(see Fig. 36)*. He also deduces that plastic surgery has helped a German spy take on the fake identity of Sir Evan: such surgery was a relatively new medical technique not widely used until after World War One in the treatment of facial and head injuries.[86] In *Secret*

---

86 The use of plastic surgery for disguise was also used in a number of other wartime films, including *The Strange Death of Adolf Hitler* (1943) in which a man changes his appearance in order to impersonate the Führer.

Weapon, he grasps the importance of the 'three sonic beams' that make the bombsight so accurate and therefore a covetable invention (and there are numerous shots of the bombsight being used with deadly accuracy), and in *Washington* he tells Watson of the advantages of storing information on microfilm: just one pigeon can transport 18,000 soldiers' letters home. In short, he is as conversant with cars, speedboats, intercoms, radios and aeroplanes as he used to be with the 1895 railway timetable, though technology is never allowed to overshadow the basic premise of the classic detective genre, which is that the crimes must be solved through intelligent deduction.

Sometimes old-fashioned methods are shown to be just as effective as the latest technologies. In *Secret Weapon*, Holmes tries to read what someone has written on a notepad before they tore off the page: his detailed explanation of the chemicals involved, and his use of a magic-lantern projector, call to mind his Victorian laboratory rather than 1940s methods. In *Washington* Holmes is forced to apologise to the US police for assuming that they would be as slow witted as they are in England, saying that he sometimes forgets 'the more modern scientific methods so particularly effective here in America'. The words 'method' and 'scientific' point up a contrast with bumbling England still stuck in the nineteenth century, though 'Victorian' England does score a small triumph later in the film when the US laboratory with its array of highly modern equipment fails to spot the vital clue – a fragment of antique wood – that Holmes finds simply with the aid of his magnifying glass.

This 'modern' Holmes is, in fact, more at home with technology than his Doylean original, indicating that nostalgia was key to the character's appeal in the stories. Nowhere, for example, in the Doyle canon is there a description of Holmes and Watson travelling by Underground, even though by the 1890s it was very much part of the fabric of London. In 'The Red-Headed League', Watson reports that they 'travelled by Underground' but no dialogue or action takes place while they are doing so; and in 'The Bruce-Partington Plans', they spend considerable time on the tracks or the station platforms in a hunt for clues, but never travel on the train itself. Similarly, neither Holmes or Watson are seen using the telephone in the stories: Holmes refers, in 'The Retired Colourman', to being able to obtain information through the telephone while at Baker Street; in 'The Three Garridebs', Watson looks up a name in the phone book but does not make a call; and in 'The Illustrious Client', Holmes makes a note of a telephone number.[87] Clearly, there is a telephone in the rooms (as indeed there is in the film-set), but in the stories it never rings, nor does the reader hear him make a call.[88]

A WARTIME MORALITY

Another way in which any tensions between present and past can be exposed, is through the values espoused by Holmes and Watson. Holmes' values are commonly perceived as absolute: they have little to do with the machinery of the law or with the 'English gentleman', but everything to do with a common-sense idea of justice. But Bernard Dick points to a new ambiguity in *Voice of Terror*, arguing that although the premise of the plot is Holmesian, the morality embraced by Holmes is a wartime morality, 'the morality of expediency'.[89] Dick is disturbed by Holmes' manipulation of Kitty, the East End bar girl. First Holmes rouses her to 'galvanise the rabble of Limehouse' behind the Allied cause with the promise that she will be at the head of a people's army. Then he expects her to sleep with her quarry, 'for England': 'the Nazi whom Kitty must seduce is an Englishman, and it is Holmes who arranges the seduction'.[90] This would probably go unremarked in any other character but Holmes: so fixed, however, is the notion of what audiences expect his values and conduct to be (unequivocally Victorian), that an attempt to 'update' them to less absolute standards is looked upon unfavourably.

Much of the later critical writing on the Universal series has focused on whether they were successful as 'Sherlock Holmes films', the general consensus being that the wartime setting tended to get in the way; but it is worth remembering that the films were made in the service of the war (and, in commercial terms, to feed audiences' hunger for films about the war). In this context, it is useful to revisit

---

87   Doyle, 1981, p.64 in *The Adventures of Sherlock Holmes*; Doyle, 1997, p.93 in *His Last Bow*; Doyle, 1951, pp.244, 120 and 14 in *The Case-Book of Sherlock Holmes*.

88   This is perhaps why one *Picture Show* reader, after he saw the Stoll series of Sherlock Holmes films, made and set in the 1920s, wrote to the magazine saying that he felt that the use of a telephone in *The Six Napoleons* was anachronistic because 'in the author's stories a telephone is never mentioned. An attempt at modernisation, perhaps, but for what reason?' (*Picture Show*, 16 September 1922, unpaginated).

89   Dick, 1985, p.112.

90   Dick, 1985, p.113.

the OWI guidelines cited at the beginning of this chapter and assess how the Holmes 'war' films met the criteria. Clearly their intent was to fulfil the aim of 'helping to win the war': Seymour remarked in 1987 that the closing speeches were so powerful that they made you 'want to rush right out and buy War Bonds, even today' and there is a direct appeal to Britain and America's common heritage in the figure of Holmes.[91] The pressbook for *Washington* overtly conflates Holmes and patriotism by recommending that cinemas place 'clues' in classified newspaper advertisements that, when deciphered, spell out a patriotic sentence, such as 'Sherlock Holmes says buy more bonds'. How the films met the OWI guidelines about timeliness and truth telling, however, is less certain. Because of the delay in releasing the films, particularly the 12-month delay in the UK of *Voice of Terror*, it is questionable whether, at the point of their maximum circulation, they reflected the current war situation: a year is an extraordinarily long time in the context of a fast-moving conflict. In regard to 'truth telling', could the enemy plausibly be seen as a series of errant individuals able to be brought to heel simply through the application of rational deduction by one man, even if that man was as extraordinary as Sherlock Holmes? The fact that the Dead End Kids and Abbott and Costello were seen to 'lick' the Nazis with OWI approval indicated that it was indeed plausible, though the industry's dropping of this type of plot from 1943 onwards signalled that it was not sustainable for very long.

After these three films, the series changed direction, retreating from overtly contemporary settings into a mythical kingdom of Scottish castles, swirling fog, candlelight and secret passages. Occasional references would be made to the war, but the crimes, the villains and their motivation would no longer be identifiably those of the Nazis. The studio – or audiences – may have tired of war-themed espionage films, or perhaps felt that the modernisation of Holmes had been taken too far. Steinbrunner and Michaels argue the latter, that 'the wrenching of Holmes from his familiar surroundings was felt too disturbing, and the mix did not quite work' though this is not entirely borne out by the reviews at the time.[92] Certainly there were dissenting voices: Howard Barnes in the *New York Tribune* advised

---

91 *Classic Images*, August 1987, p.46.

92 Steinbrunner and Michaels, 1978, p.105.

Universal to 'leave Sherlock Holmes in the period to which he so peculiarly belonged',[93] but for the most part the reviews were moderately accepting of the films – not great art, but exciting enough with plenty of action and what *Kinematograph Weekly* termed a 'good catch-penny for the industrial masses'.[94]

If Holmes did indeed stand for certainty in a time of uncertainty, then this was an increasingly difficult quality to sustain in a context where the enemy was not a single individual who could be brought to justice and the status quo restored – all in 70 minutes. Making Moriarty the criminal brain behind every act of wartime espionage set up fresh difficulties: Derek Longhurst points out that using him in this way revealed 'the evident fear of an organised network, an underground which might be rendered powerfully threatening to the social organism through the ruthless leadership of the deviant individualist'.[95] By 1943 almost every family in the US (as well, of course, as in Britain) had members fighting on land, sea or air – their stories, and the reassurance that it was the efforts of the 'little people' that were helping to win the war, seemed more relevant to audiences.[96] In the Holmes films so far, success had depended on a supreme being: the little people, like Kitty in *Voice of Terror*, were seen to be dispensable once their purpose had been served. There was also the issue of the war-weary audience. Biesen says that the OWI 'missed the point that Hollywood was already savvy to: propaganda in a story is more powerful and palatable when its message is unobtrusive to the viewer'.[97] Formed in June 1942, the OWI's domestic division was disbanded just one year later, though its foreign-markets arm continued throughout the war.

Genre considerations and studio preferences may of course have had more to do with the decision than audience reactions. Genres, even with the multiple tags favoured by the studios, have only a certain elasticity, beyond which they lose their identity and become harder to market in terms of setting audience expectations. While the

---

93 Quoted in Steinbrunner and Michaels, 1978, p.93.

94 *Kinematograph Weekly*, 21 October 1943, p.21.

95 Longhurst, 1989, p.59.

96 1943 saw the release of many such films including *A Stage Door Canteen*, *Cry Havoc*, *Bataan*, *Guadalcanal Diary* and *A Guy Named Joe*.

97 Biesen, 2005, p.83.

crime picture may have been in the ascendant at the time, its reliance on modernity (the gangsters, cars, guns of Barefoot's list cited earlier) made it an awkward fit with a hero from the classic detective genre, where the emphasis was on gentlemanly deduction and brainwork rather than action. Combining the two meant treading a fine line between two genres: one tied to modernity and one tied to the past. Add to this a contemporary war theme, with Nazis taking on the personae of gangsters, and the genre can become even more confused. Even the Production Code Administration noted this, remarking in their report on *Secret Weapon* that the war was 'simply background for Holmes chasing foreign agents'.[98] After these 'war' films, the writing, directing and design team began to pull the series back onto the firmer ground of detection/mystery by eliminating many of the signs of modernity and returning Holmes to more Gothic surroundings. In doing this, they were to tip the series into another generic overlap – that of the horror film, in which Universal already had a considerable track record.

---

98 PCA report by Charles Metzger, 5 May 1942.

CHAPTER FOUR

A MYTHICAL KINGDOM
THE ENCROACHMENT OF THE GOTHIC

Potts: 'Who could be ringing the church bell at this time?
Maybe it ain't a "who", maybe it's an "it".'
Priest: 'Ah, there's no such things as ghosts and monsters.'

The Scarlet Claw

After three war-themed films made in quick succession in 1942, the series veered sharply away from engaging with current events. The stories from now on, said the studio, were to be timeless: 'a kind of present-day proposition so far as modern conveniences such as telephones and automobiles are concerned, but with dialogue and characteristics strictly of the Victorian era'.[1] Or, in other words, as Barnes succinctly puts it, Holmes was to be left in an 'ahistorical neverwhere'.[2]

This chapter explores the temporally ambiguous territory into which the films strayed and the associated stretching of genre boundaries. In particular, it examines the influence of director Roy William Neill (largely overlooked in cinema history until now) whose professional pedigree lay in the horror genre, and offers detailed textual analysis of the visual language that Neill used. This visual language has been attributed erroneously to wartime economies of sets and lighting rather than to aesthetic choices, but was actually the result of the transfer of Gothic horror sensibilities to the detective genre. The outcome was that his Holmes films displayed many of the lighting, framing and camera techniques that were to be later associated with film noir. The absence/presence of the war in these films involved last-minute decisions by the studio, in some cases adding topical references to what had been purely Gothic storylines,

---

1   Barefoot, 2001, p.52.
2   Barnes, 2002, p.167.

and in others removing overt references, particularly in the patriotic speeches that close a number of the films. The war therefore becomes a 'structured absence' which can be perceived as just one of the temporal layers in the films, each layer leaving its accretion of meaning like the fingerprints of history.

In moving away from the war, Universal was part of a Hollywood-wide trend. Dorothy B. Jones of the OWI noted in an article for *Nation* magazine that in 1942, a quarter of all films released dealt primarily with the war, mostly in the form of spy movies, comedies or musicals, and in 1943 there was a further upsurge, particularly in films concerned with the 'United Nations'. It was a brief peak: by 1944 war-related output declined and by 1945, anticipating victory, filmmakers turned their attention to post-war challenges.[3] Perhaps it was simply that by 1944 audiences had become war weary. Evidence from Lant, in her book on wartime cinema in Britain, supports this argument: she discusses a mid-1940s poll in which a woman reported having just seen Bette Davis in *Now Voyager*. The woman says: 'what enjoyment what relief – *no war*. I have worked in a large office with other women in whose homes the war is ever present by the absence of husbands and sons on service and who, like myself, snatch their bit of break in a couple of hours each week at the cinema'.[4] The retreat from war themes could also have been a reaction to a complicated censorship regime: Glancy argues that this is why many films not only avoided mention of the war, but retreated into the past.[5]

The war, with the exception of the topic of the 'United Nations', was to receive short shrift in the ongoing Holmes series. None of the plots of the nine films that followed was based on the war. The narratives turned from espionage to themes that were more familiar to Doyle readers and to a Victorian sensibility: insurance-fiddles, jewel thefts, kidnaps and revenge killings.[6] Indeed, the war quickly became forgotten: in the two films released after *Sherlock Holmes in Washington*,

---

3   Quoted by Michael Renov, 1988, p.55.

4   Lant, 1991, p.23.

5   Glancy, 1999, p.206.

6   Interestingly, *Hollywood Reporter* thought that the plot of *The House of Fear*, which it acknowledged was based on Sir Arthur Conan Doyle's story 'The Adventure of the Five Orange Pips' written 50 years previously, reflected a current trend: that of films 'dealing with mass murders and the gradual elimination of the cast' (15 March 1945, unpaginated).

there were very brief allusions to war, such as the presence of convalescent servicemen at Hulstone Towers in *Sherlock Holmes Faces Death*, and the use of Hitler, Mussolini and Hirohito's faces on the targets of the fairground shooting gallery in *Spider Woman*, but nothing that impinged on the plot. The trade paper *Hollywood Reporter* noted the change, commenting in its review of *Sherlock Holmes Faces Death* that 'the master detective continues as a modern figure, but Axis spies and saboteurs are not his antagonists and probably will not be again for the duration'.[7] In the same way, the settings of the films that followed began to lose specificity and were more likely to include foggy moors, gloomy Scottish castles and night-sleeper trains than they were the topographies of London or Washington. Candlelight, oil lamps and smugglers' caves replaced electricity, guns, and speedboats, and Holmes was seen to travel by horse-and-cart or train rather than by aeroplane.[8]

If the new settings and themes were an attempt to put the character of Holmes back where he belonged, and to win over the more traditional fan, then the messages were mixed. He shed his Edwardian Norfolk jacket for a more 1940s-style suit, tweed overcoat and floppy-brimmed hat, and changed his Byronic windswept hairstyle for the same slicked-back look he had worn in the Fox films. The sitting room at Baker Street, which had tied Holmes symbolically to the 1890s, lost its prominence and in three of the nine films it does not appear at all.[9] The changes left Holmes floating in a temporally ambiguous zone that was much closer to the Victorian than the modern, but which was still hard to pinpoint. Far from being to the detriment of the series, this floating was a benefit: by veering towards Gothic mystery and horror, it drew more sure-footedly on Universal's proven talents, and by stripping away the accoutrements of modernity, it allowed for the foregrounding of expressionist production values.

This chapter will consider these points in the context of the next batch of films in the series released between 1943 and the early months of 1945: *Sherlock Holmes Faces Death*, *Spider Woman*, *The Scarlet*

---

7   *Hollywood Reporter*, 2 September 1943, unpaginated.

8   The very absence of war references can sometimes draw attention to the 'unspoken' subject, as in *The Black Cat* (1934).

9   *The Scarlet Claw*, *Pursuit to Algiers* and *Terror by Night*.

Claw, *The Pearl of Death* and *The House of Fear*. It will not, however, be simply a chronological look at the films: although such an examination does reveal a stylistic and thematic trajectory and therefore will be discussed briefly. Instead, the approach will be to examine in detail two of the films: *Sherlock Holmes Faces Death* and *The Scarlet Claw*, the first because it immediately followed *Sherlock Holmes in Washington*, thus emphasising the extent of the retreat from modernity, and the second because it typifies the Gothic ambience of this middle part of the series. The other films will be treated briefly in relation to the arguments being put forward in this chapter, but will not be subject to a detailed textual analysis. This is because *The House of Fear* bears strong visual and narrative similarities to *Sherlock Holmes Faces Death* and therefore can be considered alongside it. The remaining two films – *Spider Woman* and *The Pearl of Death* – will be discussed fully in Chapter Five because they introduced a new phenomenon, the female villain, which would come to dominate the rest of the series.

DIRECTION AND ART DIRECTION

The films under discussion in this chapter exhibit a strong consistency of style and this is probably due to two key members of the crew. The first was Roy William Neill, who by this stage in the series was established as its director and had also taken over the production role from Howard Benedict.[10] The second was art director John Goodman who was to work on eight of the films, beginning with *Sherlock Holmes Faces Death*.

Roy William Neill (b. Ireland 1887) had enjoyed a prolific directing career which began in 1917: he made more than forty silent films, and then handled a wide variety of talkies at Columbia, from boxing films like *Cock o' the Walk* (1930) in which he also acted, to the Ann Sothern comedy *Blind Date* (1934). Gradually, however, one genre began to dominate: the horror-mystery film, including *The Menace* (1932), an Edgar Wallace adaptation complete with Egyptian mummies and a Jack O'Lantern that comes to life; *The Ninth Guest*

---

10   Benedict did not return to Universal until 1946: Tom Weaver (Weaver, Brunas and Brunas, 2007, p.386) claims that Benedict had been promoted to executive producer, but his name appears on no film credits during this period. A more likely explanation is that he was absent on war service, though I have not been able to ascertain this from studio files.

(1934) where eight strangers are brought together to be murdered one by one unless they outwit their 'host'; *Black Moon* (1934) in which a New York socialite becomes a white goddess in Haiti and ends up performing human sacrifices; and *The Black Room* (1935), a Boris Karloff film about twin brothers under a curse. This emerging specialism was interrupted when, in 1935, Roy was sent to England by Thomas Ince to take the place of a director who had been killed in a car accident. He worked in the UK until 1941, for Gainsborough, Gaumont and First National, on a wide variety of genres.[11] Returning to the US, he moved to Universal, where his first film was a low-budget crime-thriller, *Eyes of the Underworld*, described disparagingly by the *New York Times* as 'strictly a job-lot production and not a very good grade at that' and by *Kinematograph Weekly* as 'sound and exciting fare for the masses'.[12] In the autumn of 1942, Neill started on the Sherlock Holmes films where he was to direct 11 in swift succession.

Goodman (b. 1901) began his art director career in 1934 and worked in a variety of genres for Paramount. His output increased exponentially when he joined Universal, working on more than 170 films in the 1940s, most notably Alfred Hitchcock's *Shadow of a Doubt* in 1943. He collaborated with Neill on a number of productions apart from the Holmes series and horror was a key element of his output, with films including *Son of Dracula* (1943), *The Mad Ghoul* (1943), *The Mummy's Curse* (1944), *Enter Arsene Lupin* (1944) and *House of Frankenstein* (1944). He did not specialise in the way Neill did, however, and continued to undertake everything from comedies to westerns. As one of Universal's top art directors, Goodman worked on all the major Abbott and Costello releases, and on Deanna Durbin's *Can't Help Singing* (1944). On the Holmes series, he took over from Jack Otterson who had been art director on all three war-themed films.[13] Jane Barnwell argues that the 'look and feel' of a film is largely determined by a triumvirate – director, art director and director of

---

11 Neill remained an Anglophile, retaining a home in the UK until his death in December 1946.

12 *New York Times*, 5 October 1942, unpaginated; *Kinematograph Weekly*, 1 October 1942, p.29.

13 Otterson was the successor to Charles D. Hall at Universal who designed the castle for *Dracula* (1932). Otterson was to return to art-direct the very last film in the Holmes series, *Dressed to Kill*.

photography – but the visual style of the Holmes series, once Neill was appointed director/producer, was more likely set by him in conjunction with Goodman.[14] These two were a consistent team, whereas even this 'gothic' mid-part of the series had three different directors of photography: George van Enger, George Robinson and Virgil Miller. The term 'art director' seems to be ill-defined in the studio system and is traditionally thought of as implying responsibility for set design and construction, but Barnwell points out that the remit can extend to composing 'each and every angle that is consequently shot'.[15] The strong similarities in lighting and framing throughout the 'gothic' films point to the conclusion that it was Neill, in conjunction with Goodman, who created their distinctive character.

AN OVERLOOKED TALENT

Despite Neill's credentials as a director, he is almost completely absent from cinema history, which is perhaps more of a reflection of critical and academic attitudes towards genre-films than it is of his talents. There has been no biography of Neill nor any detailed analysis of his techniques. Basil Rathbone paid him tribute in a 1967 public appearance at a US college – Wayne, Nebraska – when he praised both Neill's efficiency as a director, and his aesthetic sense. In terms of efficiency, he spoke of Neill being 'comparatively unknown… as sweet as they come, but a damn good disciplinarian. We didn't disobey orders on the set. We were always on time and we always knew our lines. It was thoroughly professional'.[16] Rathbone recalled that none of the films took more than 17 days to shoot, working a strict 9-to-5 routine. Neill, he said, had control over the entire production, acting as producer, director and scriptwriter – 'with a little help from a man called Millhauser'.[17] In terms of aesthetics, Rathbone described the result as 'beautifully made films – photographically, and the way they were directed and constructed', a fact which he attributed solely to Neill.[18]

---

14 Barnwell, 2004, p.46.

15 Barnwell, 2004, p.13.

16 _The Woods Runner_, May 1979, p.35. Rathbone was there to open the 'John H. Watson' reading room of the college.

17 Similar statements on Neill's uncredited scriptwriting appear on numerous websites about the Universal series but it has not been possible to determine whether they are simply repeating the version of events expressed, and possibly misremembered, by Rathbone.

The assistant director's daily reports bear out Rathbone's recollections, though the hours worked were rather longer: *House of Fear,* for example, had a 16-day schedule which meant filming seven pages of script each day. Given that the film used 23 different sets, and that sometimes three pages of script entailed as many as 13 camera set ups, this made for long days: the cast and crew rarely finished before 7pm or 8pm.[19] Despite tight schedules and budgets, Neill seemed to go beyond the brief in many ways: not just artistically, as will be discussed in detail below, but in those details that would lend the films an authenticity not often associated with B-movies. As previously noted, he had commissioned new aerial footage of Washington – a bold request in wartime – rather than rely on existing 1930s stock, and for the set of Dr Johnson's house in *Dressed to Kill*, he wrote to a London contact, Martin Murphy, asking him to take stills of the house in Gough Square ('all rooms, halls and stairways from various angles') and to provide a floor plan because, he said, 'it is very essential that we have this historic locale as authentic as possible'.[20]

Rathbone's praise of Neill did not seem to stir academic interest in his work. It was not until the mid 1970s that the quality of his output began to be noticed. This small surge of interest may be attributable to the birth of film studies as an academic discipline, but seems unlikely because it was some time before B-movies were seen as worthy of interest other than in terms of studio economics. The screening of the series on television in cut-down versions in the 1970s may have attracted attention, and of course new Holmes films and TV dramas continued to be made: the decade was notable for a number of comic productions, including *The Private Life of Sherlock Holmes* (1970), *The Adventures of Sherlock Holmes' Smarter Brother* (1975), *Elementary My Dear Watson* (TV, 1973), and the Peter Cook and Dudley Moore version of *The Hound of the Baskervilles* (1978). These may have renewed interest in earlier adaptations, though any comment was

---

18   *The Woods Runner*, May 1979, p.35.

19   Assistant director's daily report by Mort Singer and Phil Bowles, *The House of Fear* (May 1944). By this point in the series, the budgets had grown somewhat: *The House of Fear* was budgeted at 192,250 dollars compared to around 150,000 dollars for the early films (production estimate dated 8 May 1944) and this was to rise to 237,000 dollars for *Dressed to Kill* (Universal picture costs sheets dated November 1946).

20   Neill letter to Murphy, 19 December 1945.

largely restricted to fan-based publications. In 1975 Jim Harmon in *The History of Sherlock Holmes* magazine said that although the films were supposed to be B-movies[21] they 'never looked like cheaply mounted endeavours'.[22] In 1978 Ron Haydock, in *Deerstalker!*, wrote that the production values of the series exceeded those found in many A-film releases, especially the 'moody... Gothic overtones',[23] a view which was echoed in the same year by Steinbrunner and Michaels. It was 1979 before an academic article appeared. In 'A Case for Further Research' for *Focus on Film*, Paul Leggett attempted to stimulate interest in the series by praising the way Neill 'made the Holmes film move', avoiding the trap of a 'static' approach. The films were atmospheric too: Neill, he said, 'bathed his pictures in teutonic shadows' so that his films 'really have more of an affinity to the gothic thriller than they do to the detective genre'.[24] Leggett believed that Neill's work influenced the development in the 1940s of film noir and called for more research to be carried out.

No-one took up his call and Neill's talents seem to have been forgotten: this chapter seeks to demonstrate that his films do indeed have a strong link to the Gothic thriller and also that in his transference of these Gothic techniques and iconography to the detective genre, he might be usefully thought of in the context of the development of film noir.

Even at the time the films were released, reviewers noticed only their factory-production qualities. This was characteristic of the way B-movies were treated: for example, in reviewing *Meet Boston Blackie* (1941), which was to spawn a long-running detective series, *Variety's* only comment on its 'artistry' concerned the sheer lack of it.[25] B-movies, like the British quota quickies of the 1930s, were made on low budgets and the expected outcome was a low-quality product.

---

21 Although made as B-pictures, they were not always exhibited as such. An advertising flyer for the Capitol cinema in Bridgewater, for example, shows *The Scarlet Claw* as the A-feature, with *The Yellow Rose of Texas* as support (source: Arthur Conan Doyle Collection – Richard Lancelyn Green Bequest).

22 Harmon, 1975, p.4.

23 Haydock, 1978, p.134.

24 Leggett, 1979, p.26.

25 'The jumpiness of the episodes in the film is frequently startling. Either Florey (the director) has skipped the connecting links in an effort to hold down costs, or editor James Sweeney has scissored them to speed the tempo. At any rate, it's a crude job' (*Variety*, 5 March 1941, unpaginated).

According to Lawrence Napper, British reviews usually criticised the slowness of the narratives, lack of action and 'sedate' detective stories that were the mainstay of the quota quickie even though, with hindsight, it has in recent years begun to be acknowledged as an entertaining, intriguing and engaging corpus of films.[26]

B-movies were treated in much the same way: in terms of the Holmes series, *Variety* commented on 'the usual number of grisly murders and suspects, fog-shrouded marshes and deserted houses',[27] and described the scripts as 'straight-line',[28] the acting as 'okay',[29] and the genre as unsophisticated and 'obviously grooved B detective melodrama'.[30] The *New York Herald Tribune* called the films variously 'dreary', 'conventional' and 'undistinguished' and the UK trade paper *Kinematogaph Weekly* felt they were acceptable only 'for the industrial masses and the sticks'[31] – in other words, down-market films for the lower classes. This is not to say the films were disliked by the press, who clearly relished the horror attributes the series was acquiring but, because these were formula pictures, they did not look for, or expect to find, innovative qualities. Like the 'anonymous' pulp-magazine writers of the thirties, the director has been effaced: Neill is mentioned by only two contemporary journals, *Motion Picture Herald* and *Hollywood Reporter*, both of which were trade publications. *Motion Picture Herald* praised the way 'Roy William Neill left nothing to be desired in suspense, action and portrayal of the true Holmes and Watson in his direction'; commented on the photography and art direction as being 'well done',[32] and the pace of direction set by Neill as 'brisk and suspenseful, never faltering'.[33] The use of the word 'true' to describe the portrayal of Holmes and Watson is interesting, particularly as it is attributed to the direction and not, as is more usual, to the actors. *Hollywood Reporter* said nothing about the direction until

---

26   Napper, in Murphy, 1997, p.46. There were always exceptions, of course, such as the quota quickies made by Alfred Hitchcock or Michael Powell.

27   *Variety*, 24 May 1944, p.10.

28   *Variety*, 30 August 1944, p.10.

29   *Variety*, 30 August 1944, p.10.

30   *Variety*, 8 September 1943, p.16.

31   *New York Herald-Tribune*, 20 May 1944, unpaginated; *Kinematograph Weekly*, 19 October 1944, p.25.

32   *Motion Picture Herald*, 11 September 1943, p.51.

33   *Motion Picture Herald*, 2 September 1944, p.2,083.

the release of *Sherlock Holmes Faces Death*, which it described as 'first-rate Doyle, handsomely produced and suspensefully directed by Neill'.[34] It was then consistent in its praise, suggesting that *The Scarlet Claw*, was 'a [directorial] demonstration of ability which should lead to bigger assignments'.[35] When reviewing *The Pearl of Death* it remarked on the 'beautiful little touches executed by actors not known for them before, that must be credited to Neill and recorded as evidence of his artistic ability'.[36] Years later, *Hollywood Reporter* had evidently forgotten the accolades it had heaped on Neill when it described the series as 'B-budget potboilers' and 'penny dreadfuls'.

One clue to the reason most trade and consumer reviewers saw little aesthetic merit in the films lies in a comment in a *New York Post* review which reads: 'it is possible to enjoy *The Scarlet Claw* unless you are tired of the Holmes series, bored with Basil, disgruntled with the doctor, or allergic to misfits in movies, or *European standards of production*'.[38] What exactly was being implied here? The comment, its meaning presumably clear to the 1944 reader, is more ambivalent today. Did the film look 'arty' and this automatically associated it with European cinema – or was this a jibe at what was perceived as the cheaper output expected from non-Hollywood films? Whichever way we interpret the comment, it serves to set these films apart from the mainstream. Their coding as European opens them to an alternative analytic approach which is inextricably linked to the Britishness of the main characters, a quality they carry with them despite the wide range of foreign settings for the films. This is not the case with other contemporary B-movie detective series, which also featured British characters (including Tom Conway as The Falcon and George Sanders as The Saint) in global settings. The nationality of these characters went unremarked: they did not stand for Britain in the same way that Basil Rathbone did as Holmes – something due to Holmes' established status as a metonym for England. Nor did these films, in their matter-of-fact approach to art direction, exhibit any hint of expressionist technique: no critic described them as European.

34 *Hollywood Reporter*, 2 September 1943, unpaginated.

35 *Hollywood Reporter*, 24 April 1944, unpaginated.

36 *Hollywood Reporter*, 25 August 1944, unpaginated.

37 Osborne in *Hollywood Reporter*, 26 June 1992, p.9.

38 *New York Post*, 20 May 1944, unpaginated. Italics are my emphasis.

Part of the reason for the look of these films, it could be argued, is that these other detective series were firmly grounded in the modern-day world, whereas Holmes had one foot in the Victorian era – a period closely associated with the Gothic. 'Teutonic shadows' had been visible in the three films which strove so hard to place Holmes in the 1940s (one example is the shadow of a giant net hanging over the ministry office in the early part of *Voice of Terror*), but hardly prominent.[39] Loosening the ties with modernity enabled these Gothic sensibilities to come to the fore, and in the fourth film of the series the change of tone is striking. In using the term 'Gothic', I am employing both the definition given by the *Longman Dictionary of Contemporary English*, which refers to Gothic films as being those with 'ruined castles, haunted graveyards and eerie noises', and also to Lisa Hopkins' description of tales 'often set in ancient, partially ruined castles or mansions', in which the key genre marker is one of an aesthetic of violent contrasts.[40] These settings are the outward manifestation of a psychological situation which David Saliba says usually includes a helpless victim entranced by an evil victimiser with immense or supernatural powers, together with a sense of oppressiveness, fear and doom.[41]

SET ADRIFT FROM THE CONTEMPORARY

Sherlock Holmes Faces Death is as firmly planted in an English locale as its predecessor was in the United States, but the references to the contemporary which reminded us that *Washington* was set in the present day are almost entirely absent. This depiction of England in 1943 includes traumatised soldiers and signs warning that 'loose talk costs lives', but also features oil lamps, candles, mediaeval suits of armour, arcane heraldic rituals, landed gentry, butlers, ravens, clocks that strike thirteen, and talk of 'corpse lights'. The retreat from modernity could not be more obvious. Exhibitors would have been alerted to it immediately through the film's pressbook: in the section devoted to the publicity material available, the heading 'posters' uses a font that connotes horror and the image in the background shows

39 Naugrette has noted what he terms the 'neo-expressionist' aesthetic visible in *Secret Weapon* in lighting, camera angles and use of shadows (Naugrette, 2005, p.130).

40 Hopkins, 2005, p.i.

41 Saliba, 1980, pp.27–8.

stone steps, a crypt, a skull, a cross, and a coffin. A monstrous black shadow is cast on the far wall by a figure who seems to be struggling with an assailant.

In *Sherlock Holmes Faces Death* the war, instead of forming the core of the plot, has become incidental: this is not an espionage story but a serial-murder tale in which the perpetrator is greedy for the riches he discovers that the Musgrave family unwittingly possesses. The context for death, which in wartime might connote service for one's country, has been shifted into the realm of traditional whodunit. Holmes takes on the case, not to respond to a national imperative as he does in all three of the earlier films, but to help out his old friend Dr Watson. Servicemen are present merely as a bunch of eccentrics and could easily be replaced by other British stock characters without impact on the plot. Absence of an overt war narrative does not, of course, always indicate a straightforward escape from reality, and – as the patriotic end-speech makes clear – the war can be present as a 'structured absence' with analogies easily drawn between the moral dilemmas faced by the film's characters and those facing its audience. Lant reminds us that 'the war caused every fiction, no matter how apparently remote from the crisis, to be understood in its terms'.[42] Although, for example, there is an *explicit* reference to war in the Universal film *The Black Cat* (1934), in which an architect has built his home directly over a World War One battle site where the bodies had been piled twelve deep and the river had become a 'torrent of blood', the *implicit* reference lies in the house's overtly modernist design which is a continual reminder of what it has covered up. Merely the use of the word 'comrades' to describe the group of old friends in *The House of Fear* – a term not used in the Doyle story from which it is taken – could be taken as a World War One reference.

If the war-references in *Faces Death* seem an add-on to a Gothic mystery, this precisely reflects the production history of the film. Bertram Millhauser's screenplay was based on a storyline by Gerald Geraghty, who in turn based parts of the plot on the Doyle story 'The Musgrave Ritual'. Geraghty (b. 1906) appears to have been a freelance, producing storylines and screenplays for a number of studios including Republic, RKO and Columbia, and specialising in westerns. His only foray into the detective genre was in writing three screenplays for the

---

42   Lant, 1991, p.35.

Falcon in 1943 and 1944. Geraghty's storyline is notable for including all the Gothic trappings that would be used in the film, but none of the war references.[43] Crucially, too, the moral resolution of the plot is absent: in Geraghty's version, the manor is a private house, not a treatment centre for servicemen. It has the appearance of a castle and is described as a 'grim setting for murder' surrounded by 'grey mist'. Watson, visiting the manor with Holmes (not working there as a doctor, as he is in the filmed version) is spooked by the weird sounds the house makes and the suits of armour that fill its halls. More Gothic references are made in describing the crypt of the house, which has 'all the ghostlike qualities of an Egyptian tomb' with 'strange shadows in profusion'. As in the film, the village inn plays a part in the story, but its customers do not include servicemen, only local villagers who listen to the 'quaint music of the tap room'. In terms of the motive for the murders, the storyline uses Doyle's plotline about a riddle and an ancient document that will reveal the whereabouts of 'the crown of the English kings' but the secret dies with the murderer. There is no opportunity in Geraghty's storyline, as there is in the film, for the heroine to renounce her claim to riches, in favour of the 'little people'. This change in plot reveals that the film's ending, and the 'grab and greed' homily by Holmes in the closing sequence, was specifically added to appeal to a wartime morality. Thus in the filmed version, land, inheritance and class are all strong themes and the homily at the end seems to suggest that these old, outdated concepts which define Britain (certainly in the eyes of Hollywood) might be swept away with the coming of a new age. Millhauser had taken Geraghty's storyline, retained the Gothic elements, and given the story a quick wartime gloss in order to place it loosely in the present day. These changes are not enough, however, to anchor the film firmly to the 1940s.

The first clue that this film signals a change of tone is the absence of the pre-film caption reassuring viewers that Holmes is 'ageless, invincible and unchanging'. The first scene shows that there is little need of such reassurance. It starts with a close-up of a sign outside an inn, The Rat and Raven, swinging and creaking in the strong night-time wind.[44] Inside, the setting is recognisably a contemporary British

43 Geraghty, n.d.
44 The name surely indicates a Gothic reference to Edgar Allen Poe's tale.

pub with pump handles, advertisements for Truman Bitter, a pianola, and at-the-bar service (a different set to the Continental bierkeller that was used to represent an East End pub in *Voice of Terror*). It is closing time and sailors are putting down their empty glasses and getting ready to leave. But any expectation that the film will be about the war is dispelled by the antics of the pub's pet raven who pecks the hand of one of the sailors and then flies around the pub squawking 'blood'.[45] The raven, the landlord explains, 'is very fond of blood' and actually belongs to the nearby Hulstone Towers, the ancestral home of the Musgrave family. 'You'll see it when you pass the old iron gates', he tells the sailor, 'but don't loiter'. At this point, the landlord's words turn into a doom-laden voiceover as the camera cuts away to show the gateway to the manor with trees whipping in the wind, leaves swirling and a grim mansion visible in the distance. 'If those old walls could speak they'd tell you things that'd raise the hair on your head', he intones as the camera tracks slowly up the driveway. 'There's folks here abouts swear they've seen corpse lights' and have heard 'a wailing like lost souls'. If the presence of the blood-drinking raven was an indicator of the Gothic horror genre, then a supernatural dimension has now been added, something which harks back to the *Hound of the Baskervilles* but which has been absent since the start of the Universal series. This supernatural dimension will recur throughout the middle-period films, most notably in *The Scarlet Claw*, where a mythical monster is said to roam the moor, but also in *The House of Fear* where the mansion is haunted 'by the memory of evil'.

That we are now in the realm of the Gothic is made clear by the next scene, in which the interior of Hulstone Towers, despite its use as a recovery centre for servicemen, is shown to stand outside of time: it is a house of baronial splendour, complete with suits of armour, mullioned windows, a frock-coated butler, dancing shadows and an entire absence of electric light. Only the private family apartment where the Musgrave siblings argue about modern-day matters such as marriage, appears to be sited in the twentieth century and is comfortably furnished in the country-house manner. The appearance of Watson in this early scene, revealed as the doctor in charge of the

---

45 The sailor's angry reaction to the bird caused Joseph Breen of the PCA to write to Maurice Pivar at Universal to seek assurance that 'there should be no cruelty indicated to this raven where he is swept off the perch' (7 April 1943).

FIGURE 37 A severely high-angle shot makes Watson look vulnerable, like a pawn on a chessboard, in *Sherlock Holmes Faces Death*.

servicemen, does little to dispel the intimations of Gothic horror. He emerges from the library into the hall and calls out to Brunton, the butler, who is descending the stairs above. In a very high-angle shot (much higher than a point-of-view shot) which will become a characteristic of this film, we look down on Watson *(see Fig. 37)*, who is dwarfed not just by the baronial doorway but by the vast squares of the tiled hall that make him look as small as a pawn on a chessboard – a visual reference that becomes meaningful later in the film. In the library full of mediaeval-style furniture, where he and Brunton are illuminated by firelight, Brunton talks of the ghosts of previous generations of Musgraves walking the corridors. Dr Watson pooh-poohs the idea, dismissing it as rubbish – a sure indicator that he will encounter a 'ghost' before the film is over.

The Gothic ambiance is achieved in part through the nature of the locations and their restricted number. This was clearly an artistic rather than an economic choice, as each film in the Universal series was allocated a similar budget. The contrast in approach to *Washington* is worth exploring. *Sherlock Holmes Faces Death* uses three locations: the house and grounds of Hulstone Towers, 221B Baker Street, and the village inn. Modernity, therefore, does not intrude: the manor is a baronial hall, the Baker Street sitting room is a Victorian 'time warp', and the village in which the inn is situated has a mediaeval look – it is, in fact, the same much-used, standing-set village that features in the 1930s and 1940s Frankenstein films from Universal. To emphasise the Gothic atmosphere, almost all the scenes take place at night. By contrast, *Washington* features 15 different locations – including aeroplanes with aerial views of New York and Washington, Pullman cars, railway termini, American homes, a laboratory, city tours in open-top cars, hotels, antique shops and a senator's office. The majority of the scenes take place during daylight and there is only one scene in Baker Street. The result is that the mood of *Washington* is completely different and is much more akin to other contemporary detective B-series than to this mid-phase of the Universal Holmes films.

Technology, which carries connotations of modernity and rationality, played a prominent role in the three war-themed films, but is absent in *Sherlock Holmes Faces Death*. In place of a code to be cracked, such as the 'dancing men' code in *Secret Weapon*, the mystery of the 'Musgrave Ritual' lies in a riddle – something more commonly associated with mythology or fairy tale with their associations of timelessness. The only technology in the film is the unused telephone on the desk at Baker Street, the car in which Sally Musgrave arrives at the pub, and the 'listening device' used by the servicemen to eavesdrop on conversations in the next room. Even the document that is the motivation for the murders is not a modern legal paper but a royal declaration dating back several hundred years.

Two key scenes underline the extent to which Holmes and Watson have been transported to their own ahistorical time zone: the scene where Sally Musgrave recites the ritual, and the climax of the film where Holmes confronts the murderer in the candlelit crypt. For the recitation of the ritual, family and servants are gathered solemn-faced in the hall while the wind howls and the tree branches whip against the windows. Candles gutter as Sally speaks and lightning suddenly strikes the house, shattering the window and felling a suit of armour.[46] The scene could be taking place any time in the previous

---

46 These special electrical effects were devised by Ken Strickfaden whose former credits include *Bride of Frankenstein* (1935).

hundred years: there is nothing to anchor it to the 1940s, but there is a plethora of clues that tie it to the Gothic. The climactic crypt scene is similarly adrift in temporal terms: Holmes and the killer struggle in near-complete darkness, with only tombstones and an altar dimly visible in the background. It is easy to link the scene to Gothic horror (the set might have been recognisable to audiences as the one used for several scenes in the 1931 production of *Dracula*), but not to wartime Britain. The closing homily from Holmes, therefore, seems at odds with the mood of the film in a way that previous homilies did not, even though the sentiments are similar. There is no direct reference to the war, and no quotations from Churchill or Shakespeare: this speech was written by Bertram Millhauser and refers to Sally Musgrave's refusal to claim the land she now knows to be hers. The days of 'grab and greed', says Holmes, are on their way out:

> The time's coming, Watson, when we shan't be able to fill our bellies in comfort when other folk go hungry… and we shan't be able to kneel and thank God for our blessings before shining altars while men anywhere are kneeling in either physical or spiritual subjection… and God willing, we'll live to see that day.

A similar speech is delivered by Holmes at the end of *The Pearl of Death*, when Holmes refers to the villain, Giles Conover, who has just met his death:

> What's Conover? No more than a symbol of the greed and lust for power that has set men at each others' throats down through the centuries. The struggle will go on, Watson, for a pearl, a kingdom, perhaps even world dominion, until the greed and cruelty are burned out of every last one of us, and when that time comes, perhaps even the pearl will be washed clean again.[47]

The Scarlet Claw – whose working title was *Sherlock Holmes in Canada* – has a homily based on a Churchill speech given on 4 September

---

47 This same speech is used by Leslie Halliwell in his short-story version of *The Pearl of Death* which was based on Millhauser's screenplay. Halliwell, however, adds a comment by Watson, the story's narrator, after the speech: 'although a little wearied by now of Holmes's recent tendency towards speechifying, I could only nod my head at his meaning' (Halliwell, n.d.).

1941 extolling the virtues of the historical alliance between Canada and Britain:

> Canada – linchpin of the English-speaking world, whose relations of friendly intimacy with the United States on the one hand, and her unswerving fidelity to the British Commonwealth, the motherland, on the other. Canada – the link that joins together these great branches of the human family.[48]

These sentiments are easily understood in the context of the war – Canada, for example, had sustained heavy casualties in a bitter campaign in Italy beginning in September 1943. But the films themselves are divorced from present-day events and exist in a non-specified era where the war is never mentioned: the homilies therefore seem ill-fitting. The speech at the end of *The Pearl of Death* was to have tied its message closer to the war, by having the final shot of the pearl dissolve into a shot of a turning terrestrial globe, struck by sunlight and causing it to 'gleam hopefully'.[49] The decision not to do this dissolve was apparently a last-minute one and it is interesting to speculate whether it was because the lack of war-related narrative would make such an inclusion too heavy-handed. The difference with the speech that ends *Sherlock Holmes Faces Death* is that it was immediately followed by a War Bonds advertisement, making a psychological link between Sally Musgrave's selfless act and the selfless behaviour seen as an ideal outcome of the war.

Thus, though these films have ostensibly lost their temporal anchor through the lack of specific references to the war, they still reveal layers of history and meaning, from the structured absence of the present day back through to the Victorian, with its Gothic enthusiasms for an even earlier age – the mediaeval. An interesting example of this layering of history can be seen at 221B Baker Street where, in the Twentieth Century-Fox films, the initials 'VR' are visible on the wall of Holmes' sitting room next to the door. These initials, as audiences with literary knowledge of Holmes would be aware, were the result of his testing out a gun: they are bullet holes

---

48 Speech made by Churchill at Mansion House, London, 4 September 1941 (www.winstonchurchill.org).

49 Millhauser script, 28 March 1944, p.112.

FIGURE 38

A rationale is devised in *Sherlock Holmes Faces Death* to explain why a 1940s Holmes would mark the initials of a long-dead queen ('VR') on his wall.

neatly and patriotically incised in the plaster, part of Holmesian lore and entirely appropriate in a late-Victorian setting. However, even in a mythical space like 221B it was stretching plausibility for Holmes to have inscribed the initials of a queen who had died more than forty years previously: thus, in *Sherlock Holmes Faces Death*, they reappear but are given a whole new rationale. When Holmes is first seen in the film, he is testing whether a suspect could have fired his gun accurately while his hands and feet were bound. He fires from the floor to the spot on the wall next to the door, where traditionally the 'VR' was inscribed. This time, however, the target is a carefully drawn man's head and shoulders complete with jacket and tie – Holmes' bullet holes form a 'V' as he aims each shot up and down the jacket's lapel *(see Fig. 38)*. It is a strange reversal of historicism.[50]

---

50   Strangely, the 'VR' marks are visible briefly in the previous film, *Sherlock Holmes in Washington*, before their presence has been invented and 'justified' in *Sherlock Holmes Faces Death*. The 'V' could also, of course, stand for 'V for Victory', a symbol that civilians were encouraged to use by a BBC campaign launched in January 1941 – and which became, of course, Winston Churchill's trademark (www.bbc.co.uk/newswatch/history).

BLURRING THE BOUNDARIES: THE DETECTIVE FILM MEETS THE HORROR GENRE

The war was to be completely absent in the films that followed, apart from two brief visual references in *Spider Woman*, where sandbags are visible in a street scene, and where the faces of the rifle gallery targets are those of Hitler, Mussolini and Hirohito. After this, the War Bonds appeals vanish, and after *The Pearl of Death* there are no more ending homilies. The new Gothic mood, with its shifting sense of time and place, references to superstition, and use of chiaroscuro continued through *Spider Woman*, *The Scarlet Claw*, *Pearl of Death* and *House of Fear*. After *Sherlock Holmes Faces Death*, however, horror and otherness become more prominent. It is no coincidence that, immediately after this film, Neill and Goodman worked on a horror film for Universal: *Frankenstein Meets the Wolfman*. There are distinct visual similarities (and not least the presence of two of the actors from the Holmes series, Dennis Hoey and Lionel Atwill) – and in a brief comparison of the films I aim to illuminate Neill/Goodman's distinctive approach which blurred the boundaries between the detective and the horror genre and enabled them to use the same techniques in both.

In *Frankenstein Meets the Wolfman*, the indicators of time and place are as ambivalent as in the Holmes series. Such ambivalence is crucial to the classic horror genre because the source of the horror has to be 'eternal' if it is to remain a universal threat, in the same way that I would suggest the character of Holmes has to stand outside of time – indeed, to transcend it – if he is to remain a universal symbol of certainty. The film is ostensibly set in the present day, though no external events intrude upon the narrative to pinpoint this: it can be judged only by the costumes which, like the Holmes films, are an amalgam of periods, with only the heroine in overtly 1940s dress. The first part of the film takes place in Wales but there are no establishing shots and no Welsh accents – 'Wales', in fact, is a metaphor for an isolated and timeless place, as is Canada in *The Scarlet Claw* and Scotland in *The House of Fear*. Indeed, 'Wales' had already been used as the indeterminate setting for at least one horror film, Boris Karloff's *The Old Dark House* (1932).[51] The second part of *Frankenstein*

---

51 It is worth noting that none of the mid-series Holmes films takes place in the US, which had been clearly identified in *Sherlock Holmes in Washington* as being consonant with modernity. The use of locations such as Scotland and Wales also seems to draw on America's notions of its own ancestral past.

Meets the Wolfman is set in a small town in a middle-European country constructed through a folkloric imagery that again implies it is untouched by time. The town is the same standing set used in several of the Holmes films to represent England – including the inn in *Sherlock Holmes Faces Death*. It is awash with bierkellers, glockenspiel players, men in lederhosen and Tyrolean hats and women in dirndl skirts, in a kind of extended version of the opening Swiss scene of *Secret Weapon*. The iconography that pervades *Sherlock Holmes Faces Death*, including wind, swirling leaves, whipping tree-branches, mullioned windows and lightning strikes, is present throughout *Frankenstein Meets the Wolfman*. Much of the film takes place in near-complete darkness, with only low key-lights to outline the figures, and extensive use is made of shadows even in 'innocent' scenes devoid of any sinister significance. The choice of camera angles is also recognisably similar, particularly in the very high-angle shots which make the players in the drama look small and vulnerable. A key characteristic of the way shots are composed in this film and in the Holmes series is in the placing of an object in the centre foreground of the frame, with the protagonists framed on either side. In *Frankenstein Meets the Wolfman*, it is a lantern placed on a tomb, while the grave robbers work; in *The Scarlet Claw* it is a candelabra placed on a coffin, with Holmes on one side and Lord Penrose on the other; in *Sherlock Holmes Faces Death*, it is the telephone on the desk at Baker Street as Holmes and Watson discuss the case. In none of these examples is the object of any narrative significance nor does it seem to carry any particular connotation. The significance of these shots, which are characteristic of Gothic horror films but are also important precursors of film noir, will be discussed below. In his direction, Neill is also well aware of the power of the imagination and prefers his effects to be achieved through suggestion rather than literal depiction: in *Frankenstein Meets the Wolfman*, the viewer sees the reaction to the discovery of the grave robber's mutilated body, not the body itself – a technique used to great effect in *Sherlock Holmes Faces Death* when Philip Musgrave's body is discovered hidden in the boot of Sally Musgrave's car. That this is a choice of technique and not one governed by budget is evidenced in the horror film when a villager is shown a picture of Talbot, alias the wolfman – all the viewer sees is the back of the photograph as it is handed around.

As a horror film, it is to be expected that *Frankenstein Meets the Wolfman* would foreground otherness, which it does through the

FIGURE 39

The Creeper (Rondo Hatton) in *The Pearl of Death*, with his face 'underlighted' like that of Frederick March in *Dr Jekyll and Mr Hyde*.

werewolf itself, the resurrection of Frankenstein's monster, and the gypsy who tries to help Talbot. But this otherness begins to be present in the Holmes series: whereas in the war-themed films it was German spies who were coded in this way, more conventional horror-genre figures take their place as the series moves towards the Gothic: the raven in *Sherlock Holmes Faces Death*; the phosphorescent monster in *The Scarlet Claw*; the poison-dart-blowing pygmy and the 'Creeper' in *The Pearl of Death*.[52] The Creeper (Rondo Hatton) is perhaps the most overt use of horror in the series – a killer who never speaks; whose every appearance is always heralded by a mewl of terror from a nearby cat; who affects a lumbering, monster-like walk, and who is

---

52 Otherness had, of course, been present in the two earlier Twentieth Century-Fox films, but these were set in the Victorian era, a 'natural' time for Gothic iconography.

seen only in silhouette or from the rear until near the end of the film, where he turns to camera and the audience briefly sees his deformed face, described in Bertram Millhauser's script as 'an unspeakable face – underlighted like Frederick March as Mr Hyde'[53] *(see Fig. 39)*. Like all monsters, he needs no weapon but kills with his bare hands, breaking his paymaster's back at the end of the film. Then, in common with horror-film monsters, he does not live to face justice himself but is shot by Holmes, thus confirming his status as animal and as irredeemable. Steinbrunner and Michaels describe the Creeper as 'a genuine, first-class monster for a studio which took its monsters seriously' and define this film as the first in the series to stray into the horror genre, having classified the preceding films as mysteries.[54] Harmon feels that the series was already going against the trend of the times, which was for hardboiled detective stories or for tales of 'spies and black marketeers', and that turning the Holmes films into quasi-horror movies was making them 'seem like what they were not'.[55]

At the time of release, apart from one cynical comment by the *New York Times* warning readers that the only 'horror' audiences would encounter in *Spider Woman* was the title itself, the trade press did not change the terminology it had used to describe each Holmes release. Most note a softening in the modernising of the characters; that 'Sherlock Holmes' has been dropped from the titles; and that the films seem to feature a plethora of 'secret passageways, storm-swept nights... clatter-shutters etc'.[56] The word 'Gothic' is not used, and only *To-Day's Cinema* remarks on the introduction (in *The Scarlet Claw*) of what it calls 'full-bloodied narration foreign to the Conan Doyle school of crime and detection'.[57] Audiences can hardly have overlooked, however, how the films were now being marketed – in two years the lobby cards for the series had moved from depicting gangster-like villains shooting it out over a speedboat, to scenes straight out of a horror movie. The lobby card for *The House of Fear*, for instance, under title letters that drip blood, shows a Gothic mansion, fronted by a blasted tree, with a yellow moon hanging over

---

53 Millhauser screenplay, 28 March 1944, p.108.

54 Steinbrunner and Michaels, 1978, p.136.

55 Harmon, 1975, p.7.

56 *Motion Picture Herald*, 24 March 1945, p.2,374.

57 *To-Day's Cinema*, 11 August 1944, p.21.

FIGURE 40

In less than two years, the series had moved from speed-boat chases to scenes straight out of a Gothic horror film, as this Spanish poster for *The House of Fear* indicates.

the gables *(see Fig. 40)*.[58] These Universal films were not the only series to veer into Gothic horror territory: Abbott and Costello, whose features frequently shared the bill with Holmes, produced ghost stories, a Jekyll-and-Hyde tale, and a film with Boris Karloff entitled *Abbott and Costello Meet the Killer*. Crucially, however, these were all post-war films from a duo notorious for playful genre-bending: their tackling of Gothic themes indicated that any potential to scare the viewer had long gone and that the genre could therefore be made fun of. It is interesting to note that their only foray into 'making fun of'

58   This example is taken from the lobby card for the Spanish market.

the classic detective occurred in 1942 (*Who Done It?*) which perhaps speaks volumes about why the Holmes series moved into new territory after that date.

USE OF EXPRESSIONIST TECHNIQUES

The combination of full-bloodied narration and the expressionist photography of this middle set of films is at its most effective in *The Scarlet Claw* – a film directed, produced and co-written by Neill, and rated by subsequent critics as the best in the Universal series. This may be attributed to the additional control Neill had over the finished product, as the story diverged completely from the Doyle canon; the narrative parallels with *The Hound of the Baskervilles*, in the presence of the moor and a seemingly supernatural beast; and the final jettisoning of links with the present day. Certainly the Gothic cinematography, lighting and sets build an atmosphere and tension that sets this film aesthetically above others in the series. To refer to this as 'expressionist', however, would call for a definition of the term, as it is often rather loosely applied – a shorthand way of talking about the heavy use of shadows, or a 'European' look to an American film.

Webster's International Dictionary gives three definitions of expressionism, relating to fine art, theatre and music respectively. It makes clear that the movement started in art in the late nineteenth century and spread to other disciplines in the early twentieth. In art, expressionism is defined as seeking 'to depict not objective reality but the subjective emotions and responses that objects and events arouse in the artist with wide use of distortion, exaggeration, and symbolism'.[59] The dictionary does not offer a definition specific to film, though *The Macmillan International Film Encyclopedia* traces its cinematic emergence to the release of the 1920 German film *The Cabinet of Dr Caligari* and characterises it as 'extreme stylization of sets and décor as well as in the acting, lighting and camera angles'.[60] Expressionism is often viewed as a reaction to the aftermath of World War One. Some writers, including Siegfried Kracauer, interpret it as a political backlash against the bourgeois values seen to have caused Germany's downfall: expressionism, he says, combined this denial of bourgeois traditions with a faith in man's power to shape society

---

59 Webster, 1993, p.803.

60 *Macmillan International Film Encyclopedia*, 2001.

freely – 'on account of such virtues, it may have cast a spell over many Germans upset by the breakdown of their universe'.[61] Others see it as a pragmatic, low-budget way for European filmmakers to compete with Hollywood's lavish productions – using symbolism rather than expensive sets to convey mood. The political agenda of the style was short-lived, but the aesthetic qualities of expressionism began to influence Hollywood, their effects seeming particularly appropriate for the horror genre. Universal was an early adopter, largely due to the arrival at the studio in 1930 of German cinematographer Karl Freund who was responsible for *Dracula* (1931) with its moody lighting, near-total-darkness sets, and strong contrasts. *Dracula* set the house-style for Universal[62] on which Neill drew for the Holmes series: where Leggett saw Neill's work as a forerunner of film noir, he was probably seeing the early transference of expressionist techniques from the horror/monster genre into the detective/crime genre. The timing of this transference is interesting: some two years after America's entry into the war, arguably at a point when expectations of an early victory had proved unrealistic, and a darker, more uncertain future beckoned. Many of the motivations therefore for the initial emergence of German expressionism were arguably present once more, this time in America, and the use of expressionist techniques in this phase of the Holmes series can be seen both as a retreat from an unwelcome reality (capturing a bombsight or shooting a Nazi spy were not, after all, going to win the war) and an indulgence in, or negation of, the fears that the war was bringing. Lotte Eisner names these fears as being about the permeability of the world, so that at any moment 'Mind, Spirit, Vision and Ghosts seem to gush forth'[63] – she was actually writing about the post-World War One period, but her remarks are highly pertinent both to the mid-40s and to *The Scarlet*

---

61 Kracauer, 1974, p.68.

62 Marc Vernet warns against making a sweeping correlation between German émigrés and Hollywood's take-up of expressionism, saying that 'a good number of the directors and cinematographers in question have origins that have nothing to do with Germany or even Austria, and a good number... of German or related origin who are often invoked have nothing in common with expressionism' (Vernet, 1993, p.7). Thomas Elsaesser makes a similar point. In general terms they are probably right: in this specific instance, however, it does seem to have been Freund who introduced the style into Universal: it was how the (non-German) directors and cinematographers made use of it after *Dracula* which is of particular interest.

63 Eisner, 1952, p.15.

Claw. Holmes' role was to expose these fears as groundless: every 'supernatural' occurrence was proven to have a prosaic explanation, even if that explanation exposed another set of expressionist concerns – madness, obsession and violence.

'Ghosts and monsters' are introduced in the opening sequences of *The Scarlet Claw*, where villagers sit around the fire in Journet's inn listening to the tolling of the church bell, speculating that its ringer may be an 'it' rather than a person, and hearing reports of a 'weird glow' on the marshes and of sheep with their throats torn out. Two scenes later, when Holmes makes his appearance, it is made clear that the dispelling of fears of the supernatural will be the theme of the film. A signboard outside a hotel lounge announces a meeting of the Royal Canadian Occult Society: inside, Lord Penrose tells of the hundred-year-old apparition on the marshes of La Morte Rouge, while Holmes (who is among the audience) scoffs at the 'peasants' who believe in such things. The way these two sequences are handled illustrates some of the key techniques of expressionism, which Eisner identifies as a penchant for chiaroscuro and shadow, the portrayal of 'images in the mind', the overemphasis on the outline of the details of a set, the combination of mist and light, and the leaning towards violent contrast.[64] The photographs used here to illustrate the description of these two sequences are 'screen shots', as I have been conscious of Marc Vernet's warning that discussions about expressionism are often accompanied by publicity stills which do not necessarily correspond accurately to images in the film: 'it often happened that the publicity department or the set photographer would reorganise and relight the mise en scène of an action... adding a gigantic or strongly marked shadow to increase the dramatic effect'.[65]

The film opens with a shot of moorland at night, fog swirling around the bare branches of blasted trees and the sound of a bell tolling. The bell itself is revealed through a haze of mist and we see a low-angle shot of the underneath of the bell as it swings back and forth. From there, a series of establishing shots lead to a scene inside an inn. In common with the other mid-series Holmes films, the setting and time is uncertain, the bar being populated with bearded

64 Eisner, 1952, pp.17, 24, 92 and 100.

65 Vernet, 1993, p.7.

FIGURE 41 A low angle and the shadows from the flickering firelight give the café scene in *The Scarlet Claw* expressionist overtones.

rural types sitting at checked-cloth tables. Everyone is completely still and silent, frozen in mid-movement, as they listen to the bell. A postman in peaked cap and greatcoat enters and makes his way to a table: a highly effective moment because there is no incidental music, no other movement, and no sound except for the padding of his footsteps across the wooden floor. Dialogue then ensues around the table *(see Fig. 41)*. Expressionist techniques during this sequence include the further use of very low-angle shots, so that the face of the priest at the table is completely obscured by the shadow from his broad-brimmed hat; the apparent use of only one light-source – the log fire – which sends shadows flickering across the faces of the speakers; and the sharp shadow of the postman on the wall as he walks across the room. When the men leave the inn, the priest goes to the church to see who is ringing the bell. Instead of filming the scene from his point of view as he stops his horse and carriage outside the

FIGURE 42 Something – a manifestation of the priest's fears – is watching from inside the church in *The Scarlet Claw*.

church, sees that the door is open, and walks up the path to enter the building, the point of view chosen is the opposite one. The camera is inside the church, looking back through an arch-topped doorway out onto the path as the priest approaches. A candle and tabernacle are visible in the gloom of the church, but the surround of the doorway is in almost complete darkness. As the priest walks up the path, we see his carriage in silhouette parked on the roadway. To his right, 'moonlight' lights the cross-shaped outline of a gravestone and contrasts with the darkness of his flapping black soutane *(see Fig. 42)*. The choice of this shot builds considerable tension. It could be argued that this is false suspense because the implication is that someone, or something, is inside the church watching the priest, which is untrue. In expressionist terms, however, the shot could be interpreted as a manifestation of the priest's fears – what Eisner calls 'images in the mind'.

The second main sequence is the scene of the Royal Canadian Occult Society meeting at a luxury Quebec hotel. The meeting is taking place in a room that resembles a traditional, book-lined, Victorian gentleman's club, with heavy drapery, wing chairs, desks and an open fire. Outside the room, the hotel is ablaze with electric light, but inside is lit only by the firelight and a giant candelabra. There are table lamps, but they are unlit. While Lord Penrose talks, there is a slow panning shot of the room from high above. As the camera pans, the figure of Watson becomes clearly visible, partly because he is sitting near the candelabra, illuminated by its light, and partly because he is the only man wearing a pale-coloured suit, perhaps to symbolise his innocence in matters of the occult. Attention is therefore drawn to him before it is to Holmes, who is sitting next to him, in partial shadow and in dark clothing. The camera lingers on neither of the men, but continues past them to observe the other listeners in the room: like the villagers in Journet's inn, they are motionless. During the initial pan, the camera moves past a pillar which is placed in the foreground of the frame and thus momentarily divides the room: this shot, like the extreme high-angle shots, is characteristic of Neill and Goodman's work. As Lord Penrose begins to debate the mysteries of La Morte Rouge with Holmes, the editing alternates between Holmes and Watson, and Lord Penrose, the latter being filmed from just behind the shoulders of Holmes and Watson so that his face appears between the two, in a constricted space, perhaps to symbolise his plight.

WARTIME ECONOMIES – OR EARLY EXAMPLE OF FILM NOIR?

The Scarlet Claw, which is typical of the mid-series films, therefore demonstrates the expressionist techniques that had become a house style of Universal and that Neill had begun to transfer from the horror genre. The direction, camerawork and lighting, however, could also be seen as an early example of film noir. The roots of film noir in expressionism have been widely acknowledged: Nicolas Saada, for example, says that German cinema of the 1920s was the most frequently cited prototype of the visual style of film noir.[66] This does not mean, however, that such a link is straightforward, or that it is the only interpretation: Thomas Elsaesser has called the connection 'a

---

66   Saada, 2004, pp. 175–7.

self-validating tautology'.[67] He suggests other 'missing links' including the newshound genre of the 1930s in films such as *The Front Page*, but interestingly does not mention the horror genre which seems to have been overlooked as one possible evolutionary step in the birth of film noir.[68] Leggett makes a partial link, believing that Neill's ideas paved the way for film noir practitioners and, indeed, reading a description of characteristic noir lighting, shot composition and camera angles is very like reading a description of Neill's work. In their article on the genre's visual motifs, Janey Place and Lowell Peterson set out the parameters for a normal Hollywood lighting set up and compare these with the set up for a film noir. Most basic lighting set ups (to paraphrase them) use three different kinds of light: a key-light, a fill-light and a back-light. The key-light is a hard, direct light that produces sharply defined shadows; the fill-light is a diffused light that fills in the shadows created by the key; and the back-light is a direct light shining on the actor from behind which gives him/her form and adds interesting highlights. To produce an illusion of reality, a normal Hollywood set up uses 'high-key' lighting, which means that the ratio of key-light to fill-light is small. In this way, the intensity of the fill-light is great enough to soften harsh shadows. The set up for film noir is the exact opposite: the ratio of key-light to fill-light is large, creating areas of high contrast and rich black shadows. Using very small amounts of fill-light produces areas of total black: Place and Peterson say that this means the actors 'may play a scene totally in shadow' (the scene in the crypt in *Sherlock Holmes Faces Death* would be an example of this), 'or they may be silhouetted against an illuminated background' (the scene where Holmes is held at gunpoint by the murderer in *The Scarlet Claw* would be an example of this).[69] The connotations of this type of photography, say Place and Peterson, are to evoke an atmosphere of the mysterious and unknown, although it could be argued that any unsettling quality of expressionist photography is offset by the comforting presence of Holmes.

Place and Peterson also identify two other key motifs of film noir: the disruption of the compositional balance of the frame, and the use of the extreme high-angle shot. Both of these motifs are present in

---

67 Elsaesser, 2000, p.420.

68 Elsaesser, 2000, p.427.

69 Place and Peterson, 1974, p.66.

the Holmes films. In terms of the first motif, in film noir 'figures placed irregularly in the frame… create a world that is never stable or safe; claustrophobic framing devices 'separate the character from other characters', and 'objects seem to push their way into the foreground of the frame'.[70] A number of these claustrophobic framing devices have already been demonstrated: in *The Scarlet Claw*, it is the presence of a pillar which splits the room; and the shot of Lord Penrose framed between the shoulders of Holmes and Watson. Objects of no significance in themselves regularly dominate the foreground: in *Sherlock Holmes Faces Death* it is the telephone on the table at Baker Street, and in *The Scarlet Claw* it is the candlesticks placed on Lady Penrose's coffin.[71] The extreme high-angle shot is also used extensively in the Holmes films, a shot that Place and Peterson identify as 'an oppressive and fatalistic angle that looks down on its helpless victim'[72] – whether this is Watson seen emerging from the doorway of the Hulstone Towers library in *Sherlock Holmes Faces Death* or Holmes and Watson as they walk through the night-time, wind-torn grounds of Drearcliff House in *The House of Fear*.

This is not to argue, of course, that this group of Holmes films can be classified as film noir – merely that they share a number of lighting, camera-work and directorial techniques with the genre. These techniques have been shown to stem from the Gothic horror genre, which in turn draws on German expressionism. Yet, as Elsaesser points out: many Hollywood films with no German connections used expressionist lighting; and many Hollywood films made by Germans exhibited not a shred of expressionist technique. The way these techniques permeated the industry, says Elsaesser, may be attributable to a combination of influence and 'interference' (for example, expressionist directors being assigned to the 'wrong' genres, such as musical comedy).[73] Whatever the source of the influence/

---

70 Place and Peterson, 1974, p.68.

71 It is interesting to note that, once the crime is resolved, the frame is often opened up – at the end of *The Pearl of Death*, for example, Holmes and Watson stand in midshot, face to face, in front of a large mirror and Holmes holds up the pearl between his fingers. Initially, each man is 'doubled' in a rather cluttered way in the mirror. The camera then tracks in closer and closer towards the mirror until the men themselves disappear out of shot and Holmes' hand goes out of focus. As he delivers the lines about the pearl being 'washed clean', the camera shows only the two men's reflected profiles against the clear background of the mirror's glass.

72 Place and Peterson, 1974, p.68.

interference, using Gothic horror techniques for the Holmes films not only made good use of Neill and Goodman's previous experience at Universal, but was an appropriate transfer because it fitted well with the Victorian origins of Holmes. When Holmes was relatively firmly sited in the present day, such as in *Washington*, use of these techniques would have made little visual sense. It was the shift to a less-specific historical period, and the use of Gothic narratives and settings, that made it possible. Thus *Washington* has much more in common with the brightly lit, contemporary detective B-series such as *Boston Blackie*, *The Falcon* or *The Saint* than it does with *Sherlock Holmes Faces Death*. A simple comparison between the opening scene of *Meet Boston Blackie* (1941) and *The Pearl of Death* (1944) points up the difference in treatment: both films open on board a ship as it approaches port; both feature a glamorous and mysterious woman; and in both cases, the detective comes to her aid. The Boston Blackie opening sequence takes place in the daytime, uses high-key lighting with soft shadows, emphasises the glamour of the woman, and features an insouciant Blackie, in overtly contemporary dress, using standard chat-up lines to intervene in a threatening situation. The Holmes opening sequence *(see Fig. 43)* takes place at night, uses low-key lighting with rich blacks and heavy shadows, emphasises the mysteriousness of the woman, and features Holmes in a clergyman's disguise. This difference in approach cannot be attributed to wartime filming restrictions: though the Boston Blackie film was made before the rationing of studio sets and lighting, it is typical of the entire Blackie series, which is always unequivocally set in the present day.[74] Nor can it be simply a question of genre expectations – in other words, what a detective film was 'supposed' to look like – as this noirish phase of the Holmes series is unlike other contemporary detective series.[75] Biesen makes a strong argument for the emergence

---

73 Elsaesser, 2000, p.431.

74 The sequence for *The Pearl of Death* was filmed on the 'phantom stage' at Universal with a 1,500-dollar spend on constructing the deck of the steamer; there is no published information on the cost of the Boston Blackie set.

75 There is one film in Monogram's Charlie Chan series which seems to be the exception, though it was made slightly later than the films under discussion in this chapter – in 1945. A change of director from Phil Rosen to Phil Karlson (later to make his name with 1950s gritty, realistic TV crime programmes) for *Shanghai Cobra* meant a complete change of visual mood: much of the film takes place in almost complete darkness with low-key lighting and much use of noirish iconography such as the shadows of blinds and

FIGURE 43 *The Pearl of Death* uses low-key lighting and rich black tones for a noirish look.

of the noir look being a creative response to wartime restrictions, and it is true that film stock and electricity were rationed, sets were re-used (there was a wartime 5,000-dollar limit for each set constructed), and blackouts were common. 'Material limitations', she says, 'accentuated attributes that would later be considered so characteristic of film-noir style: rain, fog, smoke, mirrors (rather than ornate sets), resourceful angles, night locations, and tented or tarped back-lot shooting'.[76] Barnwell makes a similar assertion about the use of shadows and the employment of key elements being used to signify an entire location, claiming that an 'aesthetic of enclosure and

---

shutters. Unlike the Holmes films, however, the theme and setting of the film are resolutely modern without a trace of Gothic ambiance, and make use of contemporary technology and motifs such as radium-theft, plastic surgery and TV-screen jukeboxes.

76 Biesen, 2005, p.51.

claustrophobia was... born out of the restrictions of budget'.[77] Undoubtedly these limitations were a factor but do not offer the complete answer, because it would have meant all low-budget films shared this same 'look' and this was not so even within the narrow confines of the classic detective genre. Similarly, Vernet's assertion that American cinema had 'ever since the 1910s, a long and important tradition of "noir" lighting whether in gothic or detective films'[78] can certainly be demonstrated in the Gothic genre, but is a generalisation of the detective genre – perhaps he was remembering the noir effects in non-typical silent-era detective films such as the British film *The Lodger* (1926) and forgetting that this visual style then seemed to disappear during the 1930s and early 1940s.

There is, of course, more to genre than mise-en-scène: it is the combination of these visual techniques with the presence of particular themes that help to define a film. In the case of expressionism, the Gothic and film noir, a number of these themes coincide: these include an interest in polarities, a sense that the world has become unstable and unknowable, and an uncertainty about identity. The latter is particularly interesting in terms of *The Scarlet Claw*, where the murderer is discovered to be an actor who takes on, and discards, identities at will, possibly assuming several at once. He could, says Holmes, be 'familiar to the people of La Morte Rouge and quite above suspicion. He could be almost anyone'. His identity is constantly shifting, spreading uncertainty and fear through its instability.

Neill received little acclaim for the way he mapped the techniques of the horror film onto the detective genre and thus became one of the early adopters of what would later be termed film-noir aesthetics. James Naremore, for example, contends that the characteristic visual effects of the 1940s film noir 'could be immediately duplicated at every level of the industry' because they were developed in a wartime economy – in other words, they could be done on a shoestring budget because they relied on clever lighting rather than on elaborate sets. He states that 'a kind of generic cinema grew up around the "original" films', and that 'Roy William Neill's modestly budgeted *Black Angel* (1946) was almost as enjoyable as Hawks' high-profile adaptation of Raymond Chandler's *The Big Sleep* which was released

---

77 Barnwell, 2004, p.48.

78 Vernet, 1993, p.12.

to great fanfare the same year'.[79] While this praises Neill's work, it makes the assumption that Neill was merely a proficient copyist. Naremore gives an unwitting explanation for this interpretation on the next page of his book, when (not in the context of Neill) he remarks that 'cheapness… is in the eye of the beholder, and some forms of lowness are more valuable than others'.[80] Perhaps if Neill had specialised in the emerging 'hardboiled' rather than the 'classic detective' genre during the war years, he might have moved into this 'more valuable' form of B-movie lowness.

WINNING THE WAR

In the context of such a withdrawal from the present day in these mid-series films – something that could be interpreted as a box-office-induced wish for escapism, or as an ideological protest against unpleasant reality – it is interesting to conclude by looking again at the OWI's guidelines. At first glance, of the seven questions filmmakers were asked to consider, only one seems relevant: 'if this is an escape picture, will it harm the war effort by creating a false picture of America, her allies or the world we live in?' The term 'escape picture' may bring a sunnier film to mind than the Gothic world of these Holmes adventures, such as a musical or a romantic comedy, but absence of the war nevertheless constitutes a form of escape, even if only in the direction of thrills and chills. As for falsity, though the OWI undoubtedly meant this to refer to the representation of the progress of the war, it would be hard to find a more 'false' representation of England, Scotland and Canada than in this series. With the Gothic, however, hovering somewhere between past and present, suspension of disbelief is a prerequisite. Despite the lack of war themes in these films, the first question set by the OWI is also surprisingly relevant: 'will this picture help win the war?' The answer is a qualified 'yes', partly through the strong persona of Holmes, who continues to battle successfully against dark forces and is a metonym for England (and therefore for the Allies); and partly through the resonance of the homilies at the end of three of the films. These strong moral messages with their quasi-religious content, advocating an end to greed and subjection, and stressing the importance of the

---

79   Naremore, 1998, p.139.
80   Naremore, 1998, p.140.

unity of the human family, act as a counter to the fact that the war has been singularly absent from the rest of the film and introduce a patriotic appeal that seems a direct answer to the OWI's question.[81]

---

81 Of course the direct 'patriotic appeal' is one that only works if the audience for the films is on the side of the Allies. In Germany the only films in the Universal series eventually to get a release were the 'timeless' ones, from which two composite movies were created in the early 1950s: one a combination of *Spider Woman* and *The Scarlet Claw* (*Sherlock Holmes sieht dem tod ins gesicht*), and the other a combination of *The Woman in Green* and *Terror by Night* (*Sherlock Holmes gefahr lichster auftrag*). These composite films were made by re-editing the footage (Holmes begins on one case then is 'called away' to deal with another) to make a longer – and presumably A-feature – film. Though the war is ostensibly absent from the first of these pairs of films, and over by the time of the second, Holmes remains a metonym for England and a potent reminder of the victory of the Allies, and the 'reading' of the films by the German audience was presumably focused not on this, but on alternative layers of history embedded in the character and the narrative.

CHAPTER FIVE

FELINE, NOT CANINE

THE RISE OF THE FEMALE ARCH-VILLAIN

Holmes: *'Directing [these killings] is one of the most fiendishly clever
minds in all Europe today. I suspect a woman.'*

Watson: *'You amaze me, Holmes. Why a woman?'*

Holmes: *'Because the method, whatever it is, is peculiarly
subtle and cruel. Feline, not canine.'*

Spider Woman

The midpoint of the Holmes series from Universal was notable
not just for its retreat from modernity into an uncertain
timeframe, but for two other reasons: the dropping of the
'Sherlock Holmes' name from the titles and the introduction of a new
type of villain – the deadly female. Dropping the name revealed a loss
of confidence in the ability of the Holmes name to draw audiences,
perhaps because of his Victorian connotations, but the new titling
fitted well with the elements of horror being introduced into the series
– not necessarily the Gothic devices such as the 'creepy houses' of
Sherlock Holmes Faces Death and *The House of Fear*, with their aura of
mystery, but more visceral aspects of horror such as the hooked weeder
that is the murder weapon in *The Scarlet Claw*, the deformed killer who
snaps the back of his victims in *The Pearl of Death*, or the psychotic
doctor who severs the fingers of young women in *The Woman in Green*.
Introducing a new breed of villain drew to some extent on the need
for novelty but the choice of the 'deadly female' was also a reflection
of changing attitudes to women during the war. These female villains
seem to stand at the crossroads of the two genres – classic detective and
horror – and offer an interesting, and previously overlooked,
perspective on the portrayal of women in B-movies and on the
formation of the 'femme fatale' in film noir. This chapter will examine
the emergence of the deadly female, looking in detail at four films:
Spider Woman, *The Pearl of Death*, *The Woman in Green* and *Dressed to Kill*,
thus spanning the period from the midpoint of the series to its end.

It will position the portrayal of these women within the wartime context of changing social patterns which brought many more women into traditionally male areas of the workplace, a highly visible change resulting in anxieties about masculinity. These anxieties can be seen in the way the films use locations, furnishings and costume to connote that men belong to the past, while women belong to the present, and in the way the new physicality of horror is linked to women, who assume the 'monster' position traditionally occupied in horror films by a man or male-coded creature.

WOMEN IN THE DOYLE STORIES

Women had occupied a secondary role thus far in the Holmes films and, in this, accurately reflected their position in the Doyle stories. The female sex was largely irrelevant to Holmes, ruled as he was by his head rather than his heart: he granted women what David Hammer calls 'notional respect' but only in the context of his passion for justice and for the righting of wrongs.[1] In fact the 'strong aversion' that is June Thomson's description of his attitude seems more accurate – he finds women 'inscrutable, trivial, illogical and vain'.[2] Much of his energies in the Doyle stories are dedicated to saving damsels in distress,[3] yet they remain somehow outside the world he inhabits – a male world that Rosemary Jann characterises as akin to that of a mediaeval knight.[4] In Holmes' life, the world of domesticity is replaced by the rooms at 221B Baker Street and by his comfortable companionship with Watson, the only female intruding on this space being the unthreatening figure of Mrs Hudson. Watson's marriage and his subsequent separate domestic life are given little space in the stories: they happen 'off the page' and therefore do not disturb the relationship that he has with Holmes, even though the stories are narrated by Watson himself.

1 Hammer, 2000, p.70.

2 Thomson, 1995, p.15.

3 Examples include Mary Sutherland in 'A Case of Identity', Miss Turner in 'The Boscombe Valley Mystery', Lady Eva Brackwell in 'Charles Augustus Milverton', and Eugenia Ronder in 'The Veiled Lodger'.

4 Jann, 1995, p.43. It is interesting to note, in passing, the parallels between this male world and the world which would come to be inhabited by the anti-heroes of film noir, whose misogyny made them vulnerable to the manipulations of atypical, powerful and 'monstrous' women, just as Holmes would become in the Universal films.

The Doylean view of women was accurately translated to the screen in the Twentieth Century-Fox and early Universal films, perhaps learning from a previous film incarnation where Clive Brook, as a contemporary Holmes in *The Return of Sherlock Holmes* (1929) and *Sherlock Holmes* (1932), had been given a glamorous fiancée, a move that had not been critically well received, despite the fact that audiences were probably well acquainted with the Gillette stageplay which saw Holmes heading for married life as the curtain fell. Doyle had reputedly told Gillette that the playwright could 'do anything' he liked with the character of Holmes, including 'marrying him off' or 'killing him'.[5] In Act II of the play, Holmes criticises Watson for occasionally introducing an element of romance into his chronicles of their adventures which, says Holmes, is 'something like working an elopement into the fifth proposition of Euclid', but by Act IV he has succumbed to Alice Faulkner's charms.[6] The dilemma for Hollywood in bringing Holmes to the screen was that the absence of a female star or love-interest might alienate an important segment of the audience: in the US, weekly cinema attendance stood at 95 million, 47 million of whom were women.[7] In *Hound*, therefore, Fox had changed the Doyle story to supply a romance between Sir Henry Baskerville and Beryl Stapleton, which provided love interest without the need to entangle Holmes himself in a relationship. A similar subplot romance was used for *Adventures*, in which Ann Brandon is in love with solicitor Jerrold Hunter; for *Secret Weapon*, in which the scientist Tobel has a girlfriend, Charlotte; for *Sherlock Holmes Faces Death*, in which Sally Musgrave is in love with convalescent serviceman Captain Vickery; and for *Washington*, in which Nancy Partridge's fiancée is glamorous American Navy lieutenant Pete Merriam. All these portrayals of women exhibit a conventional or pre-war morality which was to change as the series progressed.

The role of the woman in *Voice of Terror* is rather different in terms of class and in terms of her place in the narrative. Kitty (her lack of

---

5   Gillette, 1974, p.x.

6   Gillette, 1974, p.84. This line by Gillette, which is intended to underline Holmes' rationality and unemotional nature, also serves to neatly bracket him with a timeless classical text and thus render him also timeless and classical.

7   Nelmes, 2003, p.33. The figures relate to 1946, the peak year for cinema attendance. In the UK, weekly attendance was 31.5 million with women representing 50 percent of the audience.

a surname is an indication of her lack of social importance) has a key part to play in the plot, but is stripped of romantic interest because her boyfriend Gavin is killed early in the film. Instead, the narrative concentrates on her 'use-value' in rallying the criminal classes against the Nazis, and on her sleeping with the enemy in order to get information – something she does at Holmes' instigation.[8] Although she is instrumental in trapping the Nazi sympathiser, she gets little credit: when she is shot, Holmes barely pauses to pay tribute to her before stepping around her corpse to deliver his Shakespearian 'East Wind' speech.[9] Kitty is a working-class woman and the underlying message in her portrayal is that these women are expendable in a way that middle-class women are not: they serve their country with their bodies, through sex or dying, whereas middle-class women, such as Sally Musgrave in *Sherlock Holmes Faces Death*, serve it with their wealth, by giving away their rights to land in favour of the 'little people'. Class was a major issue in wartime, with women from all walks of life having to work together: the Holmes films do not fit neatly into the propaganda of this period which portrayed the dissolving of class boundaries as achievable (cf. *Mrs Miniver* 1942). Although working-class women do not appear as lead characters in the series after *Voice of Terror*, class as an issue never goes away: in future it becomes much harder to 'read' and is more about passing for a different class than fixed class identities. It therefore becomes associated with female duplicity rather than with a classless society.

Until *Spider Woman*, the female characters in the Holmes films were coded as 'good' women, existing only to supply a romantic subplot, to serve Holmes' investigation, or to be rescued from their plight by him. In other words, their underlying purpose was to attract female

---

8   The Production Code Administration were insistent that Kitty be portrayed as a 'girl of the Limehouse' rather than a prostitute and that her relationship with Meade was to be shown as that of a 'fellow-criminal' rather than a mistress. 'Since Kitty is killed in the concluding scenes', said the PCA, this 'will get away from the further objectionable flavor of a woman who has indulged in a sex relationship with a spy dying gloriously' (letter from PCA to Pivar of Universal, dated 29 April 1942).

9   'Kitty' was a popular name in 1930s and 1940s films but one that connotes – along with its feline affinities – a certain triviality and was usually applied to a working-class Irish firebrand or devious manipulator. Other 'Kittys' around the same time included Kitty Frazier in *Day-Time Wife* (1939), Kitty McClouen in *Ladies Day* (1943), Kitty de Mornay in *Paris Underground* (1945), Kitty March in *Scarlet Street* (1945) and Kitty Collins in *The Killers* (1946).

audience interest to what was primarily a male genre. At all times, they were of minor narrative importance and never challenged the screen presence of Holmes and Watson. Arguably their main role in the Universal films was a purely visual one – to tie the action to the present day through their costume, which was always uncompromisingly contemporary, something that could not be said of the clothes worn by Holmes and Watson, nor those worn by the non-romantic-interest women such as Mrs Monteith, the housekeeper in *The House of Fear*. As the 'good woman' disappeared in favour of the female villain, their fashion-plate role grew in importance and their character began to be overtly coded through their clothes.

To say that the Doyle stories only allowed women to exist on the periphery of Holmes' world is to ignore one important female character, Irene Adler, who appears in 'A Scandal in Bohemia'. She is important because she serves as the model for the new breed of female which begins to inhabit the Holmes films from *Spider Woman* onwards. 'There was but one woman to him', says Watson, 'and that woman was Irene Adler'.[10] Adler is a retired opera singer of renowned beauty with a 'soul of steel' and 'the mind of the most resolute of men'.[11] She becomes the mistress of the King of Bohemia, but when he reveals that he never intended to marry her, she retains a photograph of the two of them to ensure that he can never marry anyone else without bringing disgrace on his family. Blackmail is not her aim, as she refuses to sell the photograph: she wants justice for the way she has been treated. Holmes is hired by the King of Bohemia to retrieve the photograph. Through a series of ruses, he finds where the picture has been hidden, only to discover that Adler has outmanoeuvred him, fleeing for the Continent and leaving in the hiding place a note addressed to 'Sherlock Holmes'. She is portrayed as a mirror image of Holmes, quick-witted, ruthless and daring, and just as clever at disguise. Holmes' love of showmanship is also evident in Adler: when walking down Baker Street dressed as a young man, she is not content with passing for a youth, but embellishes this by boldly calling out: 'goodnight, Mr Sherlock Holmes'. At the end of the story, when she leaves him the note, she cannot resist an additional

10   Doyle, 'A Scandal in Bohemia', p.9 in *The Adventures of Sherlock Holmes*, 1981.
11   Doyle, 'A Scandal in Bohemia', p.18 in *The Adventures of Sherlock Holmes*, 1981.

flourish – the inclusion of a photograph of herself, with the thought that he might like to keep it. Indeed, that is exactly what he does, and the way he speaks of her is in tones of frank admiration. He is to use the same tone in talking about Adrea Spedding in *Spider Woman* and Naomi Drake in *The Pearl of Death*. The morality of these characters, however, is different – these women are not a straight transfer from the 'Irene Adler template' to the screen because they undergo a moral shift. If Irene Adler is a mirror image of Holmes, the women in the films are the mirror image of Professor Moriarty. Adler threatened the King with exposure, using the photograph as evidence. But when she fell in love with someone else, she gave the King her word that she would never use the photograph against him. Doyle played with the idea of the beautiful feminine exterior that belies a powerful, masculine mind, but redeemed her at the end. Adler may have a 'soul of steel' but it is not a black soul – she commits no crime and commands no band of underworld figures. The difference between Adler and the women of the Universal films is one of the spirit of the times.

WOMEN IN THE WARTIME WORKFORCE

Around the time that Holmes was tracking down Tobel's bombsight, and rooting out the source of the 'voice of terror', a huge societal shift was occurring. Some three-million women in the US, who would otherwise have remained at home, took jobs. A further million young women gave up their education early to enter the workforce.[12] With so many men away fighting, and with manufacturers turning to war production, their labour was crucial. Women were encouraged through advertising campaigns in the US and Britain to enter professions previously reserved for men: to take just one example, by the early 1940s, between 15 and 25 percent of the workers in American shipyards were women.[13]

Although this was a highly visible demographic change easily attributable to the war, its seeds had been sown much earlier – all the war did, arguably, was to increase the momentum and to make the female workforce visible. According to Erin Smith, by 1930 in the US 'half of all single women and a quarter of all female adults were in the

12 Figures from Renov, 1988, p.35.
13 Schindler, 1979, p.88.

paid workforce… increasingly working side by side with men'.[14] This was not a situation with which everyone was comfortable. Rhona Berenstein says that what had been known at the turn of the century as 'new women' began by the early 1930s to be described 'in a range of popular discourses as vixens intent on overturning social mores. In an effort to save modern womanhood from ruin, educated women were urged to return to the safety of marriage and maternity lest their independence (from men) destroy the traditional fabric of American culture'.[15] Mostly, however, the media attempted to ignore the presence of women in the workforce. Hardboiled pulp-fiction magazines, for example, which had huge sales among the working class in the US, featured stories that promulgated a nostalgic picture of the workplace and the 'appropriately subordinate women that went with it'.[16] Working women, other than in traditional 'feminine' occupations such as nursing and teaching, had also been largely absent from newspapers, magazines, radio programmes and films, perhaps because these were male-run institutions that tended to portray women as wives and mothers. Even in the world of crime films, women were more likely to be 'the gangster's moll or the girl waiting patiently for the hero to reform or die' than to be the perpetrator of the crime.[17] Interestingly, this portrayal of women echoes Victorian notions of femininity, where men operated in the public sphere and women in the domestic sphere – a construction worth bearing in mind in relation to the Holmes films because of his inescapable association with the Victorian.

In terms of film, a wives-and-mothers portrayal had as much to do with the rigours of the Production Code as it did with the perceived womanly ideal. The Production Code, a set of guidelines introduced in 1930 and which by 1934 had the power to vet all screenplays, aimed to stop films having a detrimental effect on the morals of the audience. It sought, among other things, not to portray illicit sex as attractive, or crime as glamorous. In the pre-Code 1920s, dangerous women – vamps such as Theda Bara and Pola Negri – abounded on screen, with the same combination of allure and deviance that their

---

14 Smith, 2000, p.31.
15 Berenstein, 1996, p.16.
16 Smith, 2000, pp.12 and 30.
17 Schindler, 1979, p.105.

post-war counterparts were to display in an era when the Code's grip on the industry began to falter. Introduction of the Code meant that 'even Garbo and Dietrich… were obliged to conform to approved standards of motherhood, family responsibility and child worship'.[18] If women were portrayed as straying from these standards, then the Production Code required them to be seen to be punished.

At the beginning of the war, the retention of the image of the 'little woman' at home was not just an attractive one but a necessary motivator for troops abroad. Dick argues that women personified freedom and peace – and therefore made liberty worth defending, leading to women being mythologized in a way not seen since the Middle Ages. He acknowledges that part of this romanticism may have been due to commercial considerations, but sees no shift in on-screen attitude until the end of the war, stating that 'the dark or malefic side of woman was pretty much relegated to the dark side of the moon for the duration'.[19] Perhaps he had not been watching B-movies such as the Holmes series, or spotted the prototype of the dangerous, duplicitous woman in the shape of Brigid O'Shaughnessy in *The Maltese Falcon* (1941). Dick is not alone in attributing the rise of the femme fatale to post-war unease. Colin Schindler notes that the 'evil, grasping woman' appeared after 1947, Michael Renov dates it to after 1945 and Molly Haskell – though she treats the 1940s as a single entity – talks almost exclusively about post-war films when describing the 'evil woman'. All associate female villains with film noir or dark melodrama. Yet the tide had turned earlier than that – they were simply looking at the wrong genres. By January 1944, two years after America's entry into the War, and when adulation of the female was ostensibly still in full spate with films like *The White Cliffs of Dover* and *Since You Went Away*, Universal released *Spider Woman*, seven months ahead of the release of *Double Indemnity*, and considered a ground-breaking portrayal of the femme fatale.[20]

Although David Reid and Jayne Walker are right to note that equating the femme fatale with 'Rosie the Riveter' is too simplistic,

---

18 Haskell, 1973, p.118.

19 Dick, 1985, p.179.

20 Other films released in the same year with a femme fatale included *Woman in the Window* and *Murder My Sweet*, but these were released in November and December respectively. I can trace no such femme fatale in films from 1942 or 1943.

it is probably true that women's increased powers in the labour market and the economy were becoming too pressing for the movies to ignore any longer.[21] Introducing the 'deadly female' to the screen was a way of censuring women for taking on these new roles – as well as a shrewd commercial move. It played on male fears of impotence in the face of newly empowered women and it offered something to women cinema-goers in the form of an alluring and glamorous role model with a frisson of danger. In other words, as Mark Jancovich notes, the studios could 'have it both ways. They [could] make a spectacle of female sexuality for those audiences that would regard this as an attraction, while simultaneously seeming to condemn the sexual mores associated with such imagery for those that would be opposed to them'.[22]

The Production Code meant that the 'femme fatale' could never win in terms of the outcome of the plot but, as with the gangster movies of the early 1930s, she surely invited identification. Instead of displaying what had come to be seen as feminine traits, she was independent, strong, predatory and ruthless. She was also, Haskell argues, not a reflection of reality, but a male fantasy. The evil woman was 'playing a man's game in a man's world of crime and carnal innuendo, where her long hair was the equivalent of a gun, where sex was the equivalent of evil. And where her power to destroy was a projection of man's feeling of impotence'.[23] Antonia Lant also talks about this male fantasy in terms of the 'liability' of female sexuality during times of war, its association with 'war's destructiveness... still familiar to us through expressions such as "blonde bombshell" to describe Jean Harlow'.[24] It is, she says, a small step from the construction of 'woman versus man' to mapping this notion onto 'enemy versus Allied'.[25] It is worth remembering, however, that the term 'femme fatale' was not one that emerged during World War Two.

---

21 In Copjec, 1993, p.63.

22 Jancovich, 2005, p.44.

23 Haskell, 1973, p.191. Deborah Walker offers a different perspective, positioning the femme fatale not as a male fantasy, but as the very real outcome of a demographic imbalance where competition for the available men put pressure on women to behave in a more overtly sexual manner (Walker, 2008, unpublished).

24 Lant, 1991, p.75.

25 Lant, 1991, p.76.

According to the *Morris Dictionary of Word and Phrase* it was first used in 1912, to describe a seductive woman with an aura of charm and mystery who lures men into dangerous or compromising situations. This is an apt description of Lydia Marlowe in *The Woman in Green* who Holmes calls, somewhat admiringly, a 'femme fatale', but it has acquired a harder-edged meaning too: that of a sexual vampire, a nexus of evil who leaches away the virility and independence of her lovers.[26]

ENTER THE 'SPIDER WOMAN'

The choice of the title *Spider Woman* is an interesting one for the series' first incursion into this new territory. Although it is specifically connected with the narrative (the bite of a poisonous spider causes the victims to commit suicide), it also positions the woman as the 'new Moriarty' because it employs a metaphor commonly used to describe Holmes' old enemy who is said to sit motionless 'like a spider in the centre of a web, but that web has a thousand radiations and he knows well every quiver of each of them'.[27] A spider may be dangerous and quick to pounce, but the added dimension brought by applying the term to a woman is that of sexual allure. 'Spider woman' as a term was taken up in subsequent critical writing to mean exactly this: Scott Snyder, for example, in his 2001 article on the femme fatale in film noir calls them 'spiderwomen', as does Biesen in her 2005 book on the links between film noir and World War Two.[28] It does not, however, seem to have been in general use in the 1940s as it does not appear in slang dictionaries of the time and was not a phrase used in the pulps.[29] Until this film, the probability is that it had only been employed to indicate a repellent hybrid rather than a creature with the sexual power to lure men to their deaths.

In retrospect, it is easy to see Adrea Spedding in *Spider Woman* as a prototype of the film noir woman, but in fact she probably owes more to Roy William Neill's overlapping of the detective and horror

---

26 From Wikipedia entry for 'femme fatale'.

27 Doyle, 'The Final Problem' in *The Memoirs of Sherlock Holmes*, 1951.

28 Synder, 2001, pp. 155–68; Biesen, 2005, p. 7. The imagery of women as spiders may have its origins in Greek mythology: Arachne was punished by being turned into a spider, and The Fates, portrayed as cold, remorseless women, spun the 'thread of life' for mortals.

29 According to Erin Smith in an email to the author (3 May 2008).

genres. The fact that she, and the other evil women who will populate *The Pearl of Death*, *The Woman in Green* and *Dressed to Kill*, do not become sexually involved with the main protagonist separates them from their film noir counterparts, though the titillating publicity material implies otherwise.

Before engaging in detailed analysis of the films, it may be useful to give a brief overview of the narratives. *Spider Woman* is a quasi-horror tale that concerns a spate of 'pajama suicides' in which prominent London men throw themselves from bedroom windows in the middle of the night. The cause seems to be the disgrace of the gambling debts they have accumulated. But the 'suicides' are actually murders: having been persuaded by an attractive woman, Adrea Spedding, to sign over their life insurance policies to one of her associates in return for cash, they are then killed. The means of death is bizarre and involves a fairground pygmy who crawls through a ventilator shaft into their bedrooms, unleashing a poisonous spider whose bite drives them to leap through the window. The 'spider woman' then cashes in the life insurance policy. Holmes uses little in the way of on-screen deductive reasoning, but plays a cat-and-mouse game with the villain. He eventually secures her arrest after almost losing his life at the fairground's shooting gallery. The narrative trajectory of the film, together with the foregrounding of horror and otherness, means that it has much in common with *The Woman in Green*, a blackmail scam in which a series of working-class girls are randomly murdered and prominent men framed for the crime, convinced they committed it because they find themselves unable to account for their movements – and because they find the damning evidence of a severed finger in their pocket. The scam works by means of a glamorous woman, Lydia Marlowe, luring them to her apartment and hypnotising them.[30] Holmes is similarly lured, with the object of being murdered by Moriarty, but arrests the woman and causes Moriarty to leap from the building to his death.

Dressed to Kill is a more conventional detective-genre plot which involves the attempt by a murderous criminal gang, led by a woman – Hilda Courtney – to find Bank of England printing plates that have

---

30 Hypnosis had already been used as a theme in a 1944 Charlie Chan film, *Meeting at Midnight*, and one of the key moments – with Chan apparently hypnotised and being lured to step off the parapet of a tall building – is replicated in *The Woman in Green*.

been hidden somewhere in London by the man who stole them. Now a prisoner in Dartmoor, the thief spends his days in the workshop making musical boxes. To pass on to his associates the whereabouts of the plates, he changes the tune in a series of the boxes, forming a code that reveals the address. Holmes uses deductive reasoning to crack the code: when the gang finds the hiding place, Holmes is already there and they are arrested. The narrative trajectory of the film is very similar to *The Pearl of Death*, which concerns the theft of a famous pearl from a London museum. Having to stash the pearl quickly on his exit from the museum, the thief (Giles Conover) presses it into the still-wet plaster of one of a line of Napoleon busts in a nearby workshop. He and his accomplice, Naomi Drake, then have to trace and retrieve the correct bust – with Holmes endeavouring to get there first. Holmes nearly dies at the hands of a monstrous member of the gang, but arrests Drake, and shoots the 'monster'.

Underlying each of these narratives are a number of common themes which provide an insight into how the deadly female is portrayed. Among these (examined in detail below) are the use of costume to symbolise character, the centrality of disguise/performance in the construction of female identity, the pragmatic use of sexual allure, and the dichotomy between on- and off-screen personae. These themes serve as important components in the establishment of the 'deadly female' as an archetype. Firstly, however, it is productive to examine the way that the portrayal of women in these films reveals tensions between past and present, and between genres. Temporal tensions are evident in the way men, by inhabiting Victorian settings, are shown as belonging to the past, while women, by inhabiting contemporary spaces, are shown as belonging to the present. Genre tensions are evident in the 'mirroring' of the hero-victim, in this case Holmes, and the female 'monster', a device borrowed from the horror genre.

TEMPORAL TENSIONS: A GENDER DIVIDE

The way that women are shown to inhabit or embody the present day, while men are coded as belonging to the past, perhaps reveals male fears of their uncertain position – or their redundancy – in the new world that would emerge after the war.[31] From the start of the

---

31 This is true of all the Holmes films in the Universal series, not just those with a female villain.

Universal series, Holmes and Watson's rooms at 221B Baker Street had been presented as a Victorian space, with the studio anxious to ensure that the present day should only intrude when they step through the front door, but by the time of *Spider Woman*, this tension between past and present becomes gender-based, echoing that between Holmes and his female adversary.[32]

In *Spider Woman*, Holmes and Watson move through the following locations in addition to their Victorian rooms in Baker Street: rural Scotland, an idyll that is symbolic of the past; the rented room at Langdon Flats where Holmes hopes to trap the killer, a Victorian interior with dark wooden panelling and heavy furniture; and the house where spider-specialist Matthew Ordway lives, which has a wholly Victorian interior. In addition, when Holmes is presumed drowned, it is the British Museum, a place for the display of 'past' artefacts, which Watson arranges to receive his possessions. In contrast, the spaces in which Spedding moves are quintessentially modern, such as the brightly lit casino, and her elaborately designed apartment with its pale furniture, huge chandeliers and exotic decor. It is interesting that, though Holmes meets her in both of these locations, he does so in disguise ('not Holmes'). When he confronts her as himself, it is on his home territory at 221B Baker Street, an environment in which she is out of place, something that is signified by the way she tries to destroy it with a smoke bomb. In fact the scene is a deliberate inversion of the domestic: though she is accompanied by a child described as her nephew, he is not a normal boy but a sinister, mute creature, and it is in his sweet wrapper that the smoke bomb is concealed.[33] The scene in the fairground arcade at the end of the film is more ambivalent, the fairground itself and the people who work in it – the fortune tellers, exotic dancers and freak-show performers – belonging to a 'timeless' world of folklore. The issue here seems to be more about performance and otherness than about past/present, even though the set is crowded with extras in contemporary dress, through whose ranks the overcoated Holmes,

---

32 Obviously, these spaces are not exclusive to each sex, otherwise the protagonists would never meet, so it is the sense of 'belonging' to particular locations that is significant.

33 Vivian Sobchack notes that 'ironic domesticity' often runs through film noir, giving as an example the scene in *Double Indemnity* where Phyllis Dietrichson shops in a supermarket while discussing her husband's murder with Walter Neff (V. Sobchack, 1998, p.144).

Watson and Lestrade wander as if they exist in another time zone.

The gender differences are less marked in *The Pearl of Death*, with Naomi Drake moving in much the same locations as Holmes. It is notable, however, that the pearl's rightful owner, to whom Holmes delivers it, is the Royal Regent Museum – both its name and the date of its founding, written in Roman numerals on the doorpost, evoking an earlier age. The museum was established in 1832 and the decor and furnishings of the curator's office are entirely from that era even though the action is supposed to be taking place in 1944. This might be expected in a public area of the museum, but not in its 'back offices'. This remains a male space: it is from here that Conover steals back the pearl, without Naomi Drake present. As well as scenes at 221B Baker Street, there is another key scene which is redolent of the past: Holmes and Watson's visit to the plaster-figure workshop, where old, non-mechanised skills are still in use.

The Woman in Green begins with a meeting at police headquarters where top detectives discuss what to do about the 'finger murders' – the meeting room is darkly panelled in wood, with a large library of old, leather-bound books filling one wall. When the next blackmail victim wakes from his hypnotism in a stranger's bedroom, it is in Victorian surroundings with a brass bed and mahogany furniture: his subsequent suicide takes place in his own home, a baronial mansion redolent with High Gothic style. As well as their rooms at Baker Street, Holmes and Watson also inhabit other spaces which evoke the past, including the Mesmer Club, which resembles a Victorian gentleman's club. Lydia Marlowe's territory, on the other hand, is the Pembroke House nightclub, with its sophisticated modern interior, ablaze with electric light, and its contemporary-sounding music. Although Holmes is present in this setting *(see Fig. 44)*, he and his policeman colleague are clearly out of place, something that is conveyed by the way they keep their tweed overcoats on while they drink at the bar: everyone else is in evening dress. Marlowe's flat is a complete contrast to the male spaces – a vast, elegant room, with white furniture, a white piano, a uniformed maid and electrically operated curtains. Holmes' not-belonging in this space is conveyed by the fact that he comes to the flat only to be hypnotised (in other words, to be 'not there') and, indeed, this is where he very nearly meets his death. A similar crossing into the other's territory is made when Marlowe visits the Mesmer Club. To demonstrate her non-

FIGURE 44 To indicate that they do not belong in this nightclub setting in _The Woman in Green_, Holmes and the policeman keep on their overcoats throughout the scene.

belonging in this male, Victorian environment, she wears completely inappropriate attire – the equivalent of Holmes' tweed overcoat at Pembroke House – arriving in a fur coat, with huge diamond earrings and a diamond-ornamented hat.

Dressed to Kill follows a similar pattern. The film opens with establishing shots (using what looks like a very old 'stock' photograph, implying more temporal ambiguity) of Dartmoor prison where the thief is making musical boxes: it is a Victorian building. There are lengthy scenes in the auction rooms where the musical boxes are being sold, in which the audience follows the attempts of 'Stinky' Emery to buy them, Courtney's henchman to trace them, and the follow-up visit of Holmes and Watson: auctions are strongly linked with antiques and therefore with the past. Stinky is associated with the past in the same way, through his avid collecting of antique artefacts, particularly Victorian automata. The (male) buskers of London also inhabit a quasi-Victorian past with their basement bar still lit by gas, and even the place where the thief has hidden the Bank of England plates evokes the past: it is Dr Samuel Johnson's house, now a museum. By contrast, Hilda Courtney's house is in a highly fashionable Mayfair square and is a vast apartment with light-coloured furniture, the obligatory grand piano, and classical styling. Both Hilda and the woman who runs the gift-shop are shown to interact with the past only in terms of consumerism – artefacts from the past are bought and sold by them, rendering the past as some sort of commodity.

This analysis clearly indicates that men are shown to inhabit the Victorian era, and women the present. Although this tension is most easily observed in terms of Holmes and Watson – and indeed is necessary in order to preserve their distinctive '1895 bubble' – it arguably goes further than it needs to. Producer Howard Benedict said that stepping out of 221B would mean stepping into the modern world, but the distinctions are blurred and embrace other male characters in the films too. These associations with the past, particularly in terms of interiors, are unlikely to have connoted good taste, as Victorian design was not highly regarded in the mid-1940s either in the US or the UK. Design magazines from the period immediately preceding the war could, perhaps, be expected to champion the new over the old, and would therefore provide unreliable evidence to substantiate this assertion: more telling is the way the British quickly developed a taste for the pared-down style of Utility Furniture which was introduced and heavily promoted in 1942. It was the antithesis of the Victorian which, in the public's view, was 'past it'.[34] It may, however, have engendered a certain nostalgia in its association with a more settled time: novelist Barbara Pym, for example, writing in 1941, has her narrator remark that these are days when 'Victorian objects are comforting relics of a period when the upper middle classes lived pleasant, peaceful lives and wars were fought decently in foreign countries'.[35]

---

34 Gainsborough studios in the UK, of course, built considerable success in transporting viewers back to a bygone age – but it should be noted that this was more commonly a Georgian or Regency past rather than a Victorian one, and sufficiently temporally distant to be thought attractive.

35 Pym, 1990, p.371.

GENRE TENSIONS: A PHYSICALITY OF HORROR

The incursion of gothic settings and themes into the middle films of the series, attributable to Roy William Neill's horror-movie sensibilities, drew the films into new territory which, as the series progressed, became less about devices which played on the imagination such as haunted castles, shadows and ancient riddles, and more about a physicality of horror. This was counter to the trend at the time even in the horror genre – the monster-populated Gothic horror films which were the hallmark of Universal in the 1930s had given way to a psychological approach, led principally by RKO (Val Newton's horror unit in particular), in which the horror was merely suggested: examples are *Cat People* (1942), *I Walked With a Zombie* (1943), *The Ghost Ship* (1943), *The Seventh Victim* (1943) and *The Body Snatcher* (1945).[36] The trend was also noticed by the *New York Times*: when reviewing *Double Indemnity* in 1944, they remarked on the 'new horror cycle' that was 'psychological'.[37] In these films, the physically monstrous had been replaced by 'humans who [had] lost their moral compass'.[38] This accords well with the development of the Holmes series at Universal in terms of the female villains, but the visceral aspects took the series further into a borderline zone between genres, and the resulting tension is evident in Universal's advertising campaigns for the films.

Multiple genre tags might be construed as Universal's attempt to attract a wider range of cinema-goers, but these changes involved the films' content, not just their marketing: the shift was noticed by the critics, who described them as 'flesh-creeping', 'gruesome', 'hardly suitable for the youngsters' and as 'a collection of horror items'.[39] If Universal had had their way, there would have been more for the critics to comment on: the original idea for *The Woman in Green*, for example, called for the mutilation of eight-year-old girls, something

---

36 Lewton said his films were successful because they featured 'normal' people coming into contact with the strange, as opposed to the 'run-of-the-mill weird films' which were populated by 'European nobles... mad scientists, man-created monsters' (quoted by Newman, 1999, p.65).

37 Quoted in Biesen, 2005, p.191.

38 Karina Wilson on www.horrorfilmhistory.com (13 January 2008).

39 *Monthly Film Bulletin*, January 1944, p.6 and, November 1944, p.130; *Kinematograph Weekly*, 19 October 1944, p.25; and *The New York Post*, 19 October 1944, unpaginated.

that the PCA felt violated the Code. The script was changed to refer to young adult women.[40] The horror in these films derives from the tangible: poisonous spiders, severed fingers, perverted doctors, hypnotism, pygmies, a deformed killer, a mute child, grotesque sideshows at the fair, and secret compartments in coffins. Many, though not all, of these horror elements are strongly associated with the female characters and become their 'attributes': in the spider woman's case, the identification is complete – she has even taken on their name. In all cases, they represent an otherness that is to be feared and that somehow equates with the female. For example, when a man hypnotises Watson at the Mesmer Club in *The Woman in Green*, it is done for entertainment and the outcome is laughter. When a woman hypnotises Sir George, his surrender of control and implied seduction results in his death.[41] The monstrosity of the women may be covered by surface glamour, but it is these 'attributes' that hint at the true nature that lies behind the mask: the scene at the fairground in *Spider Woman* is particularly revealing in this respect with its 'Dolly Dumpling' fat-woman freakshow, Wanda the fake fortune teller, the pygmy ('Bongo from the Congo') shut in a suitcase, and the pseudo-Hawaiian dancing sisters. An earlier Holmes film – *The Sign of Four* starring Arthur Wontner and released in 1932 – features a similar fairground scene emphasising otherness: the difference, however, is that none of the featured performers or freaks are women.

In *Spider Woman*, *The Woman in Green* and *Dressed to Kill*, the woman has taken the place traditionally occupied by the horror-film monster, which raises the interesting issue of what role, therefore, Holmes fulfils.[42] There are three main protagonists in classic horror: the monster, the heroine who is both attracted and repelled by it, and the largely ineffectual hero who is nevertheless united with the heroine at the end of the film. Using Berenstein's theory of 'mirroring' in the horror genre, it could be argued that Holmes fulfils the role of the heroine in these 'deadly female' films, and Watson the ineffectual hero. This use of mirroring also serves to distinguish these

---

40 Breen letter to Universal quoted by Andy Demsky, www.basilrathbone.net.

41 With the duping of Sir George, the woman's 'otherness' strikes at the traditional class structure and reveals it as permeable.

42 *The Pearl of Death* is slightly different as it features a male monster not under the woman's control.

particular films and their protagonists, from film noir. Mirroring is, of course, also present in the classic detective film and there is a certain amount of this in Holmes' relationship with Moriarty in the three films in which he appears.[43] Moriarty is cunning, ruthless and resourceful like Holmes, and there is a mutual satisfaction in their dealings with each other. The mirroring of Holmes and the deadly females, however, goes further than this – they share Holmes' love of disguise; they exercise command with the same authority as Holmes; they remain calm, smiling and in perfect control even in times of extreme danger; and they combine allure and repulsion in a way that Moriarty does not.

One typical instance of mirroring occurs near the beginning of *Spider Woman*, in a scene at Spedding's flat, where a close two-shot reveals her reclining on a sofa reading the paper, her half-brother Norman on a chair close by. The manner of the two characters and their dialogue resemble scenes at Baker Street between Holmes and Watson. Spedding's languid air, her reading out of announcements in *The Times*, her quest for 'amusement' and her obvious position of power (she reclines while Norman sits hunched forward on the chair by her side) recall Holmes. Norman here is her 'Dr Watson', moving quickly to light her cigarette, giving buffoonish replies to her questions, and willingly taking her orders. The only indication at this stage that this 'mirroring' may be an ironic one is the placement in the foreground of a pair of Regency-style porcelain figurines, depicting a couple in courtly stance – a foretaste of what will be their distinctly uncourtly behaviour.[44]

Spedding's exoticism is shown to mirror that of Holmes – when he dresses as the Indian soldier Rajhni Singh, in turban, beard and skin-darkening makeup, Spedding appears in a sari and Indian headdress *(see Fig. 45)*. The disguises used by Naomi Drake and Hilda Courtney mirror those of Holmes in that they all use lower-class disguises in order to move invisibly through London. There is further mirroring in all the 'deadly female' films in the form of verbal

---

43 *Adventures, Secret Weapon,* and *The Woman in Green.*

44 The Production Code Administration were worried that Norman was characterised as a 'pansy type' and asked for the relationship between Adrea and Norman to be clarified, hence the positioning of him as her half-brother (Breen letter to Pivar of Universal dated 10 May 1943).

FIGURE 45 Not exactly disguise, but certainly a performance: the costume of Adrea Spedding (Gale Sondergaard) mirrors that of Holmes in this scene from *Spider Woman*.

swordplay, sometimes disguised as mutual seduction, that takes place between Holmes and the women. What is interesting about this dialogue is that it has exactly the same content and tone as the dialogues that Holmes has with Moriarty. The fact that his conversation is with a woman, however, removes the usual irony and gives it a sexual edge instead. In *Secret Weapon*, Holmes discusses the best way for Moriarty to kill him – an almost identical conversation happens between Holmes and Spedding in *Spider Woman* where he urges her to find a more imaginative method than merely tying him to the back of the targets in the shooting gallery. 'Ingenious, but uninspired', he says. 'It lacks the personal touch'. A smiling Spedding is happy to oblige, pointing out that 'perhaps Dr Watson will be your executioner'. At the end of *The Woman in Green*, he is denied such a speech with Lydia Marlowe because he is pretending to be hypnotised, so his remarks to Moriarty seem like a displaced conversation with Marlowe, particularly as he has earlier referred to her as 'a female Moriarty'. He says: 'we shall walk through the gates of eternity hand in hand – what a charming picture that would make'. His self-confessed admiration for Spedding, Marlowe and Courtney suggests that he has been pleased to meet his match – in both senses of the term. When he arrests Hilda Courtney, for example, she remarks on his cleverness: 'praise from you is indeed gratifying', he replies. And as Spedding walks away with Inspector Lestrade, her composure intact despite having just been arrested (arm-in-arm with the policeman, as if going on a date rather than going to a cell), Holmes looks longingly after her. 'A remarkable woman', he says, 'as audacious and deadly as one of her own spiders'.

The series is not consistent in its mirroring: if it were, the genre tensions would be less noticeable. *The Pearl of Death*, for example, which has a much more conventional detective-genre narrative than *Spider Woman* or *The Woman in Green*, exhibits a horror-influenced trajectory in terms of the way it portrays the relationship between Naomi Drake and the Creeper. As with conventional horror-film monsters, the Creeper is attracted to the woman with what Barnes describes as a 'King-Kong-like admiration', but the film shies away from giving them a scene together, which would be crucial in the horror genre.[45]

In addition to associating women with horror-genre monsters, and showing them as embodiments of the present and future of society, the films also highlight a number of other shared traits, which are discussed below.

COSTUME AS OVERT SYMBOLISM

In all Hollywood movies, the female lead's costume makes a statement both about the character being played and about the star's own screen persona. In the Holmes films it also offers a guide to the period in which the films are set, as opposed to the costume of the two male leads which drift between the Edwardian and the contemporary. Given that these are wartime films, the costume also offers an aspirational or fantasy 'fashion-plate' to audiences unable to buy the luxurious clothes worn by the female lead. In *Spider Woman* and *Dressed to Kill*, however, the costumes are given an unusual

---

45 Barnes, 2002, p.108.

FIGURE 46 Spedding's costume in *Spider Woman* features a claw-like diamante design to indicate her predatory nature.

amount of emphasis, particularly in terms of character symbolism.[46] The fact that costume features in the title of two of the films (*Dressed to Kill* and *The Woman in Green*) speaks volumes about its importance.

At the first appearance of Adrea Spedding, the audience is unaware that this is the villain of the film, and her costume is coded accordingly, though the fact that she is played by Gale Sondergaard – by then typecast as a glamorous schemer – provides a non-diegetic clue. She wears a flowing jersey dress and flowers in her hair, and is only seen in recumbent, feminine posture, talking about seeking out 'amusement'. This is the only scene in which her costume will be hard to 'read'. Her next appearance is at a casino *(see Fig. 46)* where she has lured a distinguished Indian soldier (Holmes in disguise) in order to dupe him of his life insurance. She wears a severely cut dark

---

46 The costume designer for the Universal series was Vera West who specialised in women's costumes and worked on more than 135 films during the five-year span of this series.

FIGURE 47 Overt symbolism in *Spider Woman*: Spedding wears a hat with a phallic fur ornament, and drapes animal skins around her shoulders like trophies.

dress dominated by large, claw-like diamante ornamentation on its front, and a hat with the veil down, creating a spider-web effect across her face. The claw-shaped ornamentation is a direct reference to Holmes' analysis of the so-called suicides and his deduction that the murders are 'feline'. The audience is now in no doubt that the 'amusement' she seeks is murder and that this is the spider woman of the title.[47] Later in the film, when she visits Holmes at 221B Baker Street, the film further reveals – and, indeed, celebrates – her predatory nature through her costume: over her sharp dark suit she wears an enormous fur stole, the heads and legs of the animals hanging limply down over her shoulder like a collection of trophies or scalps. The implication is that Holmes will be the next 'trophy' she collects.[48] Her dark pillbox hat is surmounted by an extraordinary

---

47 Stella Bruzzi (1997, p.129) argues that the duplicity of the femme fatale is traditionally signalled through 'the persistent alteration of her look, her changeable wardrobe becoming a straightforward metonym for her untrustworthiness'.

48 The same fur-stole symbolism was subsequently used by villainous women in late 1940s noirish thrillers such as Marsha Peters (Ella Raines) who arranges for her lover to murder her husband in *Impact* (1949).

phallic fur ornament, sticking up erect from the crown – symbolism does not come much more overt than this *(see Fig. 47)*. At no time, incidentally, does Spedding appear in the costume featured on the posters – a black strapless evening dress slit to the thigh – which might be alluring but does not convey the necessary 'male' authority essential to the character. This type of straight-forwardly glamorous portrayal is left to Lydia Marlowe in *The Woman in Green*, perhaps because her only role is to seduce and hypnotise her upper-class victims ('women's work') leaving Moriarty to frame them for murder.

A similar 'spider woman' approach is taken with Hilda Courtney, the deadly female of *Dressed to Kill*, whose costume also includes over-sized fur stoles with the animals' heads and legs intact; and phallic symbolism in manly suits and hats: she even sports a 'victorious' feather in her hat in the scene when she has left Holmes for dead. In her first appearance, when she makes a late-night visit to musical-box collector Julian 'Stinky' Emery, she wears the costume that appears on the posters, an evening dress and massive white fur wrap: exactly the type of costume that Sarah Berry points out was 'an omnipresent signifier of feminine luxury throughout the 1930s' but which – like the fox-fur stoles – was a sign of ostentation by the mid-40s.[49] This wrap is almost taken from her: as Stinky is stabbed in the back by one of Courtney's henchmen, he grabs hold of its end, pulling it off her shoulders and onto the floor with him. On leaving, she retrieves it by tugging at it, pulling it out calmly from under the corpse and putting it once more around her shoulders before striding out of his apartment. That the stole is a symbol of her authority and power is underlined when Courtney regains it, but leaves Stinky's corpse with its bald head exposed, his toupée lying alongside. On the one hand, the wearing of these excessive fur clothes is an appropriation of male power, but in Freudian terms it also serves as a fetish – a substitute for, and a displacement of, the real sexual object.[50] This was a period when film was beginning to engage with Freudian ideas (somewhat later than the world of fine art: for example, Surrealist Meret Oppenheim had exhibited her fur-covered cup and saucer in 1936), so the fetishism and excess displayed here are likely to have been conscious choices on the part of the director

---

49 Berry, 2000, p.49.

50 Freud, 1977, p.65.

and/or costume designer. They make an interesting contrast to the austerity and restraint of the world in which Holmes traditionally moves.

The costume of these female villains forms a sharp contrast with the 'good' women in the films – such as the unobtrusive tailored suits, discreet jewellery and modest make-up of the victim's daughter in *The Woman in Green*, and of the gift-shop owner in *Dressed to Kill*. It is interesting to note that these clothes code them not just as 'good', but also as powerless.

THE CENTRALITY OF DISGUISE/PERFORMANCE

The use of disguise and performance is characteristic of the detective genre: in every film in the Fox/Universal series, Holmes disguises himself in order to further the investigation (as a pedlar, a lascar seaman, a variety-show entertainer, an antique buyer, an antiquarian book-seller, a clergyman, a postman and so on). The male villains often adopt pseudonyms, or pretend to be someone they are not, but only in one film (*The Scarlet Claw*) is the use of disguise by the male villain essential to the plot. In the films featuring female villains, however, disguise and performance is central to the way they are presented. This ties the films more to the horror genre: Berenstein describes horror as 'a genre that trades in the masking and unmasking of creatures and celebrates the discovery that characters are not what they seem'.[51] The disguises used by the women are linked to issues of class and to passing for a class that is not their own.

When Holmes first sees the glamorous woman he later knows to be Lydia Marlowe (*The Woman in Green*), he remarks that she is 'not born to the purple, but giving an excellent imitation of it', a remark which could equally apply to any of the other female villains of the series. Their sustained 'performance' seems to be an upper-middle-class one, though their true class origins are revealed in little gestures unseen by the other protagonists, such as the way Naomi Drake puts two fingers into her mouth and emits a loud whistle to summon her associates.[52] Their preferred tactical disguise, however, is that of the

---

51 Berenstein, 1996, p.8.

52 A similar device is used to betray Vivian Vedder's real origins in *Terror by Night*. Despite her haute couture and the upper-class manner she adopts at the coffin-makers, she lets slip an 'ain't it?' phrase that makes it clear that this is all a performance.

lower classes. For example, much as Irene Adler, in 'A Scandal in Bohemia', chose the dress of a young ostler in which to stalk Holmes, Drake disguises herself as a Cockney washer-up (Bertram Millhauser's screenplay describes her as 'a slattern, in draggle-tailed cotton dress and dirty apron'), a poor match-girl, then a respectable, rather bookish shop assistant in tortoiseshell-framed glasses. Her sustained performance is of a character similar to Adrea Spedding – moneyed, fashionable and outwardly respectable, though not quite the 'lovely, starry-eyed, young' woman as Millhauser's description of her first appearance on the cross-Channel ship would indicate. This turns out to be yet another performance.

Spedding's disguises are slightly different from those assumed by Naomi Drake and Hilda Courtney because they seem to absorb her whole persona, unlike mere clothes or accents she puts on and takes off at will. She is, therefore, much more identifiable as a figure with its origins in the horror genre rather than the detective genre. Berenstein argues that one of the genre's most insistent promises is to 'confront spectators with... on-screen characters who embody role-play as a thematic and selling ploy intended to elicit complex and contradictory viewer responses'.[53] Spedding's 'performance' is consummate, but the viewer is always aware of its artificiality because the underlying evil nature of the character remains visible throughout. Her sexual allure is always tinged with danger, though this is attributable mainly to Gale Sondergaard's acting rather than to the script: Sondergaard has said in an interview with Boze Hadleigh of *Scarlet Street* that 'the characterisation was up to me: she was never intricately conceived'.[54] She never wears a 'disguise' as such and, indeed, is scornful of Holmes' disguise as an Indian, which she easily sees through: 'I hate disguises', she says. That the whole of her life is dedicated to giving a performance is made obvious in the scene in her apartment *(see Fig. 48),* the interior of which has strong theatrical connotations, with all the accoutrements of a stage including a backdrop and a proscenium arch framed by heavy curtains. It is also referred to explicitly by Holmes in the scene where she visits him at 221B Baker Street. Arriving with her 'nephew', she tells Holmes that she is 'playing nurse today'. His reply is: 'I'm sure you'll give an exceptional performance'.

---

53 Berenstein, 1996, p.35.
54 *Scarlet Street*, No. 11, 1993, unpaginated.

FIGURE 48 Spedding's whole apartment, in *Spider Woman*, looks like a theatrical set.

SEXUAL ALLURE

The main weapon in the armoury of these predatory females is sexual allure, just as it is with their emerging film noir counterparts – though there are specific differences. The first is that the viewer is privy to the duplicity of the Holmes women from the start, whereas the duplicity of the femme fatale of the film noir, such as Phyllis Dietrichson in *Double Indemnity* or Brigid O'Shaughnessy in *The Maltese Falcon*, is hidden both from the audience and from the male lead for much of the film. Dietrichson is established as a femme fatale from her first, fetishised appearance, in a shot of her shoes as she descends the staircase, but it's not until the 28th minute that her wish to have her husband killed is made explicit, and not until the 75th minute that it is apparent that she has killed in the past. The fact that O'Shaughnessy's appearance is not fetishised in the same way makes her motives even harder to read: from the beginning her story does not quite ring true, but neither Sam Spade, nor the audience, can quite put their finger on the duplicity. The second difference between the predatory female of the Holmes films and the film noir women is that Holmes does not become sexually entangled, partly perhaps because this would stretch the credibility of his character too far, and partly because such an entanglement would not fit with the genre – to stay within the classic detective genre, the detective should always remain detached. The films do play with the notion of entanglement: for example, in the seduction scene when Holmes visits Spedding's home in *Spider Woman*, and in his double-entendre conversation with Lydia Marlowe at the Mesmer Club in *The Woman in Green*, where she advocates his 'giving in' to hypnotism. These scenes give an intriguing glimpse into a usually absent aspect of Holmes, but the character is redeemed by the revelation that what appears to be mutual seduction is actually subterfuge – a point visually underlined by the fact that Holmes is in disguise (and therefore 'not really Holmes') for one of these scenes.

The women's sexuality is linked to their power, and it is this link which is designed to discomfort. Gregory Mank describes the 'definite and striking sexuality' of Adrea Spedding as 'making her villainy all the more delectable – and dangerous'.[55] This association of sexuality with black-hearted villainy brings the women much closer to the horror genre: monsters in horror films are, as Berenstein points out, 'simultaneously repulsive and desirable'.[56] The analogy with cats draws attention to this combination of attraction and danger, with its unspoken allusion to the familiars of witches, and sets up a series of polarities between female/male, other/self, feline/canine, faithless/faithful, scheming/stupid.[57] The women's power is of a languid variety – like felines, they stretch and purr and like nothing more than some gentle badinage, though when it comes to killing or maiming, they do not sully their hands. Hilda Courtney may be 'dressed to kill' – she is posed with a gun on the poster, the weapon an incongruous addition to her glamorous fur-clad depiction – but she never does so. She leaves that to her chauffeur. Even at the denouement, when the gang finally discover the hiding place of the banknote printing plates, it is her henchmen who pick the lock on the bookcase, remove the plates and even cut the string that ties them – all Courtney does is unwrap the package.

---

55 Mank, 1999, p.304.

56 Berenstein, 1996, p.19.

57 It is well-trodden ground: *The Cat and the Canary*, in which Gale Sondergaard also starred, includes the line 'Have you ever seen a man who thought he was a cat? A woman, yes, but a man – no'.

RECONCILING THE ON- AND OFF-SCREEN PERSONAE

Whereas the pressbooks for the series sought to conflate the on-screen characters of Holmes and Watson with the actors who played them, portraying them as very English, gentlemanly, patriotic, given to stopping for afternoon tea, and so on, the opposite is true of the way the pressbooks dealt with the 'deadly females'. For example Evelyn Ankers, who played Naomi Drake in *The Pearl of Death*, was a staple figure in Universal horror films, signing to the studio in 1941 and appearing as the leading lady in *The Wolf Man* (1941), *Captive Wild Women* (1943), *The Ghost of Frankenstein* (1942), *The Mad Ghoul* (1943), *Weird Woman* (1944), and *Son of Dracula* (1943), roles which would influence the way she was perceived by audiences in this film, used to seeing her as monstrous villain or frightened victim. The pressbook, however, does not characterise her as a horror-genre actress, stressing the variety of films she has appeared in, from those of Abbott and Costello to Deanna Durbin, and headlining a picture of Rathbone, Bruce and Ankers as a 'pretty problem for Sherlock'. The photograph *(see Fig. 49)* shows Holmes and Watson in a head-and-shoulders shot, in their costumes for the film, looking obliquely out of the frame. Behind them is a deeply shadowed full-length 'star' shot of Ankers standing against a wall, lit as if caught in a spotlight, and wearing a pale, full-length dress with billowing sleeves and ruffled bodice. Her hair hangs loose and falls across one eye. The caption below says: 'Sherlock Holmes and his friend Doctor Watson face their prettiest and toughest problem in Universal's "The Pearl of Death". Basil Rathbone is seen as the famous detective, Nigel Bruce as Watson and Evelyn Ankers as the lovely conundrum'. Despite her villainy in the film, the star persona prevails over the character in the use of the words 'prettiest' and 'lovely'.

The pressbook for *The Woman in Green* similarly distances the actress, Hillary Brooke, from the character. It remarks on the charm that she adds to the film, even though the sole motivation for her 'charm' is blackmail. It stresses her rationality, saying that she has never encountered a hypnotist, and although the film makes no reference to the occult, the pressbook finds it necessary to add that she has never attended a seance, or met a medium – in fact she doesn't believe in such things. 'Why [she] should suggest lethal ladies to casting directors is one of those things which make Hollywood a permanent question mark to the rest of the world', it says, because 'she is not the

Pretty Problem for Sherlock

Sherlock Holmes and his friend, Doctor Watson, face their prettiest and toughest problem in Universal's "The Pearl of Death." Basil Rathbone (L) is seen as the famous detective, Nigel Bruce as Watson, and Evelyn Ankers as the lovely conundrum.   (Mat 21)

FIGURE 49 In the pressbook for *The Pearl of Death*, Evelyn Ankers as Naomi Drake is billed as the 'lovely conundrum' rather than as a black-hearted villain.

sort of person you would expect to portray a blackmailing hypnotist'. The nearest the pressbook comes to character–actor conflation is quoting Brooke as saying 'I like playing... cold dames... [and] heavies, the heavier the better'. Her previous good-girl roles in Holmes films (she had played Sally Musgrave in *Sherlock Holmes Faces Death* and Jill, the Ministry driver assigned to Holmes in *Voice of Terror*), are not mentioned.

Likewise, Patricia Morison is carefully distanced from her character Hilda Courtney in *Dressed to Kill*, with the pressbook's emphasis being solely on her war work as a singer, and the fact that she was one of the first of the USO group to go overseas to give concerts to servicemen. Gale Sondergaard was equally active in the war effort, well known for selling war bonds across America, in the uniform of the Women's Ambulance and Defense Corps. Whether this side of her persona was promoted in the pressbook is a matter for speculation, as no copy of the pressbook exists in any of the major collections or film libraries in the US or UK. What audiences were likely to remember, however, was her chilling on-screen persona: her role as the sinister housekeeper Miss Lu who keeps a cat as her 'familiar' in the comedy-thriller *The Cat and the Canary* (1939), or as Abigail Doone in the mystery-thriller *The Black Cat*, a Universal film in which she played opposite Basil Rathbone.[58]

Audiences seem to have been quite capable of holding contradictory ideas about these stars: their on-screen villainous performance, and their off-screen idealised portraits. Berenstein is right to state that the divide between these portrayals 'engages spectators as active agents in the construction and comprehension of the inherent contradictions and complexities of cinematic discourses',[59] but it is also true that such an emphasis on wholesomeness in the pressbooks dilutes potentially worrying aspects of the on-screen character and demonstrates that they are merely a performance. Off-screen, the norms of society prevail.

Though there is a broad trajectory in the series in terms of the way women are portrayed, there are films from the later period that do not conform to this trend: there are no 'deadly females' in *Pursuit to Algiers*, for example, and the woman in *Terror by Night* who is transporting a coffin by train and who seems straight out of the Spedding, Drake or Courtney mould (complete with claw-like nails), is actually a red herring *(see Fig. 50)*. Even the inclusion of a woman villain in *Dressed to Kill* was something of an afterthought by the studio. The story outline submitted by Frank Gruber in June 1945,

---

58 The association of women with the 'feline' was clearly prevalent at this time – Jacques Tourneur's film *Cat People* was released in 1942 involving a plot-line about a woman who fears she will turn into a panther when sexually aroused.

59 Berenstein, 1996, p.79.

FIGURE 50 A publicity shot implies villainy in *Terror by Night*, but Vivian Vedder (Renée Godfrey) is strictly a red herring.

under the working title *Prelude to Murder,* was for a plot about diamond smuggling, with the woman the victim and not the perpetrator. It was five months later when Leonard Lee wrote the treatment that Hilda Courtney made her appearance, though her prominence was still not at that stage reflected in the title of the film.[60] I would suggest that it is significant that both Lee and Gruber were prominent pulp-fiction writers before they became screenwriters.[61]

The portrayal of women in these films may have been influenced by wartime discourses about women in the workplace and fears that they 'no longer knew their place', but it is important to remember that the films' purpose was entertainment: Berenstein reminds us that 'narrative cinema is a fantasy scenario, a confirmation of, and temporary release from, the subjectivities engaged in by spectators in their everyday lives'.[62] The pressbooks are a good indicator that audiences knew how to hold contradictory ideas about on- and off-screen personae – and the very fact that these were genre films, usually tagged as thriller-chillers, served to distance from 'reality' any notions about the way the women were portrayed. Indeed, the whole femme fatale concept is an artificial construct (Jean Baudrillard calls it 'the projective artefact of male hysteria')[63] and, as such, who better to see that the femme fatale is outwitted and brought to justice than a figure who personifies Victorian values?

This chapter has therefore established that women in the Universal series were introduced initially to provide a secondary-plot 'love interest' that would appeal to female cinema-goers without compromising the emotional detachment crucial to Holmes' character. During the course of the series, their portrayal began to change: they were no longer the role-model 'wives and mothers' that critics perceived as being exclusively the mood of the times, but were shown as clever, black-hearted villains, gaining pleasure from the entrapment and killing of their male victims. This role took the series into horror-genre territory – a visceral horror which was against the

---

60 Gruber story outline, 14 June 1945; Lee treatment, 16 November 1945.

61 Tom Weaver remarks on the 'pulp-like' characters that began to be introduced from *Spider Woman* onwards (Weaver, Brunas and Brunas, 2007, p.386).

62 Berenstein, 1996, p.47.

63 Baudrillard, 1999, p.119.

prevailing trend. In these later films, the traditional horror-genre trope of the 'mirroring' of monster and victim was used to present the woman as the alluring/repulsive monster, with Holmes taking the place usually occupied by the female victim. Though the films are temporally ambiguous, a clear gender divide is shown to exist whereby men occupy the past and women occupy the present, although the connotations of this implied disturbance to the 'social order' are negated by the fact that, at the end of each film, Holmes defeats the female villain and with it, presumably, the vision of a female-dominated future.

THE END OF THE SERIES

Dressed to Kill marked the end of the Holmes series at Universal. A number of theories have been put forward as to why it was not continued, with most commentators saying that Rathbone had become frustrated with being typecast, making it difficult for him to find new parts: indeed, Rathbone himself, in his autobiography, cites this as the reason.[64] A more practical reason might have been that the two stars' contracts had come to an end. A letter from Joe Lawler of Universal's publicity department to a member of the Baker Street Irregulars confirms this. Dated 9 October 1946, it says that the series had been discontinued and that after *Dressed to Kill* (released five months earlier) 'the studio's contractual relations with the principals, Rathbone and Bruce, expired'.[65] Universal would have been unlikely to simply substitute another Holmes and Watson or another director after such a long run – Roy William Neill died suddenly in December 1946. I can find no evidence to suggest, as Gavin Collinson does, that Universal was 'assiduously arranging for more of the same fayre' and attempting to change Rathbone's mind when they were thwarted by Neill's death.[66] Rathbone never really did escape the yoke of being Sherlock Holmes: he was still doing product-endorsement advertising dressed as Holmes right through the 1950s, as this advertisement *(see Fig. 51)* for Booth's Gin demonstrates. On stage and screen, he may have longed for more Shakespearean parts but they did not materialise: 'I could not find a

---

64 Rathbone, 1997, p.180.

65 Lawler letter to Skidmore, 9 October 1946.

66 Collinson, n.d., p.6.

FIGURE 51

In 1958 Rathbone was still endorsing products as Holmes, clad not in his Universal costume, but in the Victorian costume from the Twentieth Century-Fox films.

play or anyone willing to consider me for one… because of my seven years' identification with Sherlock Holmes'.[67] He also resigned from the radio show, though this continued right through until Nigel Bruce's death in 1953, with Tom Conway taking the part of Holmes, perhaps indicating that the listeners' imagination can readily accommodate a change of voice, while still maintaining their own 'image' of Holmes. That same year, Rathbone took Holmes to the stage in a play written by his wife Ouida: possibly inspired by William Gillette's 30-year success on stage, he plunged 110,000 dollars of his own money into the venture and fund-raised among all his contacts, including Adrian Conan Doyle.[68] The show closed after only three

---

67 Rathbone, 1997, p.191.

68 They exchanged many letters about the play (see Bibliography for full list), with Rathbone highly confident of success and delighted to have the chance to play Holmes on stage as he said 'the motion pictures and radio shows did not satisfy me. I am too much of a purist' (undated Rathbone letter to Adrian Conan Doyle). He was bitterly disappointed at the play's failure.

Broadway performances, having been savaged by the critics 'as callously', said Rathbone, 'as pulling a chair from under a child'.[69] The play, which had a contemporary setting, was leisurely, thoughtful and analytical: performance styles had changed and 'we were hopelessly outdated', said Rathbone.[70]

Rathbone had hit on the truth: with the ending of the war, the world had changed and Holmes' brand of deduction, rationality and infallibility was, for that moment, unsustainable. The crime genre itself was far from dead. In fact, in 1946 there was a proliferation of crime picture releases, due principally, according to Biesen, to the fact that Hollywood had stockpiled around 200 films that it had made during the war. This 'delayed reaction to Hollywood's booming war industry'[71] revealed a trend that had been partially hidden – the move towards the hardboiled genre, where morality and outcomes are more ambiguous than in Holmes' world, and where the detective becomes emotionally or sexually involved in the crime. It was a world that portrayed a physical rather than a cerebral masculinity; the world depicted by pulp writers like James M. Cain and Dashiell Hammett. Above all, it was an American world, one in which Vernet asserts that 'actors like William Powell, Warren William and Basil Rathbone had too English a look'.[72] Pulp-fiction themes and stories (such as in *The Postman Always Rings Twice*) had finally made it from the magazine stalls onto the screen, taking advantage of the post-war relaxation in the Production Code, which was to be seriously dented by the social realism films of the mid-1940s such as *The Lost Weekend* (1946) about alcoholism, and finally crumble in the wake of *The Man With the Golden Arm* (1951) with its drug-addicted hero. Instead of facing 'the enemy without', the world was facing 'the enemy within', a scenario where the values that Holmes represents could be of little help.[73]

This 'Americanisation' of Hollywood caused a leader writer on *The Times* in 1945 to express nostalgia for Hollywood's image of life

---

69 Rathbone letter to Adrian Conan Doyle, 1 November 1953.

70 Rathbone, 1997, p.213.

71 Biesen, 2005, p.123.

72 Vernet, 1993, p.23.

73 The public's taste for the hardboiled was already on the wane by this time. In 1950 Zanuck told his directors and producers at Twentieth Century-Fox that audiences no longer wanted pictures of violence, suffering and brutality peopled by unsympathetic characters or psychopaths (Behlmer, 1993, p.194).

in Britain, in an article that echoed Graham Greene's comments about the 'lost London' of fogs, cobbles and hansom cabs. This picture of nostalgia could be said to be equally Victorian:

> What a loss it is, never again to see that enchanted or at any rate transmogrified land, wrapped almost all year round in a dense fog.... It was a land which we had all learned to love.... The only traffic [its policemen] were called on to regulate was an occasional hansom cab. Its aristocracy... lived in castles of the very largest size... [and] the lower orders, a cheerful lot, wore gaiters in the country but in London, being mostly costers, dressed in a manner that befitted this calling... The Army, except of course in war-time, consisted almost entirely of senior officers, most of them in the Secret Service. There were two universities, one at Oxford and the other at Cambridge. Cricket and football were not much played and possibly as a consequence – there was a great deal of crime.[74]

It would be another 13 years before Holmes returned to the cinema screen in Britain or the US. The gap was rather less dramatic than it sounds because, in common with many wartime films, the series was re-released after the war, which casts some doubt on the theory that it had become out of touch with the times, unless of course it was viewed for its nostalgia factor.[75] It is not easy to establish the context in which the films were re-released, because post-war paper restrictions meant there was little newspaper advertising for cinemas. In Spain, however, there is evidence that *The Adventures of Sherlock Holmes* (*Sherlock Holmes Contra Moriarty*) was screened in Barcelona in September 1947, *Sherlock Holmes Faces Death* (*Sherlock Holmes Desafia a la Muerte*) in December 1947, *The Pearl of Death* (*Perla Maldita*) in January 1948 and *The Woman in Green* (*El Caso de las Dedos Cortados*) in July 1949 – possibly their first showing in the country. The character was also present on television. In Britain in 1951, Alan Wheatley played Holmes in a series of six live programmes, the same year that two one-off Holmes dramas were broadcast: *The Man with*

---

74 Quoted by Morley, 2006, p.205.
75 Universal's theatrical reissue rights were acquired in an exclusive 10-year deal in 1947 by Realart Pictures, owned by B-movie producer Jack Broder.

the Twisted Lip starring John Longdon, and *The Mazarin Stone* starring Andrew Osborn. In the US, Rathbone himself made a brief re-appearance as Holmes on screen in a CBS show in 1953: *The Adventure of the Black Baronet* was part of the 'Suspense' series and was scripted by Adrian Conan Doyle and mystery-writer John Dickson Carr. Also on US television in the mid 1950s was a series of 39 Holmes mysteries directed by Sheldon Reynolds and starring Ronald Howard as Holmes and H. Marion Crawford as Watson.

When a new cinema-screen Holmes was born in 1959, with Hammer's version of *The Hound of the Baskervilles*, the setting was Victorian – and would continue to be so through all the subsequent 1960s BBC TV-series spin-offs, the parody films of the 1970s, the Granada TV series of the 1980s, and almost all adaptations right through to 2008.

CONCLUSION

*'A bridge between the disorderly experience
of life and a dream of order'*
Stephen Knight on Holmes[1]

his book has examined the tensions inherent in the way
Twentieth Century-Fox and Universal re-constructed an
identity for Sherlock Holmes, making him at the same time
the man of Arthur Conan Doyle's stories and the product of a
particular historical moment – the years of World War Two in Europe.
Analysis of the mise-en-scène and the discourse surrounding the films
showed that these tensions exhibited themselves in two principal ways:
in generic and historical ambiguity. In the course of this analysis, the
question of what Universal termed the 'unchanging' nature of Holmes
was addressed to determine whether, and in what ways, Holmes was
indeed still 'the same' as the original Doyle creation. The aim was to
establish what Holmes symbolised for audiences at that time and why
he was still deemed 'necessary' half a century after his first appearance.
In defining his appeal, it was helpful to look beyond the iconography
that conventionally identified him, at the qualities he represented, the
core of which was 'certainty in a time of uncertainty'. The symbolic
date with which Holmes is associated is 1895, a year perceived
nostalgically both by the original readers of the Doyle stories, and the
wartime audiences of the films, as being one of stability. Because
Holmes emanated from this world of 1895, and indeed is master of it,
he offered audiences in Britain and the US the confidence that the
Allies would prevail and that the precious elements of their shared
cultural heritage would not be swept away or destroyed.

In examining generic tensions, it became clear that the classic
detective story of literature, which Todorov identified as static and
cerebral, changed to a more action-oriented approach when bringing
the detective to the screen. There was a clear parallel between the
way genre writing and genre films had been largely considered
unworthy of serious critical attention: this lay in the traditional
centrality of the 'author' who in genre works is often effaced. Genre

---

1   Knight, 1980, p.105.

films therefore, unless retrospectively appropriated for a new genre category, such as film noir, had in the main only been analysed as exemplars of commercial studio practice and not as artistic products in their own right. Genre categorisation can be much richer and more complex than a retrospective taxonomic exercise reliant on the film alone: contemporary audiences derived their genre expectations from a wide range of studio-based material including posters, presspacks, trailers, advertisements and press reviews; and whereas hindsight tends to give single-label genre categories to films, multiple-label categories were in use at the time of release.

There was a distinct generic evolution in the Holmes series, both in the mise-en-scène and in the way the series was promoted: it crossed boundaries into costume drama, espionage, Gothic chiller, and horror, but was constrained in this evolution by the necessity of portraying the 'old Holmes' that would meet audience expectations. Generic tensions were partly attributable to industry pressures, such as the perceived need for studios to be seen to support the war effort; commercial pressures, such as the emerging challenge from the hardboiled genre and the desire to appeal to a wider audience; and societal pressures such as the unease about newly empowered women in the workplace. Espionage stories, for example, enabled Holmes to be mobilised for the war effort, providing endorsement for America's decision to enter the war by highlighting Britain and America's common heritage and becoming the 'acceptable face' of Britain. The move into Gothic chillers mirrored a wider trend in the cinema from 1944, when the public seemed to want an escape from war movies: guns, speedboats and microfilm made way for spooky houses, haunted moors and ancient rituals. With this change of atmosphere and setting, director Roy William Neill introduced expressionist lighting and cinematography in what could be seen as a transfer from the Gothic horror film: identifying its use in this series opens up a fresh perspective on the development of film noir. Gothic settings drew on Universal's 1930s track record as a horror-genre specialist and presaged the final evolutionary phase of the series, into visceral horror where the 'monster' was a deadly female. These 'spider women' of the later films combined allure and danger, used their sexuality as a power base, and practised disguise as expertly as Holmes. Throughout these incursions into other generic territories, the studio always kept enough of the classic detective genre conventions to maintain

Holmes' credibility as the ultimate thinking machine who relied on intellect and deduction rather than brute force, who was ruled by his head, not his heart, and who offered the reassurance that he would solve the crime and restore the status quo.

Temporal tensions, which were expected to be evident in the Universal films, can also be seen in the 'Victorian' films from Twentieth Century-Fox, in costume, sets and character behaviour. Although on-screen dates gave the exact year in which the films were set, the past that was evoked was a non-specific one. The costume of the romantic leads, as is conventional in period drama, was an amalgam of the contemporary and the Victorian; the sets featured Regency design, a style undergoing a revival in the 1930s, rather than the 'high Victorian' style that might be associated with Holmes; and contemporary ideas of Victorian mores led to the inclusion of scenes such as a seance. A temporal divide was shown between the city, which was coded as modern and rational, and the countryside, which was portrayed as a primitive site of superstition. When the series moved to Universal, a careful balance was struck between bringing Holmes confidently into the present day and not losing sight of the 'old' Holmes: this resulted in, among other things, the construction of his sitting room as a Victorian time warp and a choice of costume that was always slightly out of step with the contemporary, making it clear he emanated from another era. Holmes was shown to be at home with all the paraphernalia of modernity, demonstrating his understanding of microfilm, wire-tapping devices, soundwave monitors and bombsights, but often made the major breakthrough with Victorian devices, such as his magnifying glass or a magic lantern projector. In effect, he and Watson existed in these films in a kind of 'bubble', inside which it was always '1895'. After the third war-themed film, set mostly in the contemporary surroundings of Washington DC, the studio perhaps thought they had stretched Holmes too far. Temporal anchors were almost completely absent from the next phase of films, which utilised 'timeless' settings such as a moor, an isolated house, or a village miles from civilisation where modernity could be kept at a distance. Set-dressing in many instances made it hard to see in what period the action was taking place: the interiors of a number of houses, for example, were furnished like baronial halls, with suits of armour and mullioned windows, and were lit only by candles. Towards the end of the series, modernity intruded once again, this time to make a specific gender-based point: that women belonged to the present (and, by implication, the future), while men belonged to the past. The spaces in which Holmes and the other men moved were Victorian; the spaces in which the women villains moved were contemporary.

In this series, Holmes underwent generic and temporal shifts that certain audience segments may have interpreted as a betrayal of the Doyle creation; yet Holmes as a character had been subject to constant evolution, right from the moment that Sidney Paget drew the first picture of Holmes in a deerstalker for *The Strand* magazine, or William Gillette stepped onto stage with a calabash pipe. Despite these accrued layers, and even when audiences had to suspend disbelief at the prospect of a reincarnated Holmes fighting the Nazis, the essence of Rathbone's portrayal still evidently accorded with the Holmes of their imagination. The resilience of Holmes as a character can be judged from the fact that actor after actor has assumed the role, yet audiences were, and are, prepared to consider each as a potential embodiment of the 'real Holmes'.[2] Michel Houllebecq believes that each new representation, pastiche or parody is only tolerated because 'all the while in our hearts we nourish the impossible dream that the central core, the very heart of the myth, would continue'.[3] This indicates an unfulfilled yearning and it is no coincidence that Houllebecq, in the same essay, draws analogies between religion and detective fiction, calling such fiction 'theist'. A similar analogy is made by Cecil Day Lewis (writing in 1942 under the pseudonym Nicholas Blake) who says that with hindsight, society will connect the rise of crime fiction with the decline of religion, the formality of the form being akin to religious ritual: he refers to the detective as a 'higher power' who 'with a flourish of trumpets', solves the mystery and separates the goats from the sheep.[4] This religious analogy may also explain why surges in Holmes' popularity seem to have occurred when the world order was under threat: the period, for example, in which more people than ever flocked to see William Gillette on stage as Sherlock Holmes was his farewell tour of 1929–1930, the years of the Great Depression.

---

2   More than 100 actors in 200 productions to date.

3   Houllebecq, 2006, p.38.

4   'Blake' in Haycraft, 1942, p.xxi.

Although the evolution of Holmes in the years since the release of *Dressed to Kill* lies outside the scope of this book, it is productive to make brief reference to it, not least because the series has been repeatedly shown on television, and released on video, so that this particular construction of Holmes has co-existed with subsequent portrayals. In the 62 years since 1946, Holmes has remained a presence in three principal ways: in direct representations, in fan culture, and as a cultural reference to suggest particular qualities. He has not been off the cinema screen, television schedules or the stage in Britain or the US for any prolonged period, and the Doyle books have never been out of print. Fan culture continues to probe every aspect of the character, from pastiche novels, fictional biographies, and commentaries on the Doyle canon, to the proliferation of Holmesian societies (in excess of 200) around the globe. London still exploits its association with Holmes: at Baker Street, there is a statue, a museum and shops selling memorabilia and his silhouette appears on the tiles of the Underground station. It is, however, the day-to-day cultural references to Holmes that demonstrate how embedded he has become in the (inter)national psyche: in a typical month in the national press in Britain, Holmes is mentioned every other day, his name often invoked to describe desirable behaviour, such as an ability to see to the heart of the matter. On the street, too, people in 2007 proved as familiar with Holmes as were their 1946 counterparts in a Mass Observation survey.[5] Not a single article in the press survey, and only one person in the street surveys, mentioned that Holmes was fictional. An idea of the extent of his immanence can be judged by carrying out a Google search on the words 'Sherlock Holmes': the result is a listing of some 10,400,000 websites.[6] No other fictional character matches Holmes in terms of international recognition, longevity, and number and variety of appropriations: those named by Christopher Frayling – Dracula, Frankenstein and Jekyll and Hyde – may initially seem comparable, but they have not enjoyed the transmedia success of Holmes.[7] Like these characters, Holmes is a Victorian and is carefully positioned as one, even when outwitting

---

5   Mass Observation Survey report number 2,427, 1946; author's surveys, August and September 2007.

6   As at 16 May 2008.

7   Frayling, 1996, p.13.

the Führer in 1942 or being dug up out of the ice in the twenty-second century.[8] Such are his ties to the Victorian (and presumably the appeal of the Victorian to audiences) that 48 of the 62 film and TV adaptations since the Twentieth Century-Fox/Universal series (1946–2008) have set him in his 'true' period of the 1890s.[9]

Somerset Maugham believed that Holmes' longevity was attributable to the way Doyle gave his character a limited set of 'marked idiosyncrasies' which he then 'hammered into the minds of his readers with the same pertinacity as the great advertisers use to proclaim the merits of their soap, beer or cigarettes'.[10] Yet the stories were actually merely the starting point for endless re-presentations of these same idiosyncrasies which, though they have been added to over the years and set against many shifting contexts, have not altered what could be described as the central core that is Holmes: the assurance of certainty in times of uncertainty. He remains, as Knight puts it, in his book on form and ideology in crime fiction, 'a bridge between the disorderly experience of life and a dream of order'.[11]

I have sought to demonstrate in this book that the consideration of films in conjunction with their surrounding discourse yields a richer and more historically accurate analysis than treating them in isolation. This is particularly relevant to genre studies: the Holmes films show that the aesthetic content of B-movies, largely disregarded unless seen to break the mould, is as worthy of examination as the films' production context. The value of primary sources in making such an examination, to create new knowledge and re-interpret existing accounts, is paramount. Obviously in a study with a specific focus, there are many avenues which I have not been able to explore but which would benefit from further research: one example would be to widen the examination of the portrayal of deadly women in wartime films and investigate to what extent they were a parallel or precursor of the film-noir woman. Another would be to explore in more detail the imaging of Victorian London in these and other Holmes films, particularly in the choice of a core group of 'signs' that

---

8   *Sherlock Holmes in the Twenty Second Century*, 1999.

9   In these statistics, I have counted series, such as the Granada Television series starring Jeremy Brett, as a single adaptation.

10 Maugham, 1967, p.160.

11 Knight, 1980, p.105.

have come to summarise the nineteenth-century city. Another would be a more wide-ranging analysis of the films of Roy William Neill, whose output has been largely overlooked to date. In terms of Sherlock Holmes, this is the first academic book to examine his portrayal on screen: given the number of times he has been adapted for the cinema, there is certainly scope for many more such investigations.

BIBLIOGRAPHY OF WORKS CITED

BOOKS

SIR ARTHUR CONAN DOYLE:

Doyle, Arthur Conan (1951) *The Memoirs of Sherlock Holmes*. London: Penguin. Includes 'The Final Problem'.
— (1951) *The Case-Book of Sherlock Holmes*. London: Penguin.
Includes 'The Adventure of the Illustrious Client', 'The Adventure of the Retired Colourman', 'The Adventure of the Three Garridebs' and 'The Adventure of the Veiled Lodger'.
— (1955) *The White Company*. London: John Murray.
— (1981) *The Adventures of Sherlock Holmes*. London: Penguin.
Includes 'The Boscombe Valley Mystery', 'A Case of Identity', 'The Five Orange Pips', 'The Red-Headed League' and 'A Scandal in Bohemia'.
— (1981) *The Return of Sherlock Holmes*. London: Penguin.
Includes 'The Adventure of Charles Augustus Milverton'.
— (1981) *The Memoirs of Sherlock Holmes*. London: Penguin.
Includes 'Silver Blaze' and 'The Adventure of the Yellow Face'.
— (1981) *The Hound of the Baskervilles*. London: Penguin.
— (1982) *The Adventures of Sherlock Holmes*. London: Penguin.
Includes 'The Man with the Twisted Lip' and 'The Adventure of the Noble Bachelor'.
— (1982) *The Sign of Four*. London: Penguin.
— (1997) *His Last Bow*. London: Penguin.
Includes 'His Last Bow' and 'The Adventure of the Bruce-Partington Plans'.
Gillette, William (1974) *Sherlock Holmes*. California: Helen Halbach.
Lycett, Andrew (2007) *Conan Doyle: The Man Who Created Sherlock Holmes*. London: Weidenfeld and Nicolson.
Pearson, Hesketh (1943) *Conan Doyle, His Life and Art*. London: Methuen.

SHERLOCK HOLMES IN CONTEXT:

Austin, Bliss (1945) *A Baker Street Folio*. New York: Baker Street Irregulars.
Bunson, Matthew (1995) *The Sherlock Holmes Encyclopaedia*. London: Pavilion.
Eyles, Allen (1986) *Sherlock Holmes: A Centenary Celebration*. London: John Murray.
Frayling, Christopher (1996) *Nightmare – the Birth of Horror*. London: BBC.
Hammer, David (2000) *Yonder in the Gaslight*. Toronto: The Battered Silicon Despatch Box.
Jann, Rosemary (1995) *The Adventures of Sherlock Holmes: Detecting Social Order*. New York: Twayne.
Keating, H.R.F. (1979) *Sherlock Holmes: The Man and His World*. London: Thames and Hudson.
Kestner, Joseph (1997) *Sherlock's Men: Masculinity, Conan Doyle and Cultural History*. Vermont and Aldershot: Ashgate Press.

Payne, David (1992) _Myth and Modern Man in Sherlock Holmes: Sir Conan Doyle and the Uses of Nostalgia_. New York: Gaslight Publications.

Pearson, Roberta (1997) 'It's Always 1895: Sherlock Holmes in Cyberspace' in Cartmell, Deborah; Hunter, I.Q. et al. (eds), _Trash Aesthetics: Popular Culture and its Audience_. London: Pluto Press.

Quindlen, Anna (2006) _Imagined London_. Washington DC: National Geographic.

Starrett, Vincent (1942) _Two Sonnets_. Ysleta: Edwin B. Hall.

Sugarman, Sally in Putney, Charles et al. (eds), (1996) _Victorian Sleuth to Modern Hero_. Metuchen NJ: Scarecrow.

Thomson, June (1995) _Holmes and Watson: A Study in Friendship_. New York: Carroll and Graf.

Tracy, Jack (1977) _The Encyclopaedia Sherlockiana_. London: New English Library.

Waal, Ronald de (1974) _The World Bibliography of Sherlock Holmes and Dr Watson_. New York: Bramball House.

SHERLOCK HOLMES FILMS:

Barnes, Alan (2002) _Sherlock Holmes on Screen: the Complete Film and TV History_. Richmond: Reynolds and Hearn.

Davies, David Stuart (1976) _Holmes of the Movies_. London: New English Library.

Druxman, Michael (1975) _Basil Rathbone: His Life and his Films_. New Jersey: A.S. Barnes.

Haydock, Ron (1978) _Deerstalker! Holmes and Watson on Screen_. Metuchen NJ: Scarecrow.

Lejeune, Anthony (ed.) (1991) _The CA Lejeune Film Reader_. Manchester: Carcanet.

Nollen, Scott Allen (1996) _Sir Arthur Conan Doyle at the Cinema_. Jefferson NC: McFarland.

Parkinson, David (ed.) (1993) _Mornings in the Dark: the Graham Greene Film Reader_. Manchester: Carcanet.

Pohle, Robert and Hart, Douglas (1977) _Sherlock Holmes on the Screen_. New Jersey: AS Barnes.

Pointer, Michael (1975) _The Public Life of Sherlock Holmes_. Newton Abbott: David and Charles.

Quinlan, David (1983) _The Illustrated Guide to Film Directors_. London: Batsford.

Rathbone, Basil (1997) _In and Out of Character_. New York: Limelight.

Ross, Michael (ed.) (2003) _Sherlock Holmes in Film und Fernsehen: Ein Handbuch_. Cologne: Baskerville.

Steinbrunner, Chris and Michaels, Norman (1978) _The Films of Sherlock Holmes_. US: Citadel.

Thompson, Kristin (1988) _Breaking the Glass Armor – Neoformalist Film Analysis_. Ewing NJ: Princeton University Press.

Weaver, Tom; Brunas, Michael and Brunas, John (2007) _Universal Horrors 1931– 1946_. Jefferson NC: McFarland.

DETECTIVE GENRE:

Cawelti, John G. (1976) *Adventure, Mystery and Romance: Formula Stories as Art and Popular Culture*. Chicago: University of Chicago Press.

Chandler, Raymond (1988) *The Simple Art of Murder*. New York: Vintage Books.

Everson, William (1972) *The Detective in Film*. New Jersey: Citadel Press.

Gates, Philippa (2006) *Detecting Men*. Albany NY: State University of New York Press.

Haycraft, Howard (1942) *Murder for Pleasure*. London: Peter Davies.

Houllebecq, Michel (2006) *HP Lovecraft: Against the World, Against Life*. London: Weidenfeld and Nicolson.

Knight, Stephen (1980) *Form and Ideology in Crime Fiction*. Basingstoke: Macmillan.

Leitch, Thomas (2002) *Crime Films*. Cambridge: Cambridge University Press.

Longhurst, Derek (ed.) (1989) *Gender, Genre and Narrative Pleasure*. London: Unwin Hyman.

Mandel, Ernest (1984) *Delightful Murder: A Social History of the Crime Story*. London: Pluto.

Maugham, W. Somerset (1967) *On Literature*. London: New English Library.

Parish, James Robert and Pitts, Michael (1974) *The Great Detective Pictures*. Metuchen NJ: Scarecrow.

Pitts, Michael (1979) *Famous Movie Detectives*. Metuchen NJ: Scarecrow.

Rubin, Martin (1999) *Thrillers*. Cambridge: Cambridge University Press.

Todorov, Tzvetan (1971) 'The Typology of Detective Fiction' in *The Poetics of Prose*. Ithaca and London: Cornell University Press.

OTHER RELEVANT GENRES AND GENRE THEORY:

Altman, Rick (1999) *Film/Genre*. London: BFI.

Barefoot, Guy (2001) *Gaslight Melodrama*. New York and London: Continuum.

Berenstein, Rhona (1996) *Attack of the Leading Ladies: Gender, Sexuality and Spectatorship in Classic Horror Cinema*. New York: Columbia University Press.

Eisner, Lotte (1952) *The Haunted Screen*. London: Secker and Warburg.

Elsaesser, Thomas (2000) *Weimar Cinema and After*. London and New York: Routledge.

Grant, Barry Keith (1999) *Film Genre Reader II*. Austin: University of Texas.

Hopkins, Lisa (2005) *Screening the Gothic*. Austin: University of Texas.

Kaminsky, S.M. (1985) *American Film Genres*. New York: Dell.

Klinger, Barbara (1994) *Melodrama and Meaning*. Indiana: Indiana University Press.

Kracauer, Siegfried (1974) *From Caligari to Hitler*. New Jersey: Princeton University Press.

Lacey, Nick (2000) *Narrative and Genre: Key Concepts in Media Studies*. Basingstoke: Macmillan.

Mank, Gregory M. (1999) *Women in Horror Films 1940s*. Jefferson NC: McFarland.

Naremore, James (1998) *More Than Night*. California: University of California Press.

Neale, Steve (2000) *Genre and Hollywood*. London: Routledge.

Place, Janey and Peterson, Lowell (1974) 'Some Visual Motifs of Film Noir' in Alain Silver and James Ursini (eds) (1999), *The Film Noir Reader*. New York: Limelight Editions.

Reid, David and Walker, Jayne L. (1993) 'Strange Pursuit: Cornwell Woolrich and the Abandoned City of the Forties' in Copjec, Joan (ed.), *Shades of Noir*. London: Verso.

Ryall, Tom (1998) 'Genre and Hollywood' in John Hill and Pamela Church Gibson (eds), *The Oxford Guide to Film Studies*. Oxford: Oxford University Press.

Saada, Nicolas (2004) 'The Noir Style in Hollywood' in Silver, Alain and Ursini, James (eds), *The Film Noir Reader 4*. New York: Limelight Editions.

Saliba, David (1980) *A Psychology of Fear: the Nightmare Formula of Edgar Allen Poe*. Lantham MD: University Press of America.

Schatz, Thomas (1981) *Hollywood Genres: Formulas, Filmmaking and the Studio System*. London: Random House.

Smith, Erin (2000) *Hardboiled – Working-class Readers and Pulp Magazines*. Philadelphia: Temple University Press.

Sobchack, Vivian (1998) 'Lounge Time: Postwar Crises and the Chronotype of Film Noir' in Browne, Nick (ed.), *Refiguring American Film Genres*. London: University of California Press.

Vernet, Marc (1993) 'Film Noir on the Edge of Doom' in Copjec, Joan (ed.), *Shades of Noir*. London: Verso.

STUDIOS AND THE STUDIO SYSTEM:

Balio, Tino (1993) *Grand Design: Hollywood as a Modern Business Enterprise 1930–1939*. California: University of California Press.

Barnwell, Jane (2004) *Production Design: Architects of the Screen*. London: Wallflower Press.

Behlmer, Rudy (ed.) (1993) *Memo from Darryl Zanuck: the Golden Years at Twentieth Century-Fox*. New York: Grove Press.

Berg, A. Scott (1981) *Goldwyn*. London: Ballantine.

Dick, B.F. (1997) *City of Dreams: The Making and Remaking of Universal Pictures*. Kentucky: University Press of Kentucky.

Dyer, Richard (1998) *Stars*. London: British Film Institute.

Gomery, Douglas (2005) *The Hollywood Studio System – a History*. London: BFI.

Hirschhorn, Clive (1983) *The Universal Story*. London: Octopus.

Horak, Jan-Christopher (2002) 'The Hollywood History Business' in Lewis, Jon (ed.), *The End of Cinema as we Know It*. London: Pluto.

McCarthy, Todd and Flynn, Charles (eds) (1975) *Kings of the Bs*. New York: Dutton.

Maltby, Richard and Craven, Ian (1995) *Hollywood Cinema*. Oxford: Blackwell.

Morley, Sheridan (2006) *The Brits in Hollywood: Tales from the Hollywood Raj*. London: Robson.

Ramirez, Juan Antonio (2004) *Architecture for the Screen*. Jefferson NC: McFarland.

Schatz, Thomas (1997) *Boom and Bust – American Cinema in the 1940s*. California: University of California Press.

Schatz, Thomas (1989) *The Genius of the System*. London: Faber and Faber.

Solomon, Aubrey (1988) *Twentieth Century-Fox – A Corporate and Financial History*. Metuchen NJ: Scarecrow.

Street, Sarah (2002) *Transatlantic Crossings*. London and New York: Continuum.

WARTIME FILMS, PROPAGANDA AND CENSORSHIP:

Biesen, Sheri Chenin (2005) *Blackout – World War II and the Origins of Film Noir*. Baltimore: Johns Hopkins University Press.

Cull, Nicholas John (1995) *Selling War: the British Propaganda Campaign Against American Neutrality in WWII*. Oxford: Oxford University Press.

Dick, Bernard (1985) *The Star-Spangled Screen – the American World War II Film*. Kentucky: University Press of Kentucky.

Glancy, H. Mark (1999) *When Hollywood Loved Britain: the Hollywood 'British' Film 1939–45*. Manchester: Manchester University Press.

Haskell, Molly (1973) *From Reverence to Rape*. Chicago: University of Chicago Press.

Koppes, Clayton and Black, Gregory (1990) *Hollywood Goes to War: How Politics, Profits and Propaganda Shaped World War II Movies*. California: University of California Press.

Lant, Antonia (1991) *Blackout – Reinventing Women for Wartime British Cinema*. Princeton: Princeton University Press.

Renov, Michael (1988) *Hollywood and Wartime Women – Representation and Ideology*. Ann Arbor MI: UMI Research Press.

Schindler, Colin (1979) *Hollywood Goes to War: Film and American Society 1939–52*. London: Routledge.

COSTUME:

Berry, Sarah (2000) *Screen Style*. Minneapolis: University of Minnesota Press.

Bruzzi, Stella (1997) *Undressing Cinema*. London: Routledge.

Cook, Pam (1996) *Fashioning the Nation*. London: BFI.

Costantino, Maria (1997) *Men's Fashion in the Twentieth Century*. London: Batsford.

Ettinger, Roseann (1998) *Men's Clothing and Fabrics in the 1890s*. Atglen PA: Schiffer Publishing.

MISCELLANEOUS:

Baudrillard, Jean (1999) *The Perfect Crime*. London: Verso.

Freud, Sigmund (1977) 'Unsuitable Substitutes for the Sexual Object' in *Three Essays on the Theory of Sexuality*. London: Penguin.

Kirby, Lynne (1997) *Parallel Tracks: the Railroad and Silent Cinema*. Exeter: University of Exeter Press.

Landy, Marcia (1996) *Cinematic Uses of the Past*. Minneapolis: University of Minnesota Press.

Leitch, Thomas (2007) *Film Adaptation and Its Discontents: From Gone with the Wind to The Passion of the Christ*. Baltimore: Johns Hopkins University Press.

Macmillan International Film Encyclopedia (2001) Basingstoke: Macmillan.

Napper, Lawrence (1997) 'A Despicable Tradition? Quota Quickies in the 1930s' in Murphy, Robert (ed.), *The British Cinema Book*. London: British Film Institute.

Naremore, James (2000) 'Film and the Reign of Adaptation' in Naremore, James (ed.), *Film Adaptation*. London: Athlone Press.

Nelmes, Jill (2003) *Introduction to Film Studies*. London: Routledge.

Newman, Kim (1999) *Cat People*. London: British Film Institute.

Pym, Barbara (1990) 'Goodbye Balkan Capital' in *Civil to Strangers*. London: Grafton.

Staiger, Janet (1992) *Interpreting Film*. Princeton NJ: Princeton University Press.

Stam, Robert (2000) 'Beyond Fidelity: the Dialogics of Adaptation' in Naremore, James (ed.), *Film Adaptation*. London: Athlone Press.

Torgovnick, Marianna (1990) *Gone Primitive*. Chicago: University of Chicago Press.

Webster's Third New International Dictionary (1993) US: Merriam-Webster.

PERIODICALS

Collinson, Gavin (n.d.) 'The Many Lives of Sherlock Holmes', programme notes, *National Film Theatre*, p.6.

Davis, John (1972) 'Notes on Warner Brothers' Foreign Policy 1918–1948', *The Velvet Light Trap,* no. 4, Spring pp.275–87.

Hadleigh, Boze (1993) 'Gale Sondergaard', *Scarlet Street*, issue 11.

Haralovich, Mary Beth (1979) 'Sherlock Holmes: Genre and Industrial Practice', *Journal of the University Film Association*, Spring pp.53–7.

Harmon, Jim (1975) 'Rathbone and Bruce at Baker Street', *The History of Sherlock Holmes Magazine*, no. 1.

Jancovich, Mark (2005) 'The Meaning of Mystery: Genre, Marketing and the Universal Sherlock Holmes Series of the 1940s', *Film International*, no. 17.

Kopple, David (2006) 'Monkeys, Apes, Gorillas: producer Jack Broder', from DVD liner notes to *Kid Monk Baroni*, 3 August.

Leggett, Paul (1979) 'Sherlock Holmes: a Case for Further Research', *Focus on Film,* April pp.25–7.

Naugrette, Jean-Pierre (2005) 'Sherlock Holmes et L'armé Secrete: les Nazis, Moriarty et Londres sous le Blitz', *Legeia*, July– Dec, pp.124–34.

Osborne, Robert (1992) 'Rathbone Centennial Recalls Hollywood Great', *Hollywood Reporter*, vol. 322 no. 26, 12 June p.9.

Seymour, Blackie (1987) 'Sherlock Holmes and the Secret Weapon', *Classic Images*, August p.46.

Sobchak, Thomas (1975) 'Genre Film: A Classical Experience', *Literature Film Quarterly*, vol. 3 no. 3.

Snyder, Scott (2001) 'Personality Disorder and the Film Noir Femme Fatale', *Journal of Criminal Justice and Popular Culture*, no. 8(3), pp.155–68.

Author uncredited (1942) 'Rathbone deserves a break', *Picturegoer*, 12 December p.7.

Author uncredited (1979) 'Basil Rathbone', *The Woods Runner* (Lake Superior College Michigan), May.

Author uncredited (1987) review of *Secret Weapon, Classic Images*, no. 146, August p.46.

Unnamed reader's letter (1922) 'A Sherlock Holmes Complaint', *Picture Show*, 16 September.

CONTEMPORARY REVIEWS OF THE SERIES:

The Hound of the Baskervilles:

Daily Telegraph (1939) 10 July.
Kinematograph Weekly (1939) no. 1,670, 20 April p.25.
Motion Picture Herald (1939) vol. 134 no. 13, 1 April p.28.
New York Times (1939) 25 March p.19.
Variety (1939) 29 March p.14.

The Adventures of Sherlock Holmes:

New York Times (1939) 2 September p.20.
Spectator (1940) 8 March.
To-day's Cinema (1939) vol. 53 no. 354, 20 December p.10.
Variety (1939) 6 September p.14.

Sherlock Holmes and the Voice of Terror:

Kinematograph Weekly (1943) no. 1,905, 21 Oct p.21.
Motion Picture Herald (1942) vol. 148 no. 11, 12 September p.897.
New York Times (1942) 19 September p.9.
To-day's Cinema (1943) vol. 61 no. 4,943, 15 October p.22.
Variety (1942) 9 September p.14.

Sherlock Holmes and the Secret Weapon:

Kinematograph Weekly (1942) no. 1,852, 15 October p.35.
New York Times (1943) 5 January p.15.
To-day's Cinema (1942) vol. 59 no. 4,789, 16 October p.12.
Variety (1942) 30 December p.23.

Sherlock Holmes in Washington:

Hollywood Reporter (1943) 15 March.
Motion Picture Herald (1943) vol. 151 no. 1, 3 April.

Picturegoer (1943) vol. 12, 6 February.
To-day's Cinema (1942) vol. 59 no. 4,810, 4 December.
To-day's Cinema (1948) vol. 70 no, 5,611, 18 February p.9.
Variety (1943) 31 March p.8.

Sherlock Holmes Faces Death:

Hollywood Reporter (1943) 2 September.
Motion Picture Herald (1943) 11 September p.51.
Variety (1943) 8 September p.16.

Spider Woman:

Monthly Film Bulletin (1944) vol. 11, January p.6.
New York Journal-American (1944) 15 January.
New York Times (1944) 15 January p.11.
To-day's Cinema (1944) vol. 62 no. 4,981, 14 January.

The Scarlet Claw:

Hollywood Reporter (1944) 24 April.
Kinematograph Weekly (1944) no. 1,948, 17 August p.20.
New York Herald-Tribune (1944) 20 May.
New York Post (1944) 20 May.
New York Times (1944) 19 May p.12.
To-day's Cinema (1944) vol. 63 no. 5,070, 11 August p.21.
Variety (1944) 24 May p.10.

The Pearl of Death:

Hollywood Reporter (1944) 15 August.
Kinematograph Weekly (1944) no. 1,957, 19 October p.25.
Motion Picture Herald (1944) vol. 156 no. 10, 1 September p.2,083.
New York Times (1944) 26 August p.15.
New York World Telegram (1944) 15 August.
To-day's Cinema (1944) vol. 63 no. 5,099, 18 October p.17.
Variety (1944) 30 August p.10.

The House of Fear:

Kinematograph Weekly (1945) 31 May p.20B.
Motion Picture Herald (1945) vol. 158 no. 12, 24 March p.2,374.
New York Herald-Tribune (1945) 17 March.
New York Times (1945) 17 March p.17.
To-day's Cinema (1945) vol. 64 no. 5,191, 25 May p.64.

The Woman in Green:

Kinematograph Weekly (1945) no. 1,996, 19 July p.27.
Motion Picture Herald (1945) vol. 159 no. 12, 23 June p.2,510.
To-day's Cinema (1945) vol. 65 no. 5,214, 18 July p.10.

Pursuit to Algiers:
To-day's Cinema (1945) vol. 65 no. 5,281, 19 December p.11.

Dressed to Kill:
Motion Picture Herald (1946) vol. 163 no. 8, 25 May p.3,007.

OTHER CONTEMPORARY FILM REVIEWS:

Eyes of the Underworld, Kinematograph Weekly (1942) no. 1,850, 1 Oct p.29.
Eyes of the Underworld, New York Times (1942) 5 October.
Meet Boston Blackie, Variety (1941) 5 March.

CONTEMPORARY ADVERTISEMENT TIE-INS:

Booth's House of Lords gin (1940s) Rathbone endorsement with link to series, US.
Chesterfield Cigarettes (1946) Rathbone endorsement with link to *Dressed to Kill*, US.
Stratford Pens (1945) Rathbone endorsement with link to *House of Fear*, 15 January, US.
Walker's DeLuxe Bourbon (1940s) Rathbone endorsement with link to series, US.
Booth's Gin (1959) Rathbone endorsement with link to Holmes, US.

WEBSITES

Churchill, Winston, 'Mansion House Speech 4 September 1941' [biographical information and speech extracts] <http://www.winstonchurchill.org> accessed 9 May 2008.
Demsky, Andy, 'Leaving Baker Street' [Basil Rathbone fan site] <http://www.basilrathbone.net> accessed 18 November 2008.
Erickson, Hal, 'The Adventures of Sherlock Holmes' [film reference and review site] <http://www.allmovie.com> accessed 5 May 2008.
Gillette, William, 'William Gillette as Sherlock Holmes' [audio recording of Gillette as Holmes from 1936] <http://www.youtube.com> accessed 5 May 2008.
Henry, J., 'The Story of *The Strand Magazine*' <http://www.jhenry.demon.co.uk> accessed 27 July 2004 – site no longer operational.
Wilson, Karina, 'Horror film in the 1940s' <http://www.horrorfilmhistory.com> accessed 13 January 2008.
Author uncredited, 'The BBC at War 1939–1945' [account of BBC-initiated campaign for 'V for Victory'] <http://www.bbc.co.uk/heritage/story/ww2/overseas> accessed 18 November 2008.

UNPUBLISHED SOURCES

Correspondence from Arthur Conan Doyle Collection, Richard Lancelyn Green Bequest, Portsmouth Museums:

Doyle, Adrian Conan, letters to Basil Rathbone, 12 November and 16 December 1953.

Doyle, Denis Conan, letters to Frank Orsatti, 6 December and 11 December 1940; 1 March and 16 June 1941.

Doyle, Denis Conan, letter to Basil Rathbone, 29 December 1940.

Doyle, Denis Conan, letter to Fitelson and Mayers, 30 April 1941.

Doyle, Denis Conan, letter to Myron Selznick and Co, 30 July 1941.

Fitelson and Mayers, Memorandum Opinion No. 2, February 1940.

Fitelson and Mayers, letters to Denis Conan Doyle, 26 February 1940, 6 September 1940 and 13 June 1942.

Johnson, Julian, Twentieth Century-Fox, letters to Paul Kohner, 30 November 1938, 24 December 1938, 8 July 1939 and 11 July 1939.

Kohner, Paul, letter to all major studios, 4 November 1938.

Kohner, Paul, letter to Gregory Ratoff of Twentieth Century-Fox, 12 December 1938.

Kohner, Paul, letter to Frank Orsatti, 25 January 1939.

DeLapp, Terry, Universal, report on Denis Conan Doyle meeting, 1 October 1942.

Lawler, Joe, letter from publicity department of Universal to Warren Skidmore, 9 October 1946.

Luntzel, James R., Universal, letter to Denis Conan Doyle, 18 August 1942.

Orsatti, Frank, letters to Denis Conan Doyle, 21 October, 2 December and 9 December 1940.

Rathbone, Basil, letter to Denis Conan Doyle, 17 November 1951.

Rathbone, Basil, letters to Adrian Conan Doyle, 31 January 1951, 16 January 1952, n.d., 13 January 1953, 1 November 1953 and 20 November 1953.

Selznick, Myron, telegrams to Denis Conan Doyle, 30 July 1941, 7 January 1942, 14 January 1942 and 23 January 1942.

Selznick, Myron, letters to Denis Conan Doyle, 6 August 1941 and 8 January 1942.

Stein, Jules, MCA, telegram to Denis Conan Doyle, 21 July 1941.

Ward, Emmett P., Universal, letter to Denis Conan Doyle, 22 September 1942.

Scripts, story outlines, contracts and other material from Arthur Conan Doyle Collection, Richard Lancelyn Green Bequest, Portsmouth Museums:

Geraghty, Gerald, storyline for *Sherlock Holmes Faces Death*, n.d.

Gruber, Frank, storyline for *Prelude to Murder (Dressed to Kill)*, 14 June 1945.

Gruber, Frank, screenplay for *Terror by Night*, 1 October 1945.

Halliwell, Leslie, typescript of short stories based on final screenplay of *Sherlock Holmes Faces Death* and *The Pearl of Death*, n.d.

Lee, Leonard, treatment for *Prelude to Murder (Dressed to Kill)*, 16 November 1945.

Millhauser, Bertram, screenplay, *The Pearl of Death*, 28 March 1944.

Pascal, Ernest, screenplay draft, *Hound of the Baskervilles*, 8 December 1938.

Spanish-language cinema advertising cards for *Sherlock Holmes Contra Moriarty (The Adventures of Sherlock Holmes)* September 1947, *Sherlock Holmes Desafía a la Muerte (Sherlock Holmes Faces Death)* December 1947, *Perla Maldita (The Pearl of Death)* January 1948, *El Caso de las Dedos Cortados (Woman in Green)* July 1949.

Twentieth Century-Fox, pressbooks for *The Hound of the Baskervilles* and *The Adventures of Sherlock Holmes*, 1939.

Universal Studios, typed list of Holmes films and options exercised, based on Agreement of 24 February 1942.

Universal Studios, Agreement between Universal and the Conan Doyle Estate, 24 February 1942.

Universal Studios, pressbooks for all films in series except *Spider Woman*, 1942–1946.

Author uncredited, dialogue continuity script for *Sherlock Holmes and the Voice of Terror*, 28 July 1942.

Author uncredited, dialogue continuity scripts for trailer to Sherlock Holmes and the Voice of Terror, 18 August 1942 and *Pursuit to Algiers*, 22 October 1945.

Correspondence from Cinema-TV Archives, University of Southern California:

Breen, Joseph, Production Code Administration, letters to Maurice Pivar, Universal, 23 March and 27 December 1944.

Drake, William, Twentieth Century-Fox, memo to Col. Jason Joy, 8 June 1939.

Drake, William, Twentieth Century-Fox, memo to Gene Markey, 8 June 1939.

Feld, Milton, Universal, memo to unnamed person, 31 August 1942.

Gartside, Frank T., US Dept of the Interior, letter to Universal, 29 August 1942.

Sid Leon (advertising agency), cable to Harry Ormiston, Universal, 25 August 1944.

Lloyd-Morris, Captn Harold, Twentieth Century-Fox, memos to Gene Markey, Fox, 1, 2, 5, 13 and 15 June 1939.

Markey, Gene, Twentieth Century-Fox, memos to William Drake, Fox, 1 May and 27 May 1939.

Neill, Roy William, Universal, letter to Martin Murphy, 19 December 1945.

Ormiston, Harry, Universal, letter to Maurice Bergman, 9 August 1944.

Ormiston, Harry, Universal, letter to Sid Leon (advertising agency), 4 October 1944.

Werker, Alfred, Twentieth Century-Fox, memos to Gene Markey, Fox, 1 June and 12 June 1939.

Scripts, story outlines, contracts and other material from Cinema-TV Archives, University of Southern California:

Blum, Edwin, story treatment for *The Hound of the Baskervilles*, 22 October 1938.

Blum, Edwin, original story outline for *The Adventures of Sherlock Holmes*, n.d.

Blum, Edwin, first draft continuity script for *Adventures of Sherlock Holmes*, 3 April 1939.

Blum, Edwin and Drake, William, temporary script for *The Adventures of Sherlock Holmes*, 29 May 1939; and revised script, 2–19 June 1939.

Universal, contract with Nigel Bruce, 9 February 1942.

Universal, assistant director's daily report for *Sherlock Holmes in Washington*, July 1942.

Universal, agreement with Stratford Pens, 9 July 1942.

Universal, production estimate for *Sherlock Holmes in Washington*, 13 July 1942.

Universal, assistant director's daily reports for *The Scarlet Claw*, January 1944.

Universal, production estimate for *The Scarlet Claw*, 5 January 1944.

Universal, set numbers list for *The Scarlet Claw*, 8 January 1944.

Universal, assistant director's daily reports for *The Pearl of Death*, April 1944.

Universal, production estimate for *The Pearl of Death*, 3 April 1944.

Universal, set list for *The Pearl of Death*, 6 April 1944.

Universal, assistant director's daily report for *The House of Fear*, May 1944.

Universal, production estimate for *The House of Fear*, 8 May 1944.

Universal, contract with Denis Hoey for *The House of Fear*, 11 May 1944.

Universal, production estimate for *The Woman in Green*, 11 January 1945.

Universal, press releases for *Dressed to Kill*, 26 January and 31 January 1945.

Universal, assistant director's daily reports for *Dressed to Kill*, January 1946.

Universal, set numbers list for *The Woman in Green*, 9 January 1946.

Universal, set numbers list for *Dressed to Kill*, 19 January 1946.

Universal, contract with Patricia Morison for *Dressed to Kill*, 21 January 1946.

Universal, contract with Frederic Worlock for *Dressed to Kill*, 25 January 1946.

Universal, summary of picture costs sheets for *Dressed to Kill*, November 1946.

Universal, production budget file for *Dressed to Kill*, n.d.

Zanuck, Darryl, conference report on story treatment for *The Hound of the Baskervilles*, 24 October 1938, and on first draft continuity script, 1 December 1938.

Zanuck, Darryl, conference report on story outline for *The Adventures of Sherlock Holmes*, 26 January 1939; on first draft continuity script, 19 April 1939; and on temporary script, 31 May 1939.

Correspondence from Margaret Herrick Library, Los Angeles:

Breen, Joseph, Production Code Administration, letters to Col. Jason Joy, Twentieth Century-Fox, 9 December 1938 and 16 June 1939.

Breen, Joseph, Production Code Administration, letters to Maurice Pivar, Universal, 7 April and 10 May 1943; 1 August and 11 October 1945; and 7 February 1946.

Joy, Col. Jason, Twentieth Century-Fox, letter to Joseph Breen, Production

Code Administration, 3 July 1939.

Pivar, Maurice, Universal, letter to G.M. Shurlock, Production Code Administration, 28 April 1942.

Writer unnamed, Production Code Administration, letters to Maurice Pivar, Universal, 29 April, and 6 May 1942.

Scripts, story outlines, contracts and other material from Margaret Herrick Library:

Brand, Harry, Twentieth Century-Fox, synopsis of *The Hound of the Baskervilles*, 8 August 1939.

Houghton and Durland, Production Code Administration, film analysis chart of *The Scarlet Claw*, 29 February 1944.

Houghton and Vizzard, Production Code Administration, film analysis chart of *Pursuit to Algiers*, 4 October 1945.

Metzger, Charles, Production Code Administration, synopsis of *Sherlock Holmes and the Voice of Terror*, 20 February 1942.

Metzger, Charles, Production Code Administration, report on *Sherlock Holmes and the Secret Weapon*, 5 May 1942.

Metzger, Charles and Pettijohn, Production Code Administration, film analysis chart of *Sherlock Holmes and the Voice of Terror*, 21 July 1942.

Metzger, Charles, Production Code Administration, synopsis of *The Woman in Green*, 26 December 1944.

Motion Picture Producers and Distributors of America, reports from local censor boards for *The Hound of the Baskervilles*, 6 July 1939.

Motion Picture Association reports from local censor boards, May–June 1946.

Motion Picture Producers and Distributors of America, report by local censor boards on *Sherlock Holmes and the Secret Weapon*, 7 January 1943.

Shurlock, G.M., and Mackinnon, Douglas, Production Code Administration, film analysis chart for *The Hound of the Baskervilles*, 14 March 1939.

Shurlock, G.M., and Metzger, Charles, Production Code Administration, film analysis chart of *The Adventures of Sherlock Holmes*, 8 August 1939.

Zehner, Harry, Production Code Administration, film analysis chart of *Dressed to Kill,* 25 February 1946.

Writer unnamed, Production Code Administration, film analysis chart of *Terror by Night*, 10 January 1946.

Correspondence from Twentieth Century-Fox archives at University of California Los Angeles:

Blair, Aubrey, Screen Actors Guild, letter to Fred Beetson, Motion Picture Producers Association, 14 January 1939 (box FXLR 547).

Dorn, W.B., Twentieth Century-Fox, memo to George Wasson, Fox, 22 September 1938 (box FXLR 547).

Friedman, Phil M., Fox Film Corp, memo to George Wasson, Fox, 29 March 1934 (box FXLR 1028).

Lavigne, E.C. de, Twentieth Century-Fox, memo to F.L. Metzler, Fox, 9 March 1939 (box FXLR 547).

Lavigne, E.C. de, Twentieth Century-Fox, letter to Sydney Towell, 12 May 1939 (box FXLR 547).

Schreiber, Lew, Twentieth Century-Fox, memo to George Wasson, Fox, 15 April 1939 (box FXLR 555).

Wasson, George, Fox Film Corp, letter to Sydney Towell, Fox, 25 May 1934 (box FXLR 1028).

Wasson, George, Twentieth Century-Fox, cable to E.P. Kilroe, Fox, 3 November 1938 (box FXLR 547).

Wasson, George, Fox Film Corp, letter to E.P. Kilroe, Fox, 9 October 1933 (box FXLR 1028).

Weese, A.W. de, Twentieth Century-Fox, memo to George Wasson, Fox, 8 March 1939 (box FXLR 547).

Writer unnamed, Fox Film Co, letter to E.P. Kilroe, Fox, 30 October 1933 (box FXLR 1028).

Scripts, story outlines, contracts and other material from Twentieth Century-Fox archives at University of California Los Angeles:

NBC, contract with Lady Jean Conan Doyle and Denis Conan Doyle for radio adaptations of Sherlock Holmes stories, 1 September 1936.

Twentieth Century-Fox, contracts with Basil Rathbone, Nigel Bruce, Wendy Barrie, Beryl Mercer and Barlowe Borland for *The Hound of the Baskervilles*, 25 October 1938.

Twentieth Century-Fox, shooting schedules for *The Hound of the Baskervilles*, 17 December and 22 December 1938, and 13–14 January 1939.

Twentieth Century-Fox, contract cancellation with Anita Louise for *The Hound of the Baskervilles*, 13 January 1939.

Twentieth Century-Fox, music cue-sheet for *The Hound of the Baskervilles*, 20 March 1939.

Twentieth Century-Fox, contract with Basil Rathbone for *The Californian*, 8 July 1940.

Theses:

Kennedy, Gary, *A Case of Identity: Sherlock Holmes: the Popular Character and Series Production in Hollywood 1939–45*, Canada: 1995, Carleton University, MA thesis.

Papers:

Walker, Deborah, *The Demographics of Female Criminalisation in Classic Film Noir*, paper given at Crime Cultures Conference, University of Portsmouth, July 2008.

FILMOGRAPHY

The Hound of the Baskervilles (1939)

Twentieth Century-Fox. Director Sidney Lanfield; producer Gene Markey; screenplay Ernest Pascal; DoP Peverell Marley; art director Richard Day; editor Robert Simpson. Cast includes Basil Rathbone (Holmes), Nigel Bruce (Watson), Richard Greene (Sir Henry Baskerville), Wendy Barrie (Beryl Stapleton), Lionel Atwill (Dr James Mortimer), John Carradine (Barryman), Morton Lowry (Jack Stapleton). Running time: 80 minutes.

Sherlock Holmes is called on by Dr James Mortimer, physician to the late Sir Charles Baskerville of Dartmoor. Sir Charles has died in mysterious circumstances: footprints of a 'gigantic hound' were found near the body and this, together with the ancestral legend about a supernatural beast, makes Dr Mortimer fear for the life of the new heir to the estate, Sir Henry. Holmes despatches Watson to Dartmoor to guard Sir Henry, claiming prior business in London. The moor echoes with strange cries; the hall is gloomy, the servants act suspiciously and the neighbours are eccentric; the only bright spot for Sir Henry is the presence of the attractive Beryl Stapleton, who lives nearby with her naturalist brother Jack. The threat of the hound grows: a seance aimed at getting in touch with the spirit of Sir Charles is interrupted by the howling of the 'beast' outside the window. Thinking himself abandoned by Holmes, Watson is angry to discover that the detective has been on Dartmoor all the time, disguised as an old pedlar. When the two men see the hound with their own eyes, attacking and killing a man, they fear the victim is Sir Henry; but it is an escaped convict wearing Sir Henry's cast-off clothes. The suspicious behaviour of the butler and his wife, the Barrymans, is explained: the convict is Mrs Barryman's brother, who she has been helping. With the convict dead, Holmes declares the case closed, and he and Watson pretend to leave for London. Meanwhile the villain is revealed to be Jack Stapleton, who keeps a slavering hound in the empty tomb of a ruined graveyard on the moor. Stapleton sets the hound on the scent of Sir Henry by giving it one of his boots: the hound quickly finds Sir Henry, leaping at his throat and knocking him to the ground. Holmes and Watson arrive in the nick of time and shoot the hound. Back at Baskerville Hall, Holmes denounces Stapleton who, as the illegitimate descendent of the original owner of the Hall, thought he could inherit by eliminating first Sir Charles and then Sir Henry. Stapleton makes a bid for escape and runs out onto the treacherous Grimpen Mire.

The Adventures of Sherlock Holmes (1939)

Twentieth Century-Fox. Director Alfred Werker; producer Gene Markey; screenplay Edwin Blum and William Drake; DoP Leon Shamroy and Hans Peters; art director Richard Day; editor Robert Bischoff. Cast includes Basil Rathbone (Holmes), Nigel Bruce (Watson), Ida Lupino (Ann Brandon), George Zucco (Moriarty), Alan Marshal (Jerrold Hunter), Henry Stephenson (Sir Ronald Ramsgate). Running time: 85 minutes.

Holmes' arch-rival, Professor James Moriarty, vows to pull off the crime of the century. His strategy is to give Holmes two cases to solve, knowing that Holmes' love of novelty will mean he will quickly forget the first case once he has a new puzzle to work on. He sends two letters: the first to Sir Ronald Ramsgate, constable of the Tower of London, telling him that an emerald, due to arrive at the Tower later that week will be stolen; and the second (the 'distraction crime'), a death threat in the form of a drawing, to a Lloyd Brandon. Holmes takes on both cases, but as Moriarty predicted, is much more interested in the second case because it is complex and mysterious, and because the person who asks for his help is a 'distressed maiden', Lloyd's sister Ann Brandon. Lloyd is duly murdered and Ann receives an identical death threat drawing through the mail. The clues point to a South American killer. Eager to concentrate on this case, Holmes delegates Watson to look after the Tower's emerald. Moriarty has disguised himself as a policeman, and stages a deliberately bungled theft which allows Watson to think he has saved the day. Unknown to Watson and Sir Ronald, in the confusion, Moriarty has concealed himself inside the cage where the Crown Jewels are kept – and has all the time in the world to extract the emerald and other jewels from their settings. Meanwhile, an attempt is made on Ann Brandon's life: Holmes pursues the killer, who admits that it was Moriarty who put him up to the murders. Holmes finally realises what Moriarty is doing and that the 'crime of the century' must be connected to the Tower of London. He rushes to the Tower, finds Moriarty and there is a fight on the battlements. Moriarty falls to his death.

Sherlock Holmes and the Voice of Terror (1942)

Universal. Director John Rawlins; producer Howard Benedict; screenplay Lynn Riggs and John Bright; DoP Woody Bredell; art director Jack Otterson; editor Russell Schoengarth. Cast includes Basil Rathbone (Holmes), Nigel Bruce (Watson), Evelyn Ankers (Kitty), Reginald Denny (Sir Evan Barham), Henry Daniell (Sir Alfred), Thomas Gomez (R.F. Meade). Running time: 65 minutes.

Wartime England is gripped by a series of radio broadcasts from a self-styled 'voice of terror' predicting acts of sabotage. The predictions are instantly fulfilled and the 'voice' seems to possess insider knowledge. Sir Evan Barham, head of the Intelligence Inner Council, calls in Sherlock Holmes. Holmes works on the theory that the events the voice describes have happened just a few minutes before the broadcast: the voice is probably recorded in England, then the record flown to Germany for broadcasting. An agent he has sent to Limehouse to find out who's behind the plot is murdered, so Holmes enlists the aid of the agent's girlfriend, Kitty, who rouses her fellow drinkers in a low-life bar to get behind the patriotic fight. On the trail of the enemy, Holmes and Watson walk into a trap at an old abandoned dock, and in the ensuing fight, Holmes allows the leader, Meade, to escape. He details Kitty to 'work' him: she soon becomes his mistress and he reveals his Nazi sympathies. The next 'voice' broadcast predicts an air invasion on England's 'defenceless north coast', but

Holmes' intelligence reveals that Meade is staying in a south coast village – so he heads south. He finds Meade and his followers, in SS uniform, in a ruined church, awaiting the anticipated German invasion. Meade realises that Kitty has betrayed him: he shoots her and is shot himself. Holmes reveals that the spy is Sir Evan, the head of the Council, but that the man they know as Sir Evan is an impostor. When the real Sir Evan was captured in World War I, the Germans noticed how closely he resembled one of their officers, Von Bork. After the war, it was Von Bork who returned to Britain, posing as Sir Evan with the help of plastic surgery.

Sherlock Holmes and the Secret Weapon (1942)

Universal. Director Roy William Neill; producer Howard Benedict; screenplay Edward T. Lowe, W. Scott Darling and Edmund Hartmann; DoP Les White; art director Jack Otterson; editor Otto Ludwig. Cast includes Basil Rathbone (Holmes), Nigel Bruce (Watson), Lionel Atwill (Moriarty), William Post Jnr (Tobel), Dennis Hoey (Inspector Lestrade). Running time: 68 minutes.

In a village in the Swiss Alps, Holmes – disguised as an old 'bookseller' – smuggles out a new design of bombsight which the Nazis are desperate to obtain and brings it, together with its inventor Dr Franz Tobel, back to London. To safeguard his invention, Tobel divides the bombsight into four parts and distributes them to four different Swiss-born craftsmen: he writes their names and addresses in code and leaves the information with his girlfriend Charlotte. She is to give it to Holmes should anything befall him. When Tobel disappears, Holmes opens the envelope but the note inside says only 'we meet again, Mr Holmes', revealing the enemy to be Moriarty. Examining the notepad on which Tobel wrote the coded message, Holmes deciphers it from the impression on the page beneath, but as he rushes to each address, he finds Moriarty has beaten him to it and the men are already dead. Only the fourth address is left. Moriarty appears to be first on the scene, but the 'Swiss' he has come to kill turns out to be Holmes in disguise. Moriarty captures Holmes and plans a grisly method of murdering him. As he is about to start the torture, Watson and Inspector Lestrade arrive and chase Moriarty who falls to his (presumed) death through a trapdoor intended for his pursuers.

Sherlock Holmes in Washington (1943)

Universal. Director Roy William Neill; producer Howard Benedict; screenplay Lynn Riggs and Bertram Millhauser; DoP Les White; art director Jack Otterson; editor Otto Ludwig. Cast includes Basil Rathbone (Holmes), Nigel Bruce (Watson), George Zucco (Hinkel), Gerald Hamer (Grayson). Running time: 71 minutes.

British agent John Grayson, who is carrying secret plans on behalf of the Allies, is followed on his journey from London to New York and abducted when he boards a train bound for Washington. The Home Office implore Holmes to retrieve the document before it can be used against the Allies. Holmes finds evidence that Grayson turned the document into microfilm and hid it in a matchbook; he flies to Washington with Watson to investigate, but Grayson's dead body is delivered to their hotel, packed in a trunk. The passengers on the train's club car, where Grayson was sitting, have all since had unwelcome visitors and threats, and one – a young woman – has been kidnapped. The matchbook, meanwhile, in a number of scenes, passes unwittingly from hand to hand. Holmes deduces from a piece of old wood entangled in the blanket in which Grayson's body was wrapped that it came from an antique shop – he tracks down the shop, owned by World War I secret agent Heinrich Hinkel, now known as Richard Stanley. On Hinkel's desk is his pipe and the matchbook containing the microfilm: he is unaware that he already possesses the document he so badly wants. Holmes confronts Hinkel but is captured and has to be rescued by Watson and the FBI. Hinkel escapes, carrying the matchbook. Holmes warns another of the club-car passengers, a senator, that he may be in danger, but is again caught by Hinkel at gunpoint. The US police rescue Holmes and arrest Hinkel. Holmes asks Hinkel for a light, and Hinkel unwittingly hands over the matchbook.

Sherlock Holmes Faces Death (1943)

Universal. Director and producer Roy William Neill; screenplay Bertram Millhauser; DoP Charles van Enger; art director John Goodman; editor Fred Fleitschaus. Cast includes Basil Rathbone (Holmes), Nigel Bruce (Watson), Hillary Brooke (Sally Musgrave), Dennis Hoey (Lestrade), Arthur Margetson (Sexton). Running time: 68 minutes.

Watson is working at a rest home for servicemen in Northumberland, aided by a Dr Sexton. Musgrave Manor, requisitioned from the Musgrave family, is a spooky Gothic mansion which the landlord of the local pub, The Rat and Raven, says is known for 'corpse lights' and 'wailing'. Sexton is injured in an attack by an unseen assailant and Watson seeks Holmes' help. On arrival, they find the body of Geoffrey Musgrave, oldest of the three siblings, buried under a pile of leaves. Inspector Lestrade arrives to lead the investigation and questions Sally Musgrave, her brother Philip and the butler, Brunton. The next night the Musgraves enact an old family ritual, with Sally Musgrave reciting seemingly meaningless verses that are traditionally said when one member of the line of succession has died. The mystery deepens: first the butler, Brunton, disappears, then Philip Musgrave's body is found in the boot of Sally's car. Holmes thinks the solution lies in the strange Musgrave Ritual. Spotting the references to chess pieces in the verses, and noting that the hall of the Manor has chequered tiles, he places people on the squares and attempts to act out the ritual's coded instructions. This leads him to investigate the crypt below the hall, where he finds Brunton's dead body: he has been murdered and an ancient document lies beside him. Everyone crowds down to look. Holmes lays a trap for the killer, who is revealed as Sexton. Sexton says he had plotted to marry Sally Musgrave because he had discovered she was an unwitting heir to one of the richest tracts of land in the country, as revealed by the ancient document. Holmes tells Sally that she is a rich woman, but realising that to obtain these riches, she would have to turn the 'little people' out of their homes on her land, she renounces her rights.

Spider Woman (1944)

Universal. Director and producer Roy William Neill; screenplay Bertram Millhauser; DoP Charles van Enger; art director John Goodman; editor William Austin. Cast includes Basil Rathbone (Holmes), Nigel Bruce (Watson), Gale Sondergaard (Adrea Spedding), Dennis Hoey (Lestrade), Vernon Downing (Norman Locke). Running time: 63 minutes.

Holmes is intrigued by a series of mysterious 'pyjama suicides' in which prominent men die in the night, clad only in their nightclothes. Wanting to investigate the case secretly, he feigns his own death while on a fishing holiday, deceiving even Watson. By the time he reappears, he already has an idea of the criminal mind behind the so-called suicides, speculating that it is a woman because of the subtle and cruel method employed. As all the suicides were gamblers, Holmes goes to a gambling club disguised as an Indian officer, luring the villain by placing an announcement of his 'arrival' in London. At the casino he loses heavily and threatens to take his own life. A glamorous woman, Adrea Spedding intercepts him and explains that if he is desperate for money, she can help. He can borrow the sum he needs on his insurance policy simply by naming a new beneficiary. Both protagonists see through each other's 'disguise' and Spedding decides to kill Holmes in the same way she has killed the other men. A pygmy in her employ releases a poisonous spider into Holmes' bedroom through the ventilator shaft – the bite of the spider will drive Holmes to throw himself out of the window. He outwits the murder attempt and traces the pygmy to a local fairground, but is trapped by Spedding and her gang. They tie him to the back of a shooting-gallery target where Watson, taking his turn at the sideshow, will unknowingly kill his friend. Holmes escapes and the gang is rounded up.

The Pearl of Death (1944)

Universal. Director and producer Roy William Neill; screenplay Bertram Millhauser; DoP Virgil Miller; art director John Goodman; editor Ray Snyder. Cast includes Basil Rathbone (Holmes), Nigel Bruce (Watson), Evelyn Ankers (Naomi Drake), Miles Mander (Giles Conover), Dennis Hoey (Lestrade), Rondo Hatton (The Creeper). Running time: 69 minutes.

On a sea crossing to Dover, a well-dressed woman – Naomi Drake – steals a famous pearl from its courier and asks an elderly clergyman to carry 'her camera' through customs for her. But the 'clergyman' is Holmes in disguise, there precisely to foil such a theft. He outwits her and sees that the pearl reaches its rightful destination, the Royal Regent Museum in London. Drake's criminal associate is Giles Conover, who controls a sinister killer known as the Creeper. Disguised as a museum cleaner, Conover snatches the pearl: though he is quickly caught, the pearl is gone. A series of killings ensues – in each case the victim's back is broken, reminding Holmes of the Creeper's modus operandi – and the body is found surrounded by broken china, including pieces of a bust of Napoleon. Holmes deduces that Conover had to dispose of the pearl very quickly and had run to a nearby plaster-cast workshop, put it in a bust that was drying, and flee. He traces the workshop where six such identical busts were made on that day, and the retail outlet that sold them. By this time, five owners of the busts are dead. When Conover and the Creeper arrive at the sixth address, Holmes is lying in wait for them. In the ensuing confrontation, Holmes makes the Creeper turn on Conover and kill him. Holmes shoots the Creeper, smashes the last Napoleon bust, and finds the pearl.

The Scarlet Claw (1944)

Universal. Director and producer Roy William Neill; screenplay Edmund Hartmann and Roy William Neill; DoP George Robinson; art director John Goodman; editor Paul Landres. Cast includes Basil Rathbone (Holmes), Nigel Bruce (Watson), Gerald Hamer (Alistair Ramson), Paul Cavanagh (Lord Penrose), Arthur Hohl (Emil Journet). Running time: 74 minutes.

Holmes and Watson are attending an occult society meeting in Canada at which Lord Penrose is reporting on his belief that psychic phenomena are behind a spate of sheep throat-cutting in his village of La Morte Rouge. While Holmes is arguing that there must be a rational explanation, Penrose receives a message to say that his wife has been found with her throat cut in the old village church. Holmes correctly identifies the weapon as a heavy garden weeder and tries unsuccessfully to catch out the local innkeeper, Emil Journet, as the killer. On the fog-bound moor that surrounds the village, he sees a ghostly glowing figure which runs away when he shoots at it. The only evidence left behind is a piece of phosphorescent cloth. He identifies the fabric and its owner, but it is part of a shirt given away to a gardener, Tanner. Holmes tracks down Tanner, living in an abandoned building, but he leaps through a window into a river to escape. Holmes discovers that 'Tanner' is the pseudonym of an actor, Alistair Ramson, who was convicted of the murder of a fellow actor but who had escaped from prison. Lady Penrose was an actress before her marriage: Ramson had been in love with her, but she had spurned him. He had clearly come to La Morte Rouge to exact revenge: 'Tanner' was probably just one of many disguises, and therefore he could be almost anyone in the village. Others are under threat – Judge Brisson, who was responsible for sentencing Ramson, is murdered; and the killer goes out onto the moor looking for Journet, who was his prison guard. It is then that his identity in La Morte Rouge – that of Potts the postman – is revealed. He takes the claw from his pocket ready to attack, but 'Journet' is actually Holmes in disguise. Holmes summons the waiting police and Ransom, alias Potts, drowns in the marshes.

The House of Fear (1945)

Universal. Director and producer Roy William Neill; screenplay Edmund
Hartmann and Roy William Neill; DoP George Robinson; art director John
Goodman; editor Paul Landres. Cast includes Basil Rathbone (Holmes), Nigel
Bruce (Watson), Aubrey Mather (Bruce Alastair), Dennis Hoey (Lestrade), Paul
Cavanagh (Simon Merivale), Holmes Herbert (Alan Cosgrave), Harry Cording
(Captain John Simpson). Running time: 69 minutes.

Drearcliff House, a gloomy mansion on the Scottish coast, has been bought by
Bruce Alastair for his fellow members of a London club – The Good
Comrades. All seven men, who have no next-of-kin, have taken out insurance
policies naming each other as beneficiaries. Two have already died violently
after receiving an envelope containing orange pips, the first by his car plunging
off a cliff and bursting into flames and the second by falling into the furnace
and his remains only identifiable by his cufflinks. The insurance agent,
Chalmers, suspecting an insurance scam, brings the case to Holmes. At the
village inn they learn that Drearcliff is the subject of local legend, haunted not
by ghosts but by the 'memory of evil', yet when they go to the house, they are
greeted in cheerful manner by Alastair. Despite the arrival of Holmes, and then
of Inspector Lestrade, more deaths ensue until only Alastair remains. But there
is clearly more to the serial killing than meets the eye: the local tobacconist,
who does not believe in ghosts, says he saw one of the dead men walking on
the beach at night – and is shot for his trouble. Holmes finds a secret passage
that leads from the great fireplace to an old smugglers' cave. There, he discovers
all six supposedly 'murdered' Comrades alive and well.

The Woman in Green (1945)

Universal. Director and producer Roy William Neill; screenplay Bertram
Millhauser; DoP Virgil Miller; art director John Goodman; editor Edward
Curtiss. Cast includes Basil Rathbone (Holmes), Nigel Bruce (Watson), Hillary
Brooke (Lydia Marlowe), Henry Daniell (Moriarty), Paul Cavanagh (Sir
George Fenwick), Matthew Boulton (Inspector Gregson). Running time: 68
minutes.

Senior police officers, baffled by the serial killing of young women whose
murderer removes one of their fingers, ask Holmes for his help. While having a
drink with Inspector Gregson in a smart nightclub, Holmes observes an
attractive woman leaving the club with a man who he recognises as Sir George
Fenwick. The woman, Lydia Marlowe, takes Sir George to her flat and, over
drinks and seduction, hypnotises him. Next morning, he awakes in a cheap
hotel: he finds a severed finger in his pocket, and the newspaper has a story
about a new murder. He attempts to talk to Lydia Marlowe about it, but is
intercepted by Professor Moriarty, who blackmails him. His daughter, seeing
him bury something in the garden at night, calls Holmes, but it is too late – Sir
George has been murdered. There is an unsuccessful attempt on Holmes' life
from the empty house opposite 221B Baker Street and the gunman proves to

be in a hypnotic trance. Following the hypnosis clue, Holmes attends a meeting at the Mesmer Club, spots Marlowe in the audience and, recognising her from the nightclub, presents himself as her next victim. At her flat, he is given a drug and then hypnotised. Moriarty appears with a sinister and perverted doctor, who tests Holmes' hypnotic state by pricking his neck with a scalpel. Moriarty then dictates a suicide note, and Holmes obediently writes it. He instructs Holmes to walk along a rooftop parapet, confident that he will walk straight off the end. But Holmes has substituted the 'drug' he was given for one that made him insensitive to pain. Watson and Inspector Gregson arrive; Moriarty attempts to flee, but falls off the roof to his death.

Pursuit to Algiers (1945)

Universal. Director Roy William Neill; producer Howard Benedict; screenplay Leonard Lee; DoP Paul Ivano; art director John Goodman; editor Saul Goodkind. Cast includes Basil Rathbone (Holmes), Nigel Bruce (Watson), Morton Lowry (Sanford), Marjorie Riordan (Sheila Woodbury), Martin Kosleck (Mirko), Rex Evans (Gregor), Wee Willie Davis (Gubec). Running time: 65 minutes.

Following the assassination of King Stefan of Rovenia, Holmes is asked to help ensure that his heir, Prince Nikolas, returns to the country as quickly as possible in order to avert a coup. Holmes and Watson arrange to accompany the prince on his flight to Rovenia, but at the last moment, Watson is told he will have to travel by ship. Watson boards the vessel, is assigned Sanford as his steward, and meets the other passengers, all of whom behave in a suspicious manner. En route, Watson learns that Holmes' plane has crashed over the Pyrenees, but this proves to be a trick: he soon finds that Holmes is on board with Nikolas, who will now pose as Watson's nephew. When the ship picks up three male passengers at Lisbon, there are numerous attempts on the life of Nikolas and Holmes, culminating in the men snatching Nikolas and leaving Holmes bound and gagged. When Watson arrives to untie him, Holmes reveals that 'Nikolas' was just a stooge – the real Nikolas has been posing as Sanford, the steward, for the entire voyage: the villains have captured the wrong man and have been quickly arrested. Along the way, Holmes manages to track down a stolen emerald necklace, being unwittingly carried by one of the passengers, Sheila Woodbury. He takes the necklace to return to its rightful owner and lets the woman go, even promising to send her the reward.

Terror by Night (1946)

Universal. Director Roy William Neill; producer Howard Benedict; screenplay Frank Gruber; DoP Maury Gerstman; art director John Goodman; editor Saul Goodkind. Cast includes Basil Rathbone (Holmes), Nigel Bruce (Watson), Renée Godfrey (Vivian Vedder), Alan Mowbray (Major Duncan-Bleek), Dennis Hoey (Lestrade), Mary Forbes (Lady Margaret Carstairs). Running time: 60 minutes.

Holmes is asked to help guard a famous diamond, the Star of Rhodesia, as its owner Lady Margaret Carstairs travels with it by train to Scotland. Inspector Lestrade is also on board, travelling incognito. When Lady Margaret shows Holmes the diamond, he quickly swaps it for a fake, giving Lestrade the real jewel. In the dining car, Holmes and Watson meet an old army chum of Watson's, Major Duncan-Bleek, but while they are there, Lady Carstairs' son is murdered and the diamond snatched. Everyone seems suspicious, especially Vivian Vedder, a young women transporting the body of her mother to Scotland for burial, but Holmes suspects the theft is the work of Moriarty's right-hand man Colonel Sebastian Moran, who he has never seen. Holmes almost dies when pushed from the train by an unseen assailant, and the baggage van guard is found murdered. Holmes discovers a secret compartment inside the coffin where the killer had concealed himself. The diminutive killer is seen getting his instructions from Major Duncan-Bleek – now revealed as a villain. He slugs Lestrade on the head, snatches the real diamond and is then killed in turn by the Major, who pockets the jewel. At an unscheduled stop an Inspector McDonald, of the Scottish police, boards. He arrests Duncan-Bleek, reveals him to be Colonel Sebastian Moran, and takes the diamond from him. Moran pulls the train's communication cord and an awkward fight ensues with Holmes eventually overcoming Moran and pulling his jacket over his head. McDonald leads Moran off the train. But the arrest is a ruse: McDonald is not a policeman, but an imposter and during the struggle, Holmes has substituted Lestrade for the real villain. He hides under the raincoat, gun at the ready, to arrest the 'inspector'.

Dressed to Kill (1946)

Universal. Director Roy William Neill; producer Howard Benedict; screenplay Leonard Lee; DoP Maury Gerstman; art director Jack Otterson; editor Saul Goodkind. Cast includes Basil Rathbone (Holmes), Nigel Bruce (Watson), Patricia Morison (Hilda Courtney), Edmund Breon (Stinky), Frederick Worlock (Colonel Cavanaugh). Running time: 76 minutes.

At a London auction room, three musical boxes are sold, all of the type made at a prison on Dartmoor by one of the convicts. Colonel Cavanaugh arrives too late to bid, but professes a desperate desire for the music boxes and bribes the auctioneer to tell him the names and addresses of the buyers. Holmes is consulted by an old school friend of Watson's – Julian 'Stinky' Emery – about the theft of one of his priceless collection of musical boxes: Holmes is intrigued because the box stolen was a plain and low-value one, but one which closely resembled a musical box Stinky had bought that very day from the auction room. Back at his house, Emery receives a visit from a glamorous acquaintance, Hilda Courtney, who asks him to give her, or sell her, the auction-room musical box. He refuses and is murdered. Holmes tracks down the buyers of the other two musical boxes from the auction, but is only able to obtain one: Courtney has beaten him to the third box. He believes the secret lies in the tune the boxes play and that this is connected with its maker serving time for stealing a set of Bank of England printing plates which have never been recovered. Holmes whistles the musical box tune to one of the buskers at a low-life cafe: the busker identifies the tune but says it has several notes misplaced. Holmes realises it must be a code but can crack only part of it without all three boxes. Courtney sets up a series of traps: first for Holmes, who she leaves to die, trapped in a garage full of exhaust fumes; and then for Watson so that she can retrieve the box he has hidden at 221B. She now has all the clues, whereas Holmes knows only that the plates are hidden behind the bookshelves at a Dr S's house. Listening to Watson talk about Samuel Johnson, he miraculously guesses that this is where the plates are hidden. They arrive just as Courtney has found the plates and help the police arrest the gang.

INDEX OF FILMS

INDEX OF NAMES